CliffsTestPrep®
Cisco® CCNA®

By
Todd Lammle

Wiley Publishing, Inc.

Publisher's Acknowledgments

Editorial

Acquisitions Editors: Maureen Adams and Jeff Kellum

Production Editor: Angela Smith

Copy Editor: Tiffany Taylor

Technical Editor: Patrick Bass

Production

Proofreader: Ian Golder

CliffsTestPrep® Cisco® CCNA®

Published by:

Wiley Publishing, Inc.

111 River Street

Hoboken, NJ 07030-5774

www.wiley.com

Copyright © 2007 Wiley, Hoboken, NJ

Published by Wiley, Hoboken, NJ

Published simultaneously in Canada

ISBN-13: 978-0-470-11752-1

Printed in the United States of America

10 9 8 7 6 5 4 3 2 1

WILEY

Contents

PART I

INTRODUCTION TO THE CISCO CCNA EXAM

Welcome to the exciting world of Cisco certification! You've picked up this book because you want something better—namely, a better job with more satisfaction. Rest assured that you've made a good decision. Cisco certification can help you get your first networking job, or more money and a promotion if you're already in the field.

Cisco certification can also improve your understanding of the internetworking of more than just Cisco products: You'll develop a complete understanding of networking and how different network topologies work together to form a network. This is beneficial to every networking job and is the reason Cisco certification is in such high demand, even at companies with few Cisco devices.

Cisco is the king of routing and switching, the Microsoft of the internetworking world. The Cisco certifications reach beyond the popular certifications, such as the MCSE, to provide you with an indispensable factor in understanding today's network: insight into the Cisco world of internetworking. By deciding that you want to become Cisco certified, you're saying that you want to be the best—the best at routing and the best at switching. This book will lead you in that direction.

The CCNA certification was the first in the new line of Cisco certifications and was the precursor to all current Cisco certifications. Now you can become a Cisco Certified Network Associate for the cost of a study guide, the price of a hands-on class, and the meager cost of this book, plus $125 for the test. And you don't have to stop there—you can choose to continue with your studies and achieve a higher certification, called the Cisco Certified Network Professional (CCNP). Someone with a CCNP has all the skills and knowledge they need to attempt the CCIE lab. However, because no textbook can take the place of practical experience, this book was designed to help you practice for the CCNA exam once you've finished your classroom studies.

Cisco, not unlike Microsoft or Novell, has created the certification process to give administrators a set of skills and to equip prospective employers with a way to measure skills or match certain criteria. Becoming a CCNA can be the initial step of a successful journey toward a new, highly rewarding, and sustainable career.

The CCNA program was created to provide a solid introduction not only to the Cisco Internetwork Operating System (IOS) and Cisco hardware, but also to internetworking in general, making it helpful to you in areas that aren't exclusively Cisco's. At this point in the certification process, it's not unrealistic to imagine that future network managers—even those without Cisco equipment—could easily require Cisco certifications for their job applicants.

If you make it through the CCNA and are still interested in Cisco and internetworking, you're headed down a path to certain success.

The way to become a CCNA is to pass one little test (CCNA exam 640–801). True, it's just one test, but you still have to possess enough knowledge to understand what the test writers are saying.

However, Cisco has announced a two-step process that you can take in order to become a CCNA that may be easier than taking one longer exam. These tests are:

- Exam 640–811: Interconnecting Cisco Networking Devices (ICND)
- Exam 640–821: Introduction to Cisco Networking Technologies (INTRO)

> **Understand that this book is designed to prepare you to pass the 640–801 exam, although it will likely help you pass both 640–811 and 640–821 as well.**

I can't stress this enough: It's critical that you have some hands-on experience with Cisco routers. If you can get hold of some 2500, 2600, or 2800 series routers, you're set.

One way to get the hands-on router experience you'll need in the real world is to attend one of the seminars offered by GlobalNet Training Solutions, Inc., which is owned and run by myself. The seminars are 5 days and 11 days long and will teach you everything you need to become a CCNA (or even a CCNP, CCSP, and CCVP). Each student gets hands-on experience by configuring at least three routers and two switches.

Pearson VUE/ Thomson Prometric

When ready to sit for one of the four exams, the candidate can choose to test with a Pearson VUE or Thomson Prometric authorized testing center. Generally, the decision is made based on which group offers a testing facility closest to the candidate or which one has a center with available testing slots that match the candidate's schedule. Cisco standardizes the exams so that the candidate's experience with either type of facility is roughly the same as with the other. Visit VUE at www.vue.com and Prometric at www.prometric.com to sign up for an exam and explore testing center locations, test scheduling and cancellation policies, the procedure to obtain a testing ID, and more.

Format of the Examinations	
Cisco Certified Network Associate (640–801)	Approximately 55 to 65 questions
Introduction to Cisco Networking Technologies (640–821)	Approximately 45 to 55 questions
Introduction to Cisco Networking Devices (640–811)	Approximately 40 to 40 questions

Passing Scores	
Cisco Certified Network Associate (640–801)	849
Introduction to Cisco Networking Technologies (640–821)	825
Introduction to Cisco Networking Devices (640–811)	849

Each test is a computer-based, proctored exam and is scored out of a maximum of 1000 points. The exams aren't adaptive, which means the content and length of your exam won't change dynamically based on how well you're doing. You have 90 minutes to complete each exam. You'll receive a score report at the end of the exam indicating whether you were successful and in which objectives you missed questions, if any.

Q. How can I guarantee my success when taking a certification exam?

A. There's really no guarantee that anyone will pass any exam that they take. This uncertainty is what helps make each industry certification valuable. If there were any way to guarantee success, the certification wouldn't be worth anything to employers and clients.

Q. Can I take notes or books into the exam?

A. Absolutely not. One of the ways high-stakes, proctored exams level the playing field is to standardize what everyone enters the examination room with. This includes only what the proctor gives you, which is generally scratch paper or erasable board and something to write with, all of which you must return to the proctor after your exam. It does not include your own study materials or notes, nor does it include watches with calculators or cell phones. You'll be able to check your prohibited items with the proctor before the exam and pick them up afterward.

Q. What if I am unable to keep my scheduled exam appointment?

A. Both VUE and Prometric have very liberal policies concerning canceling and postponing exams. Check their websites or call for more information, but expect quite a bit of leeway up to and including the day before your scheduled exam.

Q. What if I need a break during my exam?

A. Generally, you're permitted to leave the exam room to go to the restroom or get a drink. However, individual testing centers might differ in the way they exercise these liberties. Your exam clock continues to run while you're away, so it's in your best interest to take care of everything before sitting down to your exam.

Q. What if my exam terminal malfunctions or I have other technical difficulties during my exam?

A. You must notify your proctor immediately of any issues you have with the functionality of your exam station, such as loss of power, lockups, or input-device inoperability, all of which are very rare. Your proctor isn't allowed to answer any questions about the exam itself.

Q. What if I forget all the stuff I have to memorize for the exam?

A. It's completely legal to perform a complete brain dump onto your scratch material of all the things you're afraid you'll forget as soon as you sit down for your exam. That way, you don't have to concentrate as much on retaining everything you struggled to store away in your brain before the exam.

Q. What do I need to have with me when I arrive at the testing center?

A. Generally, you must have two picture IDs with you. These can include a driver's license, a military ID, a credit card with your picture, and a number of other official forms of picture identification. You should have any testing confirmations you received by e-mail with you as well, but feel free to leave these in your vehicle until you find them necessary to clear up any discrepancies. Normally, you won't need them.

Q. What happens if I am caught violating any of the policies governing my sitting for a certification exam?

A. Penalties are harsh for anyone caught in violation of official exam policy. You'll fail the current exam regardless of your score and forfeit any examination fees paid. You'll likely be subject to an extended delay before you'll be eligible to sit for that exam again and possibly for any exam by the same exam sponsor, which will also delay your certification. If your certification is required for employment or advancement, you can imagine the extent of the ramifications.

Q. Can I use shortcut commands on the simulation questions?

A. Absolutely. The command sh run works the same as `show running-config`, for example.

Q. Does the question mark work on the simulations?

A. Kind of. It does provide some output of possible commands, but not enough to answer the question for you.

Analysis of the Exam

The CCNA exam is one of the hardest written exams created by Cisco. The reason is that the objectives are so broad and cover such a large area of internetworking. To pass the CCNA, you really have to be prepared.

Ability Tested

The CCNA exam certifies that the successful candidate has important knowledge and skills necessary to select, connect to, configure, and troubleshoot the various Cisco networking devices. CCNA-certified professionals can install, configure, and operate LAN, WAN, and dial access services for small networks (100 nodes or fewer).

To meet the CCNA certification skill level, you must be able to understand or do the following:

- Install, configure, and operate simple-routed LAN, routed WAN, and switched Virtual LAN (VLAN) networks.
- Understand and be able to configure IP, IGRP, EIGRP, OSPF, serial interfaces, Frame Relay, IP RIP, VLANs, Ethernet, and access lists.
- Install and/or configure a network.
- Optimize WAN through Internet-access solutions that reduce bandwidth and WAN costs, using features such as filtering with access lists.

The following list gives the objectives found on Cisco's website for the CCNA 640-801 exam:

- Planning & Designing
  - Design a simple LAN using Cisco Technology
  - Design an IP addressing scheme to meet design requirements
  - Select an appropriate routing protocol based on user requirements
  - Design a simple internetwork using Cisco technology
  - Develop an access list to meet user specifications
  - Choose WAN services to meet customer requirements
- Implementation & Operation
  - Configure routing protocols given user requirements
  - Configure IP addresses, subnet masks, and gateway addresses on routers and hosts
  - Configure a router for additional administrative functionality
  - Configure a switch with VLANS and inter-switch communication
  - Implement a LAN
  - Customize a switch configuration to meet specified network requirements
  - Manage system image and device configuration files
  - Perform an initial configuration on a router
  - Perform an initial configuration on a switch
  - Implement access lists
  - Implement simple WAN protocols
- Troubleshooting
  - Utilize the OSI model as a guide for systematic network troubleshooting
  - Perform LAN and VLAN troubleshooting
  - Troubleshoot routing protocols

o Troubleshoot IP addressing and host configuration

o Troubleshoot a device as part of a working network

o Troubleshoot an access list

o Perform simple WAN troubleshooting

- Technology

o Describe network communications using layered models

o Describe the Spanning Tree process

o Compare and contrast key characteristics of LAN environments

o Evaluate the characteristics of routing protocols

o Evaluate TCP/IP communication process and its associated protocols

o Describe the components of network devices

o Evaluate rules for packet control

o Evaluate key characteristics of WANs

Basic Skills Necessary

Believe it or not, the Cisco CCNA exam has no prerequisites. However (and you knew that was coming), it's imperative that you have the knowledge listed in the "Ability Tested" section before you attempt the CCNA exam. Don't be fooled: This exam isn't easy, and taking the exam two or three times isn't out of the ordinary.

By reading this book, you'll get a good idea of the depth of knowledge needed to pass the exam.

Types of Questions You'll Find on the CCNA Exam

The CCNA 640–801 exam includes the following test formats:

- Multiple-choice single answer
- Multiple-choice multiple answer
- Router and switch simulations
- Drag-and-drop

The Multiple-Choice Format

The Cisco exam, at least as of this writing, always tells you how many right answers to pick, so you don't have to worry about a question that states "pick all the correct answers."

Sample

1. A receiving host has failed to receive all the segments that it should acknowledge. What can the host do to improve the reliability of this communication session?

   A. Send a different source port number.
   B. Restart the virtual circuit.
   C. Decrease the sequence number.
   D. Decrease the window size.

The correct answer is D. A receiving host can control the transmitter by using flow control (TCP uses windowing by default). By decreasing the window size, the receiving host can slow down the transmitting host so the receiving host does not overflow its buffers.

Simulations

In addition to multiple-choice and fill-in response questions, Cisco Career Certifications exams may include performance simulation exam items. Although it's imperative that you understand and can fix the configurations in the simulations questions, it isn't possible to have the simulations in this book.

Drag and Drop

Here is an example of a drag-and-drop question:

1. The local router's routing has been enabled with these commands:

```
Local(config)# ip route 0.0.0.0 0.0.0.0 192.168.10.1

Local(config)# ip route 172.16.0.0 255.255.255.0 192.168.20.2

Local(config)# ip route 172.16.0.0 255.255.0.0 192.168.30.3
```

Match the destination IP address in the left column to the proper next hop address on the right:

	Next hop 192.168.10.1	Next hop 192.168.20.2	Next hop 192.168.30.3
172.16.10.10			
172.16.0.33			
172.44.98.1			
172.16.41.2			
172.16.0.23			
172.2.5.6			

The answer would look like this:

Next hop 192.168.10.1	Next hop 192.168.20.2	Next hop 192.168.30.3
172.2.5.6	172.16.0.33	172.16.10.10
172.44.98.1	172.16.0.23	172.16.41.2

In this case, you write the IP address under the appropriate hop address. The top route is a default route, so any destination IP address that doesn't match the second and third line will be sent to 192.168.10.1. The difference between the second and second line is the subnet mask. The second static route has a /24 mask, which makes the second octet the subnet address. Because the third static route has a /16 mask, the third octet isn't part of the subnet. Once you determine that the third octet has to be a zero to match the second static route, the rest of the answers fall into place.

Test-Taking Tips

The CCNA test contains between 55 and 65 questions and must be completed in 90 minutes. The amount of time and the amount of questions can change per exam. You must get a score of about 85% to pass this exam, but again, each exam can be different.

Many questions on the exam have answer choices that at first glance look identical–especially the syntax questions! Remember to read through the choices carefully, because close doesn't cut it. If you get commands in the incorrect order or forget one measly character, you'll get the question wrong.

Also, never forget that the right answer is the Cisco answer. In many cases, more than one appropriate answer is presented, but the *correct* answer is the one that Cisco recommends. On the exam, it always tells you to pick one, two, or three, never "choose all that apply."

Suggested Approaches

Here are some general tips for exam success:

- Arrive early at the exam center, so you can relax and review your study materials.
- Read the questions *carefully*. Don't jump to conclusions. Make sure you're clear about *exactly* what each question asks.
- When answering multiple-choice questions that you're not sure about, use the process of elimination to get rid of the obviously incorrect answers first. Doing this greatly improves your odds if you need to make an educated guess.
- You can't move forward and backward through the Cisco exams, so double-check your answer before clicking Next because you can't change your mind.

After you complete an exam, you'll get immediate, online notification of your pass or fail status; a printed Examination Score Report that indicates your pass or fail status; and your exam results by section. (The test administrator will give you the printed score report.) Test scores are automatically forwarded to Cisco within five working days after you take the test, so you don't need to send your score to them. If you pass the exam, you'll receive confirmation from Cisco, typically within four to six weeks.

Best Practices for Prep

There are many different ways to study for and pass your Cisco CCNA exam, and hundreds if not thousands of web sites are dedicated to Cisco certification. Although this book is meant to help you practice for the exam by using only sample exam questions, it certainly isn't meant to be your only means for achieving certification. Once you've studied and learned about internetworking with Cisco routers and switches, you can then practice using the sample questions found in this book.

Be sure to check out the Cisco CCNA Prep center at `http://forums.cisco.com/eforum/servlet/PrepCenter?page=main`. You'll have to create a login, but it's simple, and the site has some good information regarding the exam as well as test preparation. In addition, check out the Cisco Certification Exam Tutorial at `www.cisco.com/web/learning/le3/learning_certification_exam_tutorial.html`. This exam tutorial shows all the types of questions on the CCNA exam as well as how to answer them, including the simulations.

Last, don't forget to check out my *Sybex CCNA Study Guide* for information on the technologies regarding internetworking and Cisco technologies. Information regarding *CCNA: Cisco Certified Network Associate Study Guide*, 5th Edition (ISBN: 0-7821-4391-1) can be found at `www.sybex.com/WileyCDA/SybexTitle/productCd-0782143911.html` and on my web site, `www.lammle.com`.

PART II

FULL-LENGTH PRACTICE TESTS

Answer Sheets for Practice Test 1

Section 1
Multiple Choice Questions

1 Ⓐ Ⓑ Ⓒ Ⓓ Ⓔ	31 Ⓐ Ⓑ Ⓒ Ⓓ Ⓔ
2 Ⓐ Ⓑ Ⓒ Ⓓ Ⓔ	32 Ⓐ Ⓑ Ⓒ Ⓓ Ⓔ
3 Ⓐ Ⓑ Ⓒ Ⓓ Ⓔ	33 Ⓐ Ⓑ Ⓒ Ⓓ Ⓔ
4 Ⓐ Ⓑ Ⓒ Ⓓ Ⓔ	34 Ⓐ Ⓑ Ⓒ Ⓓ Ⓔ
5 Ⓐ Ⓑ Ⓒ Ⓓ Ⓔ	35 Ⓐ Ⓑ Ⓒ Ⓓ Ⓔ
6 Ⓐ Ⓑ Ⓒ Ⓓ Ⓔ	36 Ⓐ Ⓑ Ⓒ Ⓓ Ⓔ
7 Ⓐ Ⓑ Ⓒ Ⓓ Ⓔ	37 Ⓐ Ⓑ Ⓒ Ⓓ Ⓔ
8 Ⓐ Ⓑ Ⓒ Ⓓ Ⓔ	38 Ⓐ Ⓑ Ⓒ Ⓓ Ⓔ
9 Ⓐ Ⓑ Ⓒ Ⓓ Ⓔ	39 Ⓐ Ⓑ Ⓒ Ⓓ Ⓔ
10 Ⓐ Ⓑ Ⓒ Ⓓ Ⓔ	40 Ⓐ Ⓑ Ⓒ Ⓓ Ⓔ
11 Ⓐ Ⓑ Ⓒ Ⓓ Ⓔ	41 Ⓐ Ⓑ Ⓒ Ⓓ Ⓔ
12 Ⓐ Ⓑ Ⓒ Ⓓ Ⓔ	42 Ⓐ Ⓑ Ⓒ Ⓓ Ⓔ
13 Ⓐ Ⓑ Ⓒ Ⓓ Ⓔ	43 Ⓐ Ⓑ Ⓒ Ⓓ Ⓔ
14 Ⓐ Ⓑ Ⓒ Ⓓ Ⓔ	44 Ⓐ Ⓑ Ⓒ Ⓓ Ⓔ
15 Ⓐ Ⓑ Ⓒ Ⓓ Ⓔ	45 Ⓐ Ⓑ Ⓒ Ⓓ Ⓔ
16 Ⓐ Ⓑ Ⓒ Ⓓ Ⓔ	46 Ⓐ Ⓑ Ⓒ Ⓓ Ⓔ
17 Ⓐ Ⓑ Ⓒ Ⓓ Ⓔ	47 Ⓐ Ⓑ Ⓒ Ⓓ Ⓔ
18 Ⓐ Ⓑ Ⓒ Ⓓ Ⓔ	48 Ⓐ Ⓑ Ⓒ Ⓓ Ⓔ
19 Ⓐ Ⓑ Ⓒ Ⓓ Ⓔ	49 Ⓐ Ⓑ Ⓒ Ⓓ Ⓔ
20 Ⓐ Ⓑ Ⓒ Ⓓ Ⓔ	50 Ⓐ Ⓑ Ⓒ Ⓓ Ⓔ
21 Ⓐ Ⓑ Ⓒ Ⓓ Ⓔ	51 Ⓐ Ⓑ Ⓒ Ⓓ Ⓔ
22 Ⓐ Ⓑ Ⓒ Ⓓ Ⓔ	52 Ⓐ Ⓑ Ⓒ Ⓓ Ⓔ
23 Ⓐ Ⓑ Ⓒ Ⓓ Ⓔ	53 Ⓐ Ⓑ Ⓒ Ⓓ Ⓔ
24 Ⓐ Ⓑ Ⓒ Ⓓ Ⓔ	54 Ⓐ Ⓑ Ⓒ Ⓓ Ⓔ
25 Ⓐ Ⓑ Ⓒ Ⓓ Ⓔ	55 Ⓐ Ⓑ Ⓒ Ⓓ Ⓔ
26 Ⓐ Ⓑ Ⓒ Ⓓ Ⓔ	
27 Ⓐ Ⓑ Ⓒ Ⓓ Ⓔ	
28 Ⓐ Ⓑ Ⓒ Ⓓ Ⓔ	
29 Ⓐ Ⓑ Ⓒ Ⓓ Ⓔ	
30 Ⓐ Ⓑ Ⓒ Ⓓ Ⓔ	

CUT HERE

Directions: For each of the following questions, select the choice that best answers the question or completes the statement.

1. Of the choices below, which one is needed for connectivity in a Frame Relay network if Inverse ARP isn't operational?

   A. `frame-relay arp`
   B. `frame-relay map`
   C. `frame-relay interface dlci`
   D. `frame-relay Imi-type`

2. Look at Figure 1-1. As soon as SwitchB was added to the network, VLAN connectivity problems began cropping up. Why?

```
SwitchA# show vtp status              SwitchB# show vtp status

VTP version                  : 2       VTP version                  : 2
Configuration Revision       : 1       Configuration Revision       : 7
Maximum VLANs supported locally : 64   Maximum VLANs supported locally : 64
Number of existing VLANs     : 8       Number of existing VLANs     : 4
VTP Operating Mode           : Server  VTP Operating Mode           : Server
VTP Domain Name              : cisco   VTP Domain Name              : cisco
VTP Pruning Mode             : disabled VTP Pruning Mode            : disabled
V2 Mode                      : disabled VTP V2 Mode                 : disabled
```

Figure 1-1

   A. Both switches are in server mode in the same domain.
   B. The revision number of SwitchB was higher than the revision number of SwitchA.
   C. SwitchA was not rebooted prior to adding SwitchB to the network.
   D. V-2 was not enabled.
   E. VTP pruning was not activated, so the new paths of the network have not been recalculated.

3. Look at Figure 1-2. Note both the IP addresses and how the network's routers are configured. Let's say the Sys Admin types in the `show ip eigrp neighbors` command from Router1 and gets the resulting output beneath the topology. Of the following, which is true?

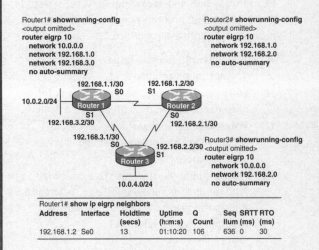

```
Router1# showrunning-config          Router2# showrunning-config
<output omitted>                     <output omitted>
router eigrp 10                      router eigrp 10
  network 10.0.0.0                     network 192.168.1.0
  network 192.168.1.0                  network 192.168.2.0
  network 192.168.3.0                  no auto-summary
  no auto-summary
```

```
Router3# showrunning-config
<output omitted>
router eigrp 10
  network 10.0.0.0
  network 192.168.2.0
  no auto-summary
```

```
Router1# show ip eigrp neighbors
Address      Interface  Holdtime  Uptime    Q      Seq  SRTT RTO
                        (secs)    (h:m:s)   Count  Ilum (ms)  (ms)

192.168.1.2  Se0        13        01:10:20  106    636  0     30
```

Figure 1-2

   A. It's normal for Router1 to show one active neighbor at a time to prevent routing loops.
   B. Routing isn't configured completely in Router3.
   C. The IP addresses aren't configured properly on the Router 1 and Router3 interfaces.
   D. The `no auto-summary` command configured on the routers prevents Router1 and Router2 from forming a neighbor relationship.

GO ON TO THE NEXT PAGE

4. Match each EIGRP item on the left with the correct interpretation on the right. (You won't use all the terms on the right.)

Neighbor table	Backup route
Topology table	Lists adjacent routers
Routing table	Contains only successor routes
Successor route	Route installed in routing table
Summary route	Holds all feasible routes in the AS
Feasible successor	

5. You're configuring a router to act as a hub within a Frame-relay hub-and-spoke topology. Why would you opt for using point-to-point subinterfaces instead of a multipoint interface?

A. It avoids split horizon issues with distance vector routing protocols.

B. Only one IP network address needs to be used to communicate with all spoke devices.

C. Point-to-point subinterfaces offer greater security than multipoint interface configuration.

D. Only a single physical interface is needed with point-to-point subinterfaces, whereas a multipoint interface logically combines multiple physical interfaces.

6. Choose two of the following that best describe the process identifier used to run OSPF on a router.

A. It's locally significant.

B. It's globally significant.

C. It's needed to identify a unique instance of an OSPF database.

D. It's an optional parameter required only if multiple OSPF processes are running on the router.

E. All routers in the same OSPF area must have the same process ID if they are to exchange routing information.

7. Correctly complete the basic switch configuration by matching each switch IOS command in the left column to its relevant function in the right column.

IP default gateway	Allows access to high-level testing commands such as `debug`
Interface vlan 1	Allows access to configuration commands that affect the systems as a whole
Hostname	Sets the system name
Ip address	Activates the interface configuration mode for vlan1
Enable	Enables the switch-management interface
No shutdown	Sets the switch-management IP address
Configure terminal	Allows the switch to be managed from remote networks

8. How would the interface clock rate be established when a router is connected to a Frame Relay WAN link using a serial DTE interface?

A. It is supplied by the CSU/DSU.

B. It is supplied by the far-end router.

C. It is determined by the `clock rate` command.

D. It is supplied by layer 1 bit stream timing.

9. Choose which of the following `show ip interface` command output options signifies a layer 1 problem.

A. Serial0/1 is up, line protocol is up

B. Serial0/1 is up, line protocol is down

C. Serial0/1 is down, line protocol is down

D. Serial0/1 is administratively down, line protocol is down.

10. Pick *two* of the following reasons why a network administrator would use access lists.

A. To control VTY access into a router

B. To control broadcast traffic through a router

C. To filter traffic as it passes through a router

D. To filter traffic that originates from a router

E. To replace passwords as a line of defense against security incursions

11. You have two routers directly connected via a serial link. One of them is made by Cisco; the other is a different brand. Choose the command you would use on a Cisco router to create a WAN connection between these two routers.

    A. `Lab(config-if)# encapsulation hdlc ansi`

    B. `Lab(config-if)# encapsulation ppp`

    C. `Lab(config-if)# encapsulation frame-relay default`

    D. `Lab(config-if)# encapsulation isdn`

12. Look at Figure 1-3. In it, you can see a new, 60-host subnet that is now part of the network. Of the options below, which one best provides a sufficient number of usable addresses while also wasting the fewest addresses?

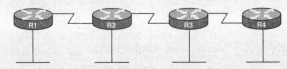

192.168.1.0/27   192.168.1.32/28   192.168.1.48/28   60 hosts

Figure 1-3

    A. 192.168.1.56/26

    B. 192.168.1.56/27

    C. 192.168.1.64/26

    D. 192.168.1.64/27

13. Choose *two* options that depict the information used by a router running a link-state protocol to create and sustain its topological database.

    A. Hello packets

    B. SAP messages sent by other routers

    C. LSAs from other routers

    D. Beacons received on point to point links

    E. Routing tables received from other link-state routers

    F. TTL packets from designated routers

14. Look at Figure 1-4. Serial0/0 isn't replying to a ping from a host on the FastEthernet0/0 LAN. What would resolve this problem?

```
BHM# show ip interface brief
Interface         IP-Address     OK?  Method Status                Protocol
FastEthernet0/0   192.168.16.1   YES  NVRAM  up                    up
Serial0/0         192.168.15.2   YES  NVRAM  administratively down  down
FastEthernet0/1   192.168.17.1   YES  NVRAM  up                    up
Serial0/1         unassigned     YES  NVRAM  administratively down  down
```

Figure 1-4

    A. Enable the serial 0/0 interface.

    B. Correct the IP address for serial 0/0.

    C. Correct the IP address for FastEthernet 0/0.

    D. Change the encapsulation type on serial 0/0.

    E. Enable auto-configuration on the serial 0/0 interface.

15. What can you accurately conclude by analyzing the router output depicted in Figure 1-5?

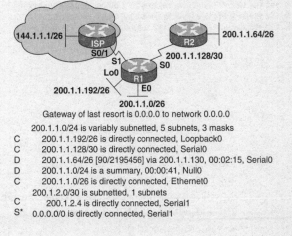

```
Gateway of last resort is 0.0.0.0 to network 0.0.0.0
     200.1.1.0/24 is variably subnetted, 5 subnets, 3 masks
C       200.1.1.192/26 is directly connected, Loopback0
C       200.1.1.128/30 is directly connected, Serial0
D       200.1.1.64/26 [90/2195456] via 200.1.1.130, 00:02:15, Serial0
D       200.1.1.0/24 is a summary, 00:00:41, Null0
C       200.1.1.0/26 is directly connected, Ethernet0
     200.1.2.0/30 is subnetted, 1 subnets
C       200.1.2.4 is directly connected, Serial1
S*   0.0.0.0/0 is directly connected, Serial1
```

Figure 1-5

    A. 200.1.1.64 is a default route.

    B. The output shows that there are three default routes.

    C. The output came from router R2.

    D. The output came from a router that has four physical interfaces.

    E. EIGRP is in use in this network.

GO ON TO THE NEXT PAGE

16. Which of the following best describes the purpose of Inverse ARP?

- **A.** To map a known IP address to a Mac address
- **B.** To map a known DLCI to a Mac address
- **C.** To map a known Mac address to an IP address
- **D.** To map a known DLCI to an IP address
- **E.** To map a known IP address to a SPID
- **F.** To map a known SPID to a Mac address

17. Look at the router table output in Figure 1-6. The corporate router receives an IP packet with a source IP address of 192.168.214.20 and a destination address of 192.168.22.3. Which of the following represents what the router will do with this packet?

```
Corp#show ip route
...
Gateway of last resort is not set

C  192.168.13.0/24 is directly connected, Serial0/1
C  192.168.14.0/24 is directly connected, FastEthernet0/0
C  192.168.15.0/24 is directly connected, Serial0/0.102
C  192.168.20.0/24 is directly connected, Serial0/0.117
R  192.168.16.0/24 [120/1] via 192.168.15.2, 00:00:05, Serial0/0.102
R  192.168.17.0/24 [120/1] via 192.168.15.2, 00:00:05, Serial0/0.102
R  192.168.30.0/24 [120/2] via 192.168.20.2, 00:00:05, Serial0/0.117
R  192.168.19.0/24 [120/1] via 192.168.20.2, 00:00:25, Serial0/0.117
R  192.168.21.0/24 [120/3] via 192.168.20.2, 00:00:25, Serial0/0.117
R  192.168.214.0/24 [120/1] via 192.168.14.2, 00:00:22, FastEthernet0/0
```

Figure 1-6

- **A.** It will encapsulate the packet as a frame relay and forward it out of Serial 0.0.117.
- **B.** It will discard the packet and send an ICMP Destination Unreachable message out interface FastEthernet 0/0.
- **C.** It will forward the packet out interface Serial 0/1 and send an ICMP echo reply message out interface Serial 0/0.102.
- **D.** It will change the IP packet to an ARP frame and forward it out as FastEthernet 0/0.

18. You're testing an ISDN circuit that uses PPP between two IP hosts. Match the indicator in the left column with the OSI layer on the right that it confirms.

The line is up.	Layer 3
A ping of the remote host is successful.	Layer 2
A telnet connection to the host is successful.	Layer 1
A dial session to the remote host is successful.	

19. Look at Figure 1-7. One of the routers has 25 hosts with one connection to the Internet through the R1 router. Which routing configurations would be the best to implement on both the R1 and ISP routers?

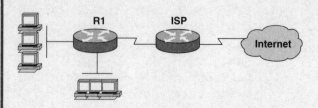

Figure 1-7

- **A.** BGP on both routers
- **B.** RIP on both routers
- **C.** Default routes on both routers
- **D.** BGP on the ISP router and a static route on R1
- **E.** A default route on R1 and a static route on the ISP router

20. Look at Figure 1-8. Which *two* of the following options depict what the output line of `show ip route` tells you?

R 10.10.10.8 [120/2] via 10.10.10.6, 00:00:25, Serial0/1

Figure 1-8

- **A.** The next routing update can be expected in 35 seconds.
- **B.** The IP address 10.10.10.6 is configured on S0/1.
- **C.** The IP address 10.10.10.8 is configured on S0/1.
- **D.** This route is using the default administrative distance.
- **E.** The 10.10.10.8 network is two hops away from this router.

21. Without a loopback interface, which of the following accurately describes what an OSPF router would use for the router ID if all OSPF routers in one area were configured with the same priority value?

    A. The IP address of the Fast Ethernet interface

    B. The IP address of the console-management interface

    C. The highest IP address among its active interfaces

    D. The lowest IP address among its active interfaces

    E. The priority value until a loopback interface is configured

22. Your VLAN with the subnet address of 172.16.4.0/22 contains hosts that must be prevented from accessing websites on the Internet. Match the options from the left column and write them on the right to fulfill this command: `access-list 156 deny protocol 172.16.4.0 mask any eq port`. (Obviously, you won't use all the options.)

23	protocol	mask	port
80			
Ip			
Tcp			
Udp			
0.0.0.3			
0.0.0.255			
0.0.3.255			
23			
80			

23. Look at Figure 1-9. What would you use to enable communication between host A and host B?

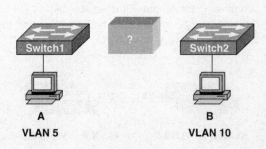

Figure 1-9

    A. A CSU/DSU connected to the switches with crossover cables

    B. A router connected to the switch with straight-through cables

    C. A router connected to the switches with crossover cables

    D. A straight-through cable only

    E. A crossover cable only

GO ON TO THE NEXT PAGE

24. Look at Figure 1-10. You have two 2950 switches that connect via ports Fa0/24 and a straight-through cable. What facts can you gain by combining the output of the `show cdp neighbor` command from both switches and the information given?

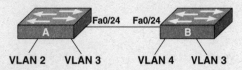

A# **show cdp neighbor**
Capability Codes: R - Router, T - Trans Bridge, B - Source Route Bridge
        S - Switch, H - Host, I - IGMP, r - Repeater, P - Phone

Device ID   Local Intrfce   Holdtme Capability Platform Port ID

A#█
_____

B# **show cdp neighbor**
Capability Codes: R - Router, T - Trans Bridge, B - Source Route Bridge
        S - Switch, H - Host, I - IGMP, r - Repeater, P - Phone

Device ID   Local Intrfce   Holdtme Capability Platform Port ID

B#█

Figure 1-10

A. Port Fa0/24 on each switch must be configured on VLAN 1 in order for the switches to see neighbor information.

B. Port Fa0/24 on each switch must be configured as a trunk port in order for neighbor information to be received.

C. The switches are not cabled properly.

D. An IP address needs to be assigned to both switches.

E. VTP is incorrectly configured on switch A.

25. On which OSI layer does the protocol operate that imparts the information you get by using the `show cdp neighbors` command?

A. Physical

B. Data link

C. Network

D. Transport

E. Application

26. Figure 1-11 depicts a corporate LAN that uses IP network 172.28.4.0/22 for all departments. All hosts use 172.28.4.1 as a default gateway address. You've been called on to address the issue of excessive broadcasts slowing network performance. What would you do to resolve the problem?

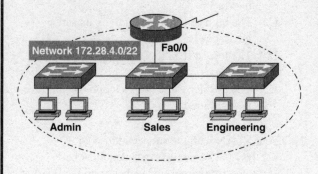

Figure 1-11

A. Implement VLANs after creating IP subnets for each department.

B. Configure each NIC and switch port to operate at full duplex.

C. Increase the number of switches in the network closet of each department.

D. Change the router-to-switch connection from Fast Ethernet to Gigabit Ethernet.

E. Configure an access control list on the router to prevent broadcast forwarding.

27. Look at Figure 1-12. Pick the two commands you must configure on the 2950 switch and the router that will permit communication between host 1 and host 2.

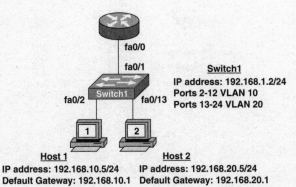

Host 1
IP address: 192.168.10.5/24
Default Gateway: 192.168.10.1

Host 2
IP address: 192.168.20.5/24
Default Gateway: 192.168.20.1

Figure 1-12

A.
```
Router(config)# interface
fastethernet 0/0
Router(config-if)# ip address
192.168.1.1 255.255.255.0
Router(config-if)# no shut
down
```
B.
```
Router(config)# interface
fastethernet 0/0
Router(config-if)# no shut
down
Router(config)# interface
fastethernet 0/0.1
Router(config-subif)#
encapsulation dot1q 10
Router(config-subif)# ip
address 192.168.10.1
255.255.255.0
Router(config)# interface
fastethernet 0/0.2
Router(config-subif)#
encapsulation dot1q 20
Router(config-subif)# ip
address 192.168.20.1
255.255.255.0
```
C.
```
Router(config)# router eigrp
100
Router(config-router)# network
192.168.10.0
Router(config-router)# network
192.168.20.0
```

D.
```
Switch1(config)# vlan database
Switch1(config-vlan)# vtp
domain XYZ
Switch1(config-vlan)# vtp
server
```
E.
```
Switch1(config)# interface
fastethernet 0/1
Switch1(config-if)# switchport
mode trunk
```
F.
```
Switch1(config)# interface
vlan 1
Switch1(config-if)# ip default
gateway 192.168.1.1
```

28. Look at Figure 1-13. In it, you can see that the switches have been configured with static VLANs. But when testing, the Sys Admin finds that VLAN 20 on SwitchA isn't connecting with VLAN 30 on SwitchB. What steps should be taken solve this problem?

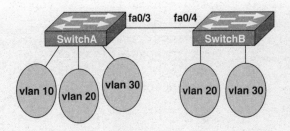

Figure 1-13

A. Configure the interconnected ports on SwitchA and SwitchB in access mode.

B. Connect the two switches with a straight-through cable.

C. Add a Layer 3 device to connect VLAN 20 and VLAN 30.

D. Configure the management VLAN with IP addresses.

E. Ensure that the VTP passwords match on both switches.

GO ON TO THE NEXT PAGE

29. Of the choices below, which *three* host addresses are valid members of networks that can be routed across the Internet?

    A. 10.172.13.65

    B. 172.16.223.125

    C. 172.62.12.29

    D. 192.168.23.252

    E. 198.234.12.95

    F. 212.193.48.254

30. Choose the command that will configure a switch port to use the IEEE standard method of adding VLAN membership information into Ethernet frames.

    A. `Switch(config)# switchport trunk encapsulation isl`

    B. `Switch(config)# switchport trunk encapsulation ietf`

    C. `Switch(config)# switchport trunk encapsulation dot1q`

    D. `Switch(config-if)# switchport trunk encapsulation isl`

    E. `Switch(config-if)# switchport trunk encapsulation ietf`

    F. `Switch(config-if)# switchport trunk encapsulation dot1q`

31. Look at Figure 1-14 with these goals in mind:

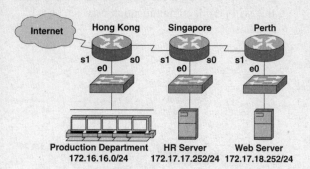

Figure 1-14

    1. Allow Telnet from the Internet to the HR server.

    2. Allow HTTP access from the Internet to the web server.

    3. All other traffic from the Internet should be blocked.

Choose the *two* access list statements you need to achieve your objective.

    A. `access-list 101 permit tcp any 172.17.18.252 0.0.0.0 eq 80`

    B. `access-list 101 permit tcp any 172.17.17.252 0.0.0.0 eq 23`

    C. `access-list 101 deny tcp any 172.17.18.252 0.0.0.0 eq 80`

    D. `access-list 101 permit tcp 172.17.18.252 0.0.0.0 any eq 23`

    E. `access-list 101 deny tcp 172.17.18.252 0.0.0.0 eq 23`

    F. `access-list 101 permit tcp 172.17.18.252 0.0.0.0 eq 23`

32. Look at the newly installed network in Figure 1-15. Host B can access the Internet, but it can't ping Host C. Why?

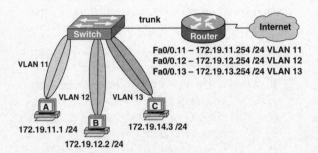

Fa0/0.11 – 172.19.11.254 /24 VLAN 11
Fa0/0.12 – 172.19.12.254 /24 VLAN 12
Fa0/0.13 – 172.19.13.254 /24 VLAN 13

172.19.11.1 /24
172.19.12.2 /24
172.19.14.3 /24

Figure 1-15

A. Host B should be in VLAN 13.
B. The address of Host C is incorrect.
C. The gateway for Host B is in a different subnet than the host is on.
D. The switch port that sends VLAN 13 frames from the switch to the router is shut down.
E. The switch port connected to the router is incorrectly configured as an access port.

33. If you needed to permit Internet access for the hosts in your network assigned addresses in the 192.168.8.0 through 198.168.15.255 range, which wildcard mask would you employ to achieve that objective?

A. 0.0.0.0
B. 0.0.0.255
C. 0.0.255.255
D. 0.0.7.255
E. 0.0.3.255

34. Of the following situations, when would multiple copies of the same unicast frame be the most likely to be relayed in a switched LAN?

A. During high-traffic periods
B. After broken links are re-established
C. When upper-layer protocols require high reliability
D. In an improperly implemented redundant topology
E. When a dual-ring topology is in use

35. You've just inserted a new router into an established OSPF network, but the networks attached to the recently added router aren't showing up in the routing tables of the other OSPF routers. By looking at the information within the partial configuration given below, what's causing this issue?

```
Router(config)# router ospf 1
Router(config-router)# network
10.0.0.0 255.0.0.0 area 0
```

A. The process id is configured improperly.
B. The OSPF area is configured improperly.
C. The network wildcard mask is configured improperly.
D. The network number is configured improperly.
E. The AS is configured improperly.
F. The network subnet mask is configured improperly.

36. Choose *two* options that best describe the steps of the OSI encapsulation process.

A. The transport layer divides a data stream into segments and adds reliability and control information.
B. The data link layer adds physical source and destination addresses and an FCS to the segment.
C. Packets are created when the network encapsulates a frame with source and destination host addresses and protocol-related control information.
D. Packets are created when the network layer adds Layer 3 addresses and control information to the segment.
E. The presentation layer translates bits into voltages for transmission across the physical link.

GO ON TO THE NEXT PAGE

37. Match and drag the security features in the column on the left to the exact security risks they help protect against in the right column. (You'll have some left over.)

Access-group	Remote access to device console
Console password	Access to the console 0 line
Enable secret	Access to connected networks or resources
CHAP authentication	Viewing of passwords
VTY password	Access to privileged mode
Service password-encryption	

38. You need to stop 172.16.1.5 from accessing the 172.16.4.0 network, but permit access to all other networks. Choose the command sequence that will properly apply this access list.

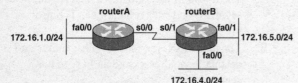

```
access-list 10 permit host 172.16.1.5
access-list 10 deny 172.16.1.0 0.0.0.255
access-list 10 permit any
```

Figure 1-16

A. `routerA(config)# interface fa0/0`
`routerA(config-if)# ip access-group 10 in`

B. `routerA(config)# interface s0/0`
`routerA(config-if)# ip access-group 10 out`

C. `routerB(config)# interface fa0/1`
`routerB(config-if)# ip access-group 10 out`

D. `routerB(config)# interface fa0/0`
`routerB(config-if)# ip access-group 10 out`

E. `routerB(config)# interface s0/1`
`routerB(config-if)# ip access-group 10 out`

39. Your security policy dictates that only one host can be permitted to dynamically attach to each interface, and if this policy is violated, the interface should immediately shut down. Choose the *two* commands you need to configure on the 2950 Catalyst switch to implement your policy.

A. `Switch1(config-if)# switchport port-security maximum 1`

B. `Switch1(config)# mac-address-table secure`

C. `Switch1(config)#Access-list 10 permit ip host`

D. `Switch1(config-if)# switchport port-security violation shutdown`

E. `Switch1(config-if)# ip access-group 10`

40. When analyzing Figure 1-17, what does the term *dynamic* mean as indicated in the output of the `show frame-relay map` command?

R1# **show frame-relay map**
Serial0/0 (up): ip 172.16.3.1 dlci 100 (0×64, 0×1840), dynamic
broadcast,, status defined, active

Figure 1-17

A. The Serial0/0 interface is passing traffic.
B. The DLCI 100 was dynamically allocated by the router.
C. The Serial0/0 interface acquired the IP address of 172.16.3.1 from a DHCP server.
D. The DLCI 100 will be dynamically changed as required to adapt to changes in the Frame Relay cloud.
E. The mapping between the DLCI 100 and the end station IP address 172.16.3.1 was learned through Inverse ARP.

41. You're troubleshooting a connectivity issue when you notice that a port-status LED on a Cisco Catalyst series switch is alternating green and amber. What does this mean?

A. The port is experiencing errors.
B. The port is administrator disabled.
C. The port is blocked by spanning tree.
D. The port has an active link with normal traffic activity.

42. You need to reconfigure a Catalyst 2950, and you must make sure the old configuration is erased. Which *two* options will ensure you're successful?

    A. Erase flash.

    B. Restart the switch.

    C. Delete the VLAN database.

    D. Erase the running configuration.

    E. Erase the startup configuration.

    F. Modify the configuration register.

43. Look at Figure 1-18. You've configured a new router and entered the `copy startup-config running-config` command on it. You power down the router and set it up at a remote location, but when it starts up, it enters the system configuration dialog shown in the figure. What's causing this to happen?

```
---System Configuration Dialog---

Would you like to enter the initial configuration dialog? [yes/no]:
% Please answer 'yes' or 'no'.
Would you like to enter the initial configuration dialog? [yes/no]: n

Would you like to terminate autoinstall? [yes]:

Press RETURN to get started!
```

Figure 1-18

    A. The network administrator failed to save the configuration.

    B. The configuration register is set to 0x2100.

    C. The boot system flash command is missing from the configuration.

    D. The configuration register is set to 0x2102.

    E. The router is configured with the boot system startup command.

44. On point-to-point networks, OSPF hello packets are addressed to which address?

    A. 127.0.0.1

    B. 172.16.0.1

    C. 192.168.0.15

    D. 223.0.0.2

    E. 224.0.0.5

45. What is the purpose of spanning tree in a switched LAN?

    A. To provide a mechanism for network monitoring in switched environments

    B. To prevent routing loops in networks with redundant switched paths

    C. To prevent switching loops in networks with redundant switched paths

    D. To manage the addition, deletion, and naming of VLANs across multiple switches

    E. To segment a network into multiple collision domains

46. Look at Figure 1-19. If all switches are set to the default priority setting, which switch will be the root bridge?

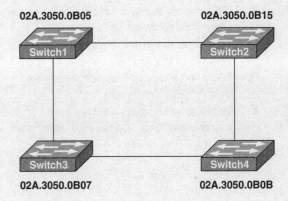

Figure 1-19

    A. Switch 1

    B. Switch 2

    C. Switch 3

    D. Switch 4

GO ON TO THE NEXT PAGE

47. Looking at Figure 1-20, why hasn't the network converged?

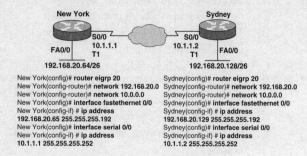

New York(config)# **router eigrp 20**
New York(config-router)# **network 192.168.20.0**
New York(config-router)# **network 10.0.0.0**
New York(config)# **interface fastethernet 0/0**
New York(config-if) # **ip address**
192.168.20.65 255.255.255.192
New York(config)# **interface serial 0/0**
New York(config-if) # **ip address**
10.1.1.1 255.255.255.252

Sydney(config)# **router eigrp 20**
Sydney(config-router)# **network 192.168.20.0**
Sydney(config-router)# **network 10.0.0.0**
Sydney(config)# **interface fastethernet 0/0**
Sydney(config-if) # **ip address**
192.168.20.129 255.255.255.192
Sydney(config)# **interface serial 0/0**
Sydney(config-if) # **ip address**
10.1.1.2 255.255.255.252

Figure 1-20

A. The `no auto-summary` command needs to be applied to the routers.

B. The network numbers have not been properly configured on the routers.

C. The subnet masks for the network numbers have not been properly configured.

D. The autonomous system number has not been properly configured.

E. The bandwidth values have not been properly configured on the serial interfaces.

48. Examine Figure 1-21. You've installed SwitchB, and you want to configure it to allow remote access from the management workstation connected to SwitchA. Choose the set of commands that will enable you to achieve this.

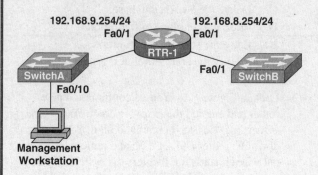

Figure 1-21

A.
```
SwitchB(config)# interface
FastEthernet 0/1
SwitchB(config-if)# ip address
192.168.8.252 255.255.255.0
SwitchB(config-if)# no shutdown
```

B.
```
SwitchB(config)# interface
vlan 1
SwitchB(config-if)# ip address
192.168.8.252 255.255.255.0
SwitchB(config-if)# ip default
gateway 192.168.8.254
255.255.255.0
SwitchB(config-if)# no shutdown
```

C.
```
SwitchB(config)# ip default-
gateway 192.168.8.254
SwitchB(config)# interface
vlan 1
SwitchB(config-if)# ip address
192.168.8.252 255.255.255.0
SwitchB(config-if)# no shutdown
```

D.
```
SwitchB(config)# ip default
network 192.168.8.254
SwitchB(config)# interface
vlan 1
SwitchB(config-if)# ip address
192.168.8.252 255.255.255.0
SwitchB(config-if)# no shutdown
```

E.
```
SwitchB(config)# ip route
192.168.8.254 255.255.255.0
SwitchB(config)# interface
FastEthernet 0/1
SwitchB(config-if)# ip address
192.168.8.252 255.255.255.0
SwitchB(config-if)# no shutdown
```

49. Choose the *three* feasible trunking modes for a switch port.

    A. Transparent

    B. Auto

    C. On

    D. Desirable

    E. Client

    F. Forwarding

50. Which *two* commands would you use to configure running OSPF, plus adding network 192.168.16.0/24 to OSPF area 0?

    A. `Router(config)# router ospf 0`

    B. `Router(config)# router ospf 1`

    C. `Router(config)# router ospf area 0`

    D. `Router(config-router)# network 192.168.16.0 0.0.0.255 0`

    E. `Router(config-router)# network 192.168.16.0 0.0.0.255 area 0`

    F. `Router(config-router)# network 192.168.16.0 255.255.255.0 area 0`

51. You've configured an interface with the access list shown. Based on the access list, which information packets in the left column would be permitted, and which packets would be denied?

Access-list 107 deny tcp 207.16.12.0 0.0.3.255 any eq http

Access-list 107 permit ip any any

Source IP 207.16.32.14, destination application: http	
Source IP 207.16.15.9, destination port 23	
Source IP 207.16.14.7, destination port 80	
Source IP 207.16.13.14, destination application http	
Source IP 207.16.16.14, destination port 53	

52. You've configured the Ethernet 0 interface of a router with address 10.64.0.1. 255.224.0.0 and the Ethernet 1 interface with address 10.96.0.1/11. Choose the *two* commands you would use to configure RIP version 1 on this router so it would advertise both networks to the neighboring routers.

    A. `Router(config)# router rip`
`Router(config-router)# network 10.0.0.0 255.224.0.0`

    B. `Router(config)# router rip`
`Router(config-router)# network 10.64.0.1 255.224.0.0`
`Router(config-router)# network 10.96.0.1 255.224.0.0`

    C. `Router(config)# router rip`
`Router(config-router)# network 10.0.0.0`

    D. `Router(config)# router rip`
`Router(config-router)# network 10.64.0.0`
`Router(config-router)# network 10.96.0.0`

53. Look at Figure 1-22, and give the reason the switch has two MAC addresses assigned to the FastEthernet 0/1 port in the switch address table.

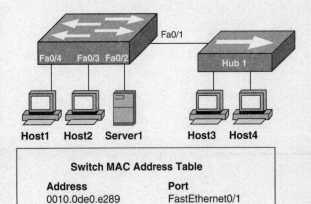

Switch MAC Address Table

Address	Port
0010.0de0.e289	FastEthernet0/1
0010.7b00.1545	FastEthernet0/1
0060.5cf4.0076	FastEthernet0/2
00e0.1e9f.3900	FastEthernet0/4

Figure 1-22

    A. Data from two of the devices connected to the switch has been sent to Host3.

    B. Data from Host3 and Host4 has been received by the switch port FastEthernet 0/1.

    C. Either Host3 or Host4 has just had the NIC replaced.

    D. Host3 and Host4 are on two different VLANs.

GO ON TO THE NEXT PAGE

54. A Class C network address has been subnetted with a /27 mask. Which of the following addresses is a broadcast address used for subnets?

    A. 201.57.78.33

    B. 201.57.78.84

    C. 201.57.78.87

    D. 201.57.78.97

    E. 201.57.78.159

    F. 201.57.78.254

55. Where are EIGRP successor routes stored?

    A. In the routing table only

    B. In the neighbor table only

    C. In the topology table only

    D. In the routing table and neighbor table

    E. In the routing table and topology table

    F. In the topology table and neighbor table

Answer Key for Practice Test 1

1. B	**15.** E	**29.** C, E, F	**44.** E
2. B	**16.** D	**30.** F	**45.** C
3. B	**17.** B	**31.** A, B	**46.** A
4. See Answer Explanation	**18.** See Answer Explanation	**32.** B	**47.** A
		33. D	**48.** C
5. A	**19.** C	**34.** D	**49.** B, C, D
6. A, C	**20.** D, E	**35.** C	**50.** B, E
7. See Answer Explanation	**21.** C	**36.** A, D	**51.** See Answer Explanation
	22. See Answer Explanation	**37.** See Answer Explanation	
8. A			**52.** C, D
9. C	**23.** B	**38.** D	**53.** B
10. A, C	**24.** C	**39.** A, D	**54.** E
11. B	**25.** B	**40.** E	**55.** E
12. C	**26.** A	**41.** A	
13. A, C	**27.** B, E	**42.** C, E	
14. A	**28.** C	**43.** A	

Answer Explanations for Practice Test 1

1. **B.** Inverse ARP is used to resolve an IP address to local DLCI number. If a router does not support IARP or is used on the network, a frame-relay map must be configured for each PVC.

2. **B.** If the revision number of the new switch is higher, then the other switches will begin taking the new switches' update, which could cause connectivity problems.

3. **B.** From the output of the `show ip eigrp neighbors` command, the administrator can see that Router3 has not found Router1 as a neighbor. This is because Router3 does not have a network statement for the 192.168.3.1 network.

4.

Neighbor table	Lists adjacent routers
Topology table	Holds all feasible routes in the AS
Routing table	Contains only successor routes
Successor route	Route installed in routing table
Feasible successor	Backup route

EIGRP creates three tables to providing routing services, unlike RIP that creates only one. The three tables are neighbor table, which lists all adjacent neighbors; the topology table that lists every link in the network, called successor routers and feasible successor router (backup routes) and the routing table, where the success routes are copied from the topology table and placed.

5. **A.** In a case where split horizon is the problem, split horizon defines the rule "it is never useful to send routing information back in the direction from which it came." With this rule in place, routing updates that come from spoke routers would never be relayed from the hub router. By implementing point-to-point links and sub-interfaces on the spoke router, the routing protocol looks at each of the sub-interfaces as separate physical links, allowing the updates to go between each point-to-point link and update the spoke routers.

6. **A, C** The OSPF process id is locally significant and identifies each individual instance of OSPF that is running, should multiple instances be running on a single router.

7.

IP default gateway	Allows the switch to be managed from remote networks
Interface vlan 1	Activates the interface configuration mode for vlan1
Hostname	Sets the system name
Ip address	Sets the switch management IP address
Enable	Allows access to high level testing commands such as debug
No shutdown	Enables the switch management interface
Configure terminal	Allows access to configuration commands that affect the systems as a whole

Switches do not need an IP address. It is very important that you remember this. IP addresses are used on a switch for management reasons only. The ip default-gateway command allows you to manage the switch from outside your local LAN or VLAN. If you do set an IP address, it would be set under the management VLAN, which by default is VLAN 1. A router or switch name is set by using the hostname command. You can set an IP address on an interface of a router or switch interface, logical or physical, by using the ip address command. The enable command allows you to access privledge mode. No shutdown enables and interface. All switch ports are enabled by default and the configure terminal command puts you into global configuration mode.

8. A. In a serial connection, only a device or the end of the cable is the DTE (router in most cases), and the other device or end of the cable is the DCE (CSU/DSU or ISP device). In this type of connection, the clock rate and control for the connection come from the DCE device.

9. C. In the interface output *Serial0/1 is down, line protocol is down*, the section *Serial0/1 is down* means that the interface is not receiving carrier detect; this is a physical layer (layer 1) problem. *Line protocol is down* means that the interface is not receiving keepalives from the remote router, which is considered a data link (layer 2) problem.

10. A, C. Access lists filter traffic as it is trying to pass through the router, and traffic generated at the router will not be filtered. Also, by placing an access list on the VTY lines, you can provide telnet security on your router.

11. B. Cisco uses the default serial encapsulation of HDLC, which is proprietary. If you have a Cisco router and a different brand of router on another side of the link, you have to use another encapsulation. One example is PPP.

12. C. Having 60 hosts on the network requires that at least 6 host bits be left from the network bits. 6 host bits will create 62 hosts on the network. Because network 192.168.1.64 is the next network, that will be the network id. With 6 host bits, that leaves 26 network bits or a /26 mask.

13. A, C. A router running a link-state protocol uses hello packets to find neighbors and form adjacencies. Once an adjacency has been formed, it will use link-state advertisement (LSA) packets to exchange topology information and updates when changes occur.

14. A. *Administratively down* means the interface must be enabled with the `no shutdown` command.

15. E. The *D* in the router output means the router is using EIGRP as a routing protocol. There are three directly connected networks attached to this router.

16. D. Inverse ARP is the automatic process of finding a DLCI from a known IP address. If this function is not available, then the mapping of the DLCI to the IP address must be done manually through the `frame-relay map` command.

17. B. Because there is no route entry for the 192.168.22.0 network, the router will discard the frame and use ICMP to tell the transmitting host (out fa0/0) that the network is unreachable.

18.

The line is up.	Layer 2
A ping of the remote host is successful.	Layer 3
A dial session to the remote host is successful.	Layer 1

A successful dial session is the Physical layer, or layer 1, the "line is up" is a Data Link, or layer 2 function, and ping is a program that runs at the Network layer, or layer 3.

19. C. Because there is only one Internet connection, and the size and complexity of the network is small, default routes are the easiest and lowest overhead options for routing data.

20. D, E. The exhibit shows an entry from a routing table. The *R* to the left of the entry means the RIP routing protocol is being run. Moving to the right, 10.10.10.8 is the network that was learned. In the brackets [120/2], 120 is the default administrative distance (AD) for RIP, and 2 is the metric; for RIP, this is given in hops, meaning the network is 2 hops or routers away.

21. C. In the election process of OSPF routers, the priority value is checked first. By default, all routers have a value of 1. If a loopback interface is configured, the interface with the highest IP address is used. If there is no loopback interface, then the active interface with the highest IP address is used.

22.

23	protocol	mask	port
80	TCP	0.0.3.255	80
Ip			
Tcp			
Udp			
0.0.0.3			
0.0.0.255			
0.0.3.255			
23			
80			

Web traffic uses HTTP, which is port 80. HTTP uses TCP at the Transport layer. Since the subnet mask is a /20, which is a block size of 4 in the third octet, the wildcard mask would be 0.0.3.255.

23. B. Because different VLANs are configured, different networks must be configured. In order to communicate from one network to another, a router is required. The router can be connected to each switch with a straight-through cable on different router interfaces.

24. C. When connecting two like devices together directly, a crossover cable must be used for them to communicate.

25. B. Cisco Discovery Protocol (CDP) is a Cisco proprietary protocol that works at the data link layer.

26. A. VLANs break up broadcast domains in layer-2 switched networks. Figure 1-11 shows all hosts in one broadcast domain, because switches do not break up broadcast domains by default.

27. B, E. By configuring logical interfaces on the router for each VLAN and then trunking the port from the switch to the router, and by using a frame-tagging encapsulation type of either 802.1q or ISL, inter-VLAN communication would occur at that router's interface.

28. C. When VLANs are configured, they provide a broadcast domain boundary or separate network. In order for a host to communicate from one network to another, a layer 3 or routing device is required.

29. C, E, F. To answer this question, the private address ranges must be known. There is a range in each class of addresses: 10.0.0.0-10.255.255.255, 172.16.0.0-172.31.255.255, and 192.168.0.0-192.168.255.255. Any of the options in these ranges will not be routed on the Internet.

30. F. There are two trunking encapsulation methods: ISL, which is Cisco propriety, and 802.1q, which is not proprietary. Use the command `dot1q` when using 802.1q.

31. A, B. The access-list statement `access-list 101 permit tcp` means that it is an extended list and will be used port numbers to filter the network. The next command is `any` and means "any source." The next command is the destination address and is specified by using the 0.0.0.0 wildcard. Finally, `eq port` tells the destination port number.

32. B. Host C's address is on the wrong network: It is on the 13 network, whereas its current IP is on the 14 network.

33. D. A wildcard is always one less than the block size. The third octet has a block size of 8, and the fourth octet has a block size of 256. This makes the mask 0.0.7.255.

34. D. If you do not have spanning-tree enabled on your switches, and you have redundant links, you will have broadcast storms and multiple frame copies.

35. C. OSPF uses an inverse mask to configure the network statement. The mask in this example should be 0.255.255.255.

36. A, D. This question is asking about Protocol Data Units (PDUs). The Transport layer creates segments and uses port number, the Network layer creates packets and uses logical addressing, the Data Link layer creates Frames and uses hardware addresses (MAC) and the Physical layer uses bits.

37.

Access-group	Access to connected networks or resources
Console password	Access to the console 0 line
Enable secret	Access to privileged mode
VTY password	Remote access to device console
Service password-encryption	Viewing of passwords

The access-group command is used to place an access-list on a router interface. The console password is used to secure the console port, the enable secret is used to secure privileged mode, the VTY password is used for securing telnet access and the service password-encryption is used to encrypt your routers passwords in the configuration.

38. D. Because a standard access list is being used in this network, you should place the access list closest to the destination network.

39. A, D. By using the `switchport port-security` command, you can implement a security policy on your Catalyst switches.

40. E. You can statically map IP addresses to your local DLCI, or IARP will dynamically learn mappings. By default, IARP is enabled.

41. A. If a port on a switch is turning from green to amber and back again, there is some type of problem with the cabling or device connected to the switch.

42. C, E. If you erase the startup-config and reload the router, you will still have the VLAN database on the switch (vlan.dat, stored in flash). You must also delete the VLAN database to restore a switch back to factory defaults.

43. A. In this example, the administrator has incorrectly used the `copy` command. The correct syntax for this is `copy "source file" "destination file"`. Because the configuration was made directly to the router, the changes were made to the running-configuration file stored in RAM. The permanent location for the configuration file is in NVRAM as the startup-configuration file. The command should have been `copy running-configuration startup-configuration`.

44. E. OSPF uses a multicast address of 224.0.0.5 to send hello packets to adjacent neighbors.

45. C. The spanning-tree protocol is used to prevent loops in the layer 2 switching topology by controlling or blocking the use of redundant links. In a layer 2 network, redundant links are not a bad thing, unless they are uncontrolled, because they provide a secondary path if the primary fails and thus eliminate single points of failure.

46. A. Switch1 has the lowest MAC address, which by default is used to find the root bridge.

47. A. The network shown in Figure 1-20 is a discontiguous network, and the `no auto-summary` command must be applied under the routing protocol.

48. C. By configuring an IP address, enabling interface VLAN 1, and then setting a default gateway with the `ip default-gateway` command, the switch will allow a remote host access for administrative purposes.

49. B, C, D. The three possible trunking modes include *on*, which means it is configured as "always" a trunk port and attempts to make the port on the far end of the segment a trunk port as well. This negotiation of trunk status is done using the dynamic trunking protocol (DTP). The next mode is *desirable*, which desires to be a trunk port send DTP frames, but can be an access port the other end will not be a trunk port. The third mode is *auto*, which becomes a trunk port if it receives DTP frames to become one; however it will not send DTP frames to change the other port.

50. B, E. When configuring OSPF to route on a network, the OSPF process must be started using the `router OSPF <process id>` command. Then, while in the router configuration mode, the `network` command can be used to add a network and enable interfaces to operate in OSPF. The `network` command in OSPF includes the network, a wildcard bit mask, and the area to which you want the network to belong.

51.

Source IP 207.16.13.14, destination application http	Permitted
Source IP 207.16.14.7, destination port 80	Permitted
Source IP 207.16.32.14, destination application: http	Denied
Source IP 207.16.15.9, destination port 23	Denied
Source IP 207.16.16.14, destination port 53	Denied

The wildcard 0.0.3.255 is a block size of 4, which means that the third octet will permit anything from 12 to 15. Also, the applicaiton is HTTP, so the access list will only permit port 80.

52. C, D. RIP, IGRP, and EIGRP are all configured the same way: with classful addresses, which means all default host bits are off. In this question, two networks are using the 10.0.0.0 classful network address. If you are studying for your CCNA exam, it would be wise to understand this type of configuration.

53. B. Multiple hosts can be connected to a switch port, by either a hub or another switch. All MAC addresses connected to that switch port will be placed into the CAM table.

54. E. With a /27 mask, the networks will increment by 32. The 201.57.78.128/27 network will have a broadcast address of 201.57.78.159.

55. E. EIGRP successor routes (the best routes) are stored in the topology table with all the other routes. Only the successor routes are then copied into the route table to be used for routing.

Answer Sheets for Practice Test 2

Section 1
Multiple Choice Questions

CUT HERE

1 Ⓐ Ⓑ Ⓒ Ⓓ Ⓔ Ⓕ	31 Ⓐ Ⓑ Ⓒ Ⓓ Ⓔ Ⓕ
2 Ⓐ Ⓑ Ⓒ Ⓓ Ⓔ Ⓕ	32 Ⓐ Ⓑ Ⓒ Ⓓ Ⓔ Ⓕ
3 Ⓐ Ⓑ Ⓒ Ⓓ Ⓔ Ⓕ	33 Ⓐ Ⓑ Ⓒ Ⓓ Ⓔ Ⓕ
4 Ⓐ Ⓑ Ⓒ Ⓓ Ⓔ Ⓕ	34 Ⓐ Ⓑ Ⓒ Ⓓ Ⓔ Ⓕ
5 Ⓐ Ⓑ Ⓒ Ⓓ Ⓔ Ⓕ	35 Ⓐ Ⓑ Ⓒ Ⓓ Ⓔ Ⓕ
6 Ⓐ Ⓑ Ⓒ Ⓓ Ⓔ Ⓕ	36 Ⓐ Ⓑ Ⓒ Ⓓ Ⓔ Ⓕ
7 Ⓐ Ⓑ Ⓒ Ⓓ Ⓔ Ⓕ	37 Ⓐ Ⓑ Ⓒ Ⓓ Ⓔ Ⓕ
8 Ⓐ Ⓑ Ⓒ Ⓓ Ⓔ Ⓕ	38 Ⓐ Ⓑ Ⓒ Ⓓ Ⓔ Ⓕ
9 Ⓐ Ⓑ Ⓒ Ⓓ Ⓔ Ⓕ	39 Ⓐ Ⓑ Ⓒ Ⓓ Ⓔ Ⓕ
10 Ⓐ Ⓑ Ⓒ Ⓓ Ⓔ Ⓕ	40 Ⓐ Ⓑ Ⓒ Ⓓ Ⓔ Ⓕ
11 Ⓐ Ⓑ Ⓒ Ⓓ Ⓔ Ⓕ	41 Ⓐ Ⓑ Ⓒ Ⓓ Ⓔ Ⓕ
12 Ⓐ Ⓑ Ⓒ Ⓓ Ⓔ Ⓕ	42 Ⓐ Ⓑ Ⓒ Ⓓ Ⓔ Ⓕ
13 Ⓐ Ⓑ Ⓒ Ⓓ Ⓔ Ⓕ	43 Ⓐ Ⓑ Ⓒ Ⓓ Ⓔ Ⓕ
14 Ⓐ Ⓑ Ⓒ Ⓓ Ⓔ Ⓕ	44 Ⓐ Ⓑ Ⓒ Ⓓ Ⓔ Ⓕ
15 Ⓐ Ⓑ Ⓒ Ⓓ Ⓔ Ⓕ	45 Ⓐ Ⓑ Ⓒ Ⓓ Ⓔ Ⓕ
16 Ⓐ Ⓑ Ⓒ Ⓓ Ⓔ Ⓕ	46 Ⓐ Ⓑ Ⓒ Ⓓ Ⓔ Ⓕ
17 Ⓐ Ⓑ Ⓒ Ⓓ Ⓔ Ⓕ	47 Ⓐ Ⓑ Ⓒ Ⓓ Ⓔ Ⓕ
18 Ⓐ Ⓑ Ⓒ Ⓓ Ⓔ Ⓕ	48 Ⓐ Ⓑ Ⓒ Ⓓ Ⓔ Ⓕ
19 Ⓐ Ⓑ Ⓒ Ⓓ Ⓔ Ⓕ	49 Ⓐ Ⓑ Ⓒ Ⓓ Ⓔ Ⓕ
20 Ⓐ Ⓑ Ⓒ Ⓓ Ⓔ Ⓕ	50 Ⓐ Ⓑ Ⓒ Ⓓ Ⓔ Ⓕ
21 Ⓐ Ⓑ Ⓒ Ⓓ Ⓔ Ⓕ	51 Ⓐ Ⓑ Ⓒ Ⓓ Ⓔ Ⓕ
22 Ⓐ Ⓑ Ⓒ Ⓓ Ⓔ Ⓕ	52 Ⓐ Ⓑ Ⓒ Ⓓ Ⓔ Ⓕ
23 Ⓐ Ⓑ Ⓒ Ⓓ Ⓔ Ⓕ	53 Ⓐ Ⓑ Ⓒ Ⓓ Ⓔ Ⓕ
24 Ⓐ Ⓑ Ⓒ Ⓓ Ⓔ Ⓕ	54 Ⓐ Ⓑ Ⓒ Ⓓ Ⓔ Ⓕ
25 Ⓐ Ⓑ Ⓒ Ⓓ Ⓔ Ⓕ	55 Ⓐ Ⓑ Ⓒ Ⓓ Ⓔ Ⓕ
26 Ⓐ Ⓑ Ⓒ Ⓓ Ⓔ Ⓕ	
27 Ⓐ Ⓑ Ⓒ Ⓓ Ⓔ Ⓕ	
28 Ⓐ Ⓑ Ⓒ Ⓓ Ⓔ Ⓕ	
29 Ⓐ Ⓑ Ⓒ Ⓓ Ⓔ Ⓕ	
30 Ⓐ Ⓑ Ⓒ Ⓓ Ⓔ Ⓕ	

Directions: For each of the following questions, select the choice that best answers the question or completes the statement.

1. Your router discovers a remote network via a static route, EIGRP, and OSPF, and all the routing protocols are set to their default administrative distance. In this situation, which route will the router use to forward data to the newly discovered remote network?

   A. The router will use the static route.
   B. The router will use the OSPF route.
   C. The router will use the EIGRP route.
   D. The router will load balance and use all three routes.

2. Look at the following diagram. You've added another router called Vine2, but no routing updates are being exchanged between it and the pre-existing Vine1 router. You look into the issue and find that other interconnectivity and Internet access for all your existing locations throughout the corporate network are working great. What must you do to isolate the problem and tweak the router configurations so they can communicate fully?

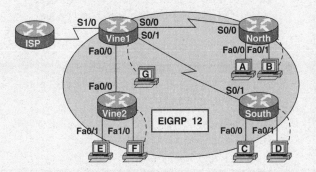

Figure 2-1

   A. Connect to the Internet router, and reload it.
   B. Connect to Vine1 and Vine2, and reload them.
   C. Connect to Vine1 and Vine2, and make sure they are both in the same autonomous system and the network statements are correctly configured on both routers.
   D. Add RIP to both routers.

3. Look at the following diagram. You can see that all your hosts are maintaining connectivity with each other. Choose *three* of the following that would be relevant to the addressing scheme likely used by this network:

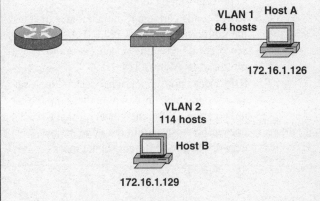

Figure 2-2

   A. The subnet mask in use is 255.255.255.192.
   B. The subnet mask in use is 255.255.255.128.
   C. The IP address 172.16.1.25 can be assigned to hosts in VLAN1.
   D. The IP address 172.16.1.205 can be assigned to hosts in VLAN1.
   E. The LAN interface of the router is configured with one IP address.
   F. The LAN interface of the router is configured with multiple IP addresses.

GO ON TO THE NEXT PAGE

4. Choose *three* of the following that accurately describe RIP.

A. RIPv1 does not support routing update authentication. RIPv2 does support routing update authentication.

B. RIPv1 does not include subnet information in routing updates. RIPv2 does include subnet information in routing updates.

C. RIPv1 does not support advertising routes across WANs. RIPv2 supports advertising routes across LANs as well as WANs.

D. RIPv1 uses hold-down timers and split horizon to prevent routing loops. RIPv2 does not require hold-down timers or split horizon to prevent routing loops.

E. RIPv1 sends periodic routing updates over the multicast IP address 224.0.0.10. RIPv2 sends periodic routing updates over the multicast IP address 224.0.0.9.

F. RIPv1 does not support a network addressing scheme in which hosts within the same major network have different subnet masks. RIPv2 does allow hosts within the same major network to have different subnet masks.

5. Look at the following diagram. Which of the following will happen if you enter these command lines into the router?

```
Napa(config)# interface
    FastEthernet 0/0
Napa(config-if)# no ip
    access-group 106 in
Napa(config-if)#
    interface Serial 0/0
Napa(config-if)# ip
    access-group 106 out
```

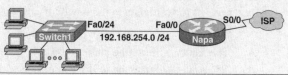

access-list 106 permit ip host 192.168.254.7 any
access-list 106 deny tcp 192.168.254.0 0.0.0.255 any eq www
access-list 106 permit ip any any
interface Fa0/0
 ip access-group 106 in

Figure 2-3

A. The change has no effect on the packets being filtered.

B. All traffic from the 192.168.254.0 LAN to the Internet is permitted.

C. Web pages from the Internet cannot be accessed by hosts in the 192.168.254.0 LAN.

D. No hosts in the 192.168.254.0 LAN except 192.168.254.7 can telnet to hosts on the Internet.

6. In a Spanning Tree topology, which of the following would you use to delimit the root port on each non-root switch?

A. Path cost

B. Lowest port MAC address

C. VTP revision number

D. Highest port priority number

E. Port priority number and MAC address

7. Which of the following is the reason you configure port security on a switch?

A. To prevent unauthorized Telnet access to a switch port

B. To limit the number of Layer 2 broadcasts on a particular switch port

C. To prevent unauthorized hosts from accessing the LAN

D. To protect the IP and MAC address of the switch and associated ports

E. To block unauthorized access to the switch-management interfaces over common TCP ports

8. Choose which IP address you would assign to Host 1 based on the following diagram.

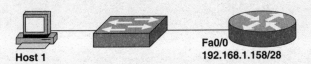

Fa0/0
192.168.1.158/28

Host 1

Figure 2-4

A. 192.168.1.143/28
B. 192.168.1.144/28
C. 192.168.1.145/28
D. 192.168.1.159/28
E. 192.168.1.160/28

9. While troubleshooting your internetwork's connection problems, you view Host1's output. Based on the following diagram, which of the following is the problem Host1's output is showing you?

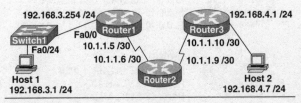

192.168.3.254 /24
Switch1
Fa0/0 Router1
Fa0/24
10.1.1.5 /30
10.1.1.6 /30
Router2
192.168.4.1 /24
Router3
10.1.1.10 /30
10.1.1.9 /30
Host 1
192.168.3.1 /24
Host 2
192.168.4.7 /24

C:\>ping 192.168.3.254

Pinging 192.168.3.254 with 32 bytes of data:

Reply from 192.168.3.254: bytes=32 time=3ms TTL=255
Reply from 192.168.3.254: bytes=32 time=3ms TTL=255
Reply from 192.168.3.254: bytes=32 time=3ms TTL=255
Reply from 192.168.3.254: bytes=32 time=3ms TTL=255

C:\>tracert 192.168.4.7

Tracing route to 192.168.4.7 over a maximum of 30 hops

1   3 ms   3 ms   3 ms   192.168.3.254
2   10.1.1.6 reports: Destination host unreachable.

Trace complete.

Figure 2-5

A. The routing on Router2 is not functioning properly.

B. An access list is applied to an interface of Router3.

C. The Fa0/24 interface of Switch1 is down.

D. The gateway address of Host1 is incorrect or not configured.

GO ON TO THE NEXT PAGE

10. Look at the following diagram. What's the best way to configure the FastEthernet0/1 ports on the 2950 model switches to achieve connectivity between all machines?

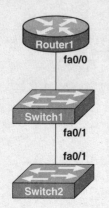

Router1
fa 0/0.1 192.168.1.1/24 VLAN 1
fa 0/0.10 192.168.10.1/24 VLAN 10
fa 0/0.20 192.168.20.1/24 VLAN 20

Switch1
IP address: 192.168.1.2/24
Ports 3-12 VLAN 10
Ports 13-24 VLAN 20

Switch2
IP address: 192.168.1.3/24
Ports 2-12 VLAN 10
Ports 13-24 VLAN 20

Figure 2-6

A. The ports only need to be connected by a crossover cable.

B. `SwitchX(config)# interface`
`fastethernet0/1`
`SwitchX(config-if)# switchport`
`mode trunk`

C. `SwitchX(config)# interface`
`fastethernet0/1`
`SwitchX(config-if)# switchport`
`mode access`
`SwitchX(config-if)# switchport`
`access vlan 1`

D. `SwitchX(config)# interface`
`fastethernet0/1`
`SwitchX(config-if)# switchport`
`mode trunk`
`SwitchX(config-if)# switchport`
`trunk vlan 1`
`SwitchX(config-if)# switchport`
`trunk vlan 10`
`SwitchX(config-if)# switchport`
`trunk vlan 20`

11. You need the 192.1.1.0/24 address to be subnetted over all three Ethernet networks that are attached to Vine1. Based on the following diagram, which of the following equals the greatest number of host addresses you can get using VLSM on all three networks collectively?

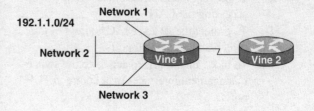

Figure 2-7

A. 126
B. 186
C. 192
D. 224
E. 250
F. 254

12. You've installed a new router in the Cabernet location, but you can't back up the IOS image of this new router to a TFTP server at the Chardonnay location. Based on the following diagram, why is this happening?

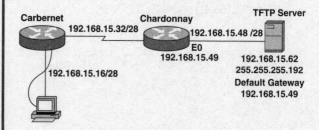

Figure 2-8

A. Incorrect default gateway of the TFTP server
B. Incorrect subnet mask of the TFTP server
C. Incorrect IP address of the TFTP server
D. Incorrect IP address on e0 of the Chardonnay router
E. Incorrect subnet mask on the Cabernet router

13. Which of these situations would cause numerous copies of the same unicast frame to be transmitted over a switched LAN?

- **A.** During high-traffic periods
- **B.** After broken links are re-established
- **C.** When upper-layer protocols require high reliability
- **D.** In an improperly implemented redundant topology
- **E.** When a dual ring topology is in use

14. Which command would you use to configure a default route to a destination network that's not listed in the routing table?

- **A.** `Router(config)# ip default-route 0.0.0.0 255.255.255.255 s0`
- **B.** `Router(config)# ip route 0.0.0.0 255.255.255.255 s0`
- **C.** `Router(config)# ip default-route 0.0.0.0 s0`
- **D.** `Router(config)# ip route 0.0.0.0 0.0.0.0 s0`
- **E.** `Router(config)# ip route any any e0`

15. Look at the following router output, and choose the answer that best describes what the term *dynamic* means in the output obtained via the `show frame-relay map` command:

```
Vine#show frame-relay map
Serial0/0 (up): ip 192.168.10.1
    dlci 16 (0x64, 0x1840), dynamic
Broadcast, status defined, active
```

Code Listing 2-1

- **A.** The Serial0/0 interface is passing traffic.
- **B.** The DLCI 16 was dynamically allocated by the router.
- **C.** The Serial0/0 interface acquired the IP address of 192.168.10.1 from a DHCP server.
- **D.** The DLCI 16 will be dynamically changed as required to adapt to changes in the Frame Relay cloud.
- **E.** The mapping between DLCI 16 and the end station IP address 192.168.10.1 was learned through inverse ARP.

16. The Winery Coop now has five branches throughout Napa and Sonoma, and they want to build a WAN to give them a completely meshed environment with a minimum of 512 kbps throughput. They also need the most cost-effective solution. Which WAN service should they choose?

- **A.** Frame Relay
- **B.** Leased lines
- **C.** ISDN BRI
- **D.** ATM
- **E.** PPP

17. Look at the following diagram. You're trying to configure the FastEthernet0/0 interfaces on the two interconnected routers, and you've configured Boundary1 without a hitch. But when you move on to configure the interface on the Sales router; you get the error message shown in the figure. Why is this happening?

```
Boundry1(config)#interface FastEthernet 0/0
Boundry1(config-if)#ip address 192.168.125.36 255.255.255.192
Boundry1(config-if)#no shutdown
Boundry1(config-if)#

Sales(config)#interface FastEthernet 0/0
Sales(config-if)#ip address 192.168.125.37 255.255.255.192
Bad mask /26 for address 192.168.125.37
Sales(config-if)#
```

Figure 2-9

- **A.** The address being applied to the Sales interface is a broadcast address.
- **B.** The Sales router needs to be configured to re-enable the use of subnet 0.
- **C.** The FastEthernet0/0 interfaces of the two routers are using different Layer 2 protocols.
- **D.** The FastEthernet0/0 interface on the Border1 router has the bandwidth improperly configured.

GO ON TO THE NEXT PAGE

18. Based on the following switch output, how would the switch have received the MAC table entry for 0012.7f4b.6882?

```
Switch#sh mac address-table
           Mac Address Table
-------------------------------------------
Vlan    Mac Address      Type        Ports
----    -----------      --------    -----
 All    0005.dccb.d740   STATIC      CPU
 All    0100.0ccc.cccc   STATIC      CPU
 All    0100.0ccc.cccd   STATIC      CPU
 All    0100.0cdd.dddd   STATIC      CPU
   1    000a.f467.9e80   DYNAMIC     Fa0/11
   1    0010.7b7f.c2b0   DYNAMIC     Fa0/11
   1    0012.7f4b.6880   DYNAMIC     Fa0/11
   1    0012.7f4b.6881   DYNAMIC     Fa0/11
   1    0012.7f4b.6882   DYNAMIC     Fa0/11
   1    0030.80dc.460b   DYNAMIC     Fa0/11
   1    0030.9492.a5dd   DYNAMIC     Fa0/2
   1    00d0.58ad.05f4   DYNAMIC     Fa0/1
Total Mac Addresses for this criterion: 12
Switch#
```

Code Listing 2-2

A. It was forwarded from an adjacent switch.
B. It was entered from the configuration mode.
C. It was acquired by a broadcast from the switch.
D. It represents a MAC address of the switch.

19. Look at the following diagram. From what you see there, which of the following switches will be elected root bridge, and why?

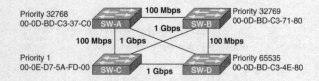

Figure 2-10

A. Switch A, because it has the lowest MAC address
B. Switch A, because it is the most centrally located switch
C. Switch B, because it has the highest MAC address
D. Switch C, because it is the most centrally located switch
E. Switch C, because it has the lowest priority
F. Switch D, because it has the highest priority

20. You're adding a new router into an OSPF network, and the networks connected to your new router aren't showing up in the routing tables of the other OSPF routers. You have the subnets 10.10.10.0/24 and 10.11.11.0/24. What will your OSPF configuration be if you want to create one network entry and place both subnets into area 0?

A. Router(config)# router ospf 1
Router(config)# network
10.0.0.0 255.0.0.0 area 0

B. Router(config)# router ospf 1011
Router(config)# network
10.0.0.0 255.255.255.0 area 0

C. Router(config)# router ospf 1
Router(config)# network
10.0.0.0 0.0.0.255 area0

D. Router(config)# router ospf 1
Router(config)# network
10.0.0.0 0.0.0.255 area 0

21. Looking at the following output, what *two* things would you expect to discover in the line of show ip route output?

```
R    192.168.10.32 [120/3] via
         192.168.10.17 00:00:23
```

A. The next routing update can be expected in 35 seconds.
B. The IP address 192.168.10.17 is configured on S0/1.
C. The IP address 10.10.10.8 is configured on S0/1.
D. This route is using the default administrative distance.
E. The 192.168.10.32 network is three hops away from this router.

22. You need to keep the hosts with the subnet address 172.16.24.0/21 in the VLAN from accessing telnet services. Which of the following would provide the missing answers in this command? (Choose three.)

```
access-list 110 deny
     protocol
172.16.24.0  mask any
     eq port
```

- **A.** Port 23
- **B.** Port 80
- **C.** Protocol IP
- **D.** Protocol TCP
- **E.** Wildcard 0.0.3.255
- **F.** mask 0.0.7.255

23. Why would you use this command?

```
ip route 0.0.0.0 0.0.0.0
     serial0/0
```

- **A.** It configures a router to send all packets out interface serial0/0.
- **B.** It configures a router to block routing updates from being sent out interface serial0/0.
- **C.** It configures a router as a firewall, blocking all unauthorized packets from exiting serial0/0.
- **D.** It configures a router to send all packets for unknown destination networks out interface serial0/0.
- **E.** It configures a router to drop all packets for which the destination network is unknown.

24. Figure 2-11 shows a host connected to a switch port with a crossover cable. Everything is configured as shown in the figure and is correct. Why can't the host communicate with other hosts on the network?

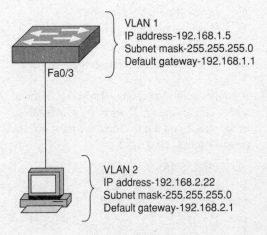

VLAN 1
IP address-192.168.1.5
Subnet mask-255.255.255.0
Default gateway-192.168.1.1

Fa0/3

VLAN 2
IP address-192.168.2.22
Subnet mask-255.255.255.0
Default gateway-192.168.2.1

Figure 2-11

- **A.** The switch port is a trunk port.
- **B.** The cable is the wrong type.
- **C.** The switch has the wrong IP address.
- **D.** STP has blocked the port.
- **E.** The switch and host are using the same subnet mask.

25. Looking at the following diagram, why did VLAN connectivity issues begin to happen right after SwitchB was added to the network?

```
SwitchA# show vtp status              SwitchB# show vtp status
VTP version                  : 2      VTP version                  : 2
Configuration Revision       : 1      Configuration Revision       : 7
Maximum VLANs supported locally : 64  Maximum VLANs supported locally : 64
Number of existing VLANs     : 8      Number of existing VLANs     : 4
VTP Operating Mode           : Server VTP Operating Mode           : Server
VTP Domain Name              : cisco  VTP Domain Name              : cisco
VTP Pruning Mode             : disabled VTP Pruning Mode            : disabled
V2 Mode                      : disabled VTP V2 Mode                 : disabled
```

Figure 2-12

- **A.** Both switches are in server mode in the same domain.
- **B.** The revision number of SwitchB was higher than the revision number of SwitchA.
- **C.** SwitchA was not rebooted prior to adding SwitchB to the network.
- **D.** V2-mode is not enabled.
- **E.** VTP pruning is not activated, so the new paths in the network have not been recalculated.

GO ON TO THE NEXT PAGE

26. You're faced with reconfiguring a Catalyst 2950. Pick *three* steps that will guarantee the old configuration is erased.

   A. Erase flash.

   B. Restart the switch.

   C. Delete the VLAN database.

   D. Erase the running configuration.

   E. Erase the startup configuration.

   F. Modify the configuration register.

27. If you were implementing VLSM on a network with a single Class C IP address, which subnet mask would you use to create the most effective point-to-point serial link?

   A. 255.255.255.0

   B. 255.255.255.240

   C. 255.255.255.248

   D. 255.255.255.252

   E. 255.255.255.254

28. You've subnetted your client's internetwork using 29 bits. You now need to configure an extended access list to control access to a whole subnetwork. To achieve this, which of the following wildcard masks should you use?

   A. 255.255.255.224

   B. 255.255.255.248

   C. 0.0.0.224

   D. 0.0.0.8

   E. 0.0.0.7

   F. 0.0.0.3

29. Look at following output, and pick the option that solves the problem of why Serial0/0 won't respond to a ping from a machine on the FastEthernet0/0 LAN.

```
Napa#sh ip interface brief
Interface   IP-Address    OK? Method Status            Protocol
Ethernet0/0 192.168.10.1  YES NVRAM  up                up
Serial0/0   192.168.15.1  YES NVRAM  administratively  down
                                     down
Serial0/1   192.168.16.1  YES NVRAM  up                up
Serial0/2   unassigned    YES NVRAM  administratively  down
                                     down
Router#
```

Code Listing 2-3

   A. Enable the Serial0/0 interface.

   B. Correct the IP address for Serial0/0.

   C. Correct the IP address for FastEthernet0/0.

   D. Change the encapsulation type on Serial0/0.

   E. Enable autoconfiguration on the Serial0/0 interface.

30. You've configured a router three different times. You tested each configuration and successfully saved each of them to NVRAM using the `copy running-config startup-config` command. Then, you typed in the **reload** command. But now, when the router restarts, it looks as though it's got the default blank configuration. What's causing this?

   A. The `boost system` commands were left out of the configuration.

   B. The NVRAM is corrupted.

   C. The configuration register setting is incorrect.

   D. The upgraded IOS just loaded is not compatible with the hardware.

   E. The upgraded configuration is not compatible with the hardware platform.

31. Look at the following diagram. Host A sends an ARP request for the MAC address of Host B, and the network's performance practically grinds to a halt. The switches reveal a huge number of broadcast frames. What's causing this?

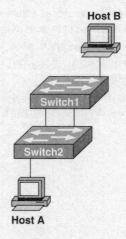

Figure 2-13

   A. The `portfast` feature is not enabled on all switch ports.

   B. The PCs are in two different VLANs.

   C. Spanning Tree Protocol is not running on the switches.

   D. Host B is down and is not able to respond to the request.

   E. The VTP versions running on the two switches do not match.

32. Why is a default route important?

   A. It is a route to be used when the routing protocol fails.

   B. It is a route configured by an ISP that sends traffic into a corporate network.

   C. It is a route used when a packet is destined for a remote network that is not listed in the routing table.

   D. It is a route manually configured for a specific remote network for which a routing protocol is not configured.

   E. It is used to send traffic to a stub network.

33. Based on the following diagram, choose *two* options that describe ports that can safely be configured with PortFast:

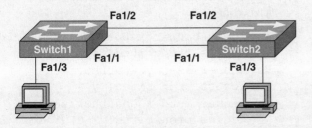

Figure 2-14

   A. Switch1 - port Fa1/2

   B. Switch2 - port Fa1/2

   C. Switch1 - port Fa1/3

   D. Switch2 - port Fa1/3

   E. Switch1 - port Fa1/1

   F. Switch2 - port Fa1/1

34. The steps in PPP session establishment occur in a specific order. Choose the correct order from these alternatives:

   A. optional authentication phase, link establishment phase, network layer protocol phase

   B. network layer protocol phase, link establishment phase, optional authentication phase

   C. network layer protocol phase, optional authentication phase, link establishment phase

   D. link establishment phase, network layer protocol phase, optional authentication phase

   E. link establishment phase, optional authentication phase, network layer protocol phase

   F. optional authentication phase, network layer protocol phase, link establishment phase

35. Look at the following diagram. You've configured this internetwork as shown, and it appears that routing has been configured improperly. Of the following configuration options, which one will give hosts on the Branch LAN access to resources on the Corp LAN with the most efficient use of bandwidth and the least burden on router processing?

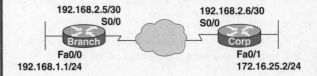

Figure 2-15

   A. `Corp(config)# ip route 192.168.`
`1.0 255.255.255.0 192.168.2.5`
`Branch(config)# ip route 172.16.`
`25.0 255.255.255.0 192.168.2.6`

   B. `Corp(config)# router rip`
`Corp(config-router)# network`
`192.168.2.0`
`Corp(config-router)# network`
`172.16.0.0`
`Branch(config)# router rip`
`Branch (config-router)#`
`network 192.168.1.0`
`Branch (config-router)#`
`network 192.168.2.0`

   C. `Corp(config)# router eigrp 56`
`Corp(config-router)# network`
`192.168.2.4`
`Corp(config-router)# network`
`172.16.25.0`
`Branch(config)# router eigrp 56`
`Branch (config-router)#`
`network 192.168.1.0`
`Branch (config-router)#`
`network 192.168.2.4`

   D. `Corp(config)# router ospf 1`
`Corp(config-router)# network`
`192.168.2.4 0.0.0.3 area 0`
`Corp(config-router)# network`
`172.16.25.0 0.0.0.255 area 0`
`Branch(config)# router ospf 1`
`Branch (config-router)#`
`network 192.168.1.0 0.0.0.255`
`area 0`
`Branch (config-router)#`
`network 192.168.2.4 0.0.0.3`
`area 0`

GO ON TO THE NEXT PAGE

36. The local router's routing has been enabled with these commands:

```
Local(config)# ip route 0.0.0.0 0.0.0.0 192.168.10.1
Local(config)# ip route 172.16.0.0 255.255.255.0 192.168.20.2
Local(config)# ip route 172.16.0.0 255.255.0.0 192.168.30.3
```

Code Listing 2-4

Match the destination IP address in the left column to the proper next hop address on the right:

172.16.10.10	Next hop 192.168.10.1
172.16.0.33	Next hop 192.168.20.2
172.44.98.1	Next hop 192.168.30.3
172.16.41.2	
172.16.0.23	
172.2.5.6	

Table 2-1

37. Choose *two* of the following options that accurately describe the tasks that the OSPF Hello protocol performs:

A. It provides dynamic neighbor discovery.

B. It detects unreachable neighbors at 90-second intervals.

C. It maintains neighbor relationships.

D. It negotiates correctness parameters between neighboring interfaces.

E. It uses timers to elect the router with the fastest links as the designated router.

38. Which type of EIGRP route entry describes a feasible successor?

A. A backup route, stored in the routing table

B. A primary route, stored in the routing table

C. A backup route, stored in the topology table

D. A primary route, stored in the topology table

39. What does a Layer 2 switch do if it receives a frame with a destination MAC address that is not found in its MAC address table?

A. The frame is dropped.

B. The frame is addressed with a broadcast MAC address and sent out all ports.

C. The frame is sent out all ports except the receiving port.

D. An ARP request is sent out all ports except the receiving port.

E. A destination unreachable message is sent back to the source address.

40. You want the phrase *"Unauthorized access prohibited!"* to show up before the login prompt when a Telnet session to a router is attempted. Choose the command that you would use to achieve this.

A. `login banner x Unauthorized access prohibited! x`

B. `banner exec y Unauthorized access prohibited! y`

C. `banner motd x Unauthorized access prohibited! x`

D. `login message "Unauthorized access prohibited!"`

E. `vty motd "Unauthorized access prohibited!"`

F. `vty 0 4 banner "Unauthorized access prohibited!"`

41. A network administrator issues the `ping 192.168.2.5` command and successfully tests connectivity to a host that has been newly connected to the network. Which protocols were used during the test? (Choose two.)

A. ARP

B. CDP

C. DHCP

D. DNS

E. ICMP

42. You've created the following access list and applied it to an interface. Which of the following are denied based on the access list? (Choose two.)

```
access-list 107 deny tcp 207.16.12.0 0.0.3.255 any eq http
access-list 107 permit ip any any
```

Code Listing 2-5

A. Source IP: 207.16.32.14, destination application: http
B. Source IP: 207.16.15.9, destination port: 23
C. Source IP: 207.16.14.7, destination port: 80
D. Source IP: 207.16.13.14, destination application: http
E. Source IP: 207.16.16.14, destination port: 53

43. Look at both the topology and configuration illustrated in the following diagram. Based on the fact that the router is configured to allow communication between the VLANs, choose the *three* IOS commands you need to configure switch port fa0/1 and establish a link with router R1 using the IEEE standard protocol:

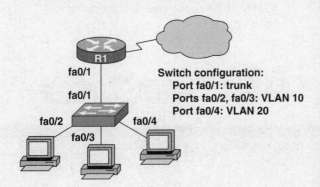

Switch configuration:
Port fa0/1: trunk
Ports fa0/2, fa0/3: VLAN 10
Port fa0/4: VLAN 20

Figure 2-16

A. `Switch(config)# interface fastethernet 0/1`
B. `Switch(config-if)# switchport mode access`
C. `Switch(config-if)# switchport mode trunk`
D. `Switch(config-if)# switchport access vlan1`
E. `Switch(config-if)# switchport trunk encapsulation isl`
F. `Switch(config-if)# switchport trunk encapsulation dot1q`

44. Look at the following diagram. You want to use NAT in that network, so choose the *two* commands you can use to apply NAT configuration to the correct interfaces:

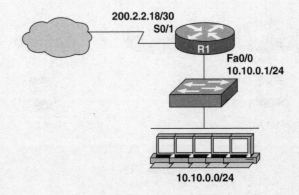

Figure 2-17

A. `R1(config)# interface serial0/1`
   `R1(config-if)# ip nat inside`
B. `R1(config)# interface serial0/1`
   `R1(config-if)# ip nat outside`
C. `R1(config)# interface fastethernet0/0`
   `R1(config-if)# ip nat inside`
D. `R1(config)# interface fastethernet0/0`
   `R1(config-if)# ip nat outside`
E. `R1(config)# interface serial0/1`
   `R1(config-if)# ip nat outside source pool 200.2.2.18 255.255.255.252`
F. `R1(config)# interface fastethernet0/0`
   `R1(config-if)# ip nat inside source 10.10.0.0 255.255.255.0`

45. Match the cable type in the left column to the task for which it's best used, in the right column:

crossover	switch access port to router
null modem	switch to switch
straight-through	PC COM port to switch
rollover	9-25 pin serial

Table 2-2

GO ON TO THE NEXT PAGE

46. Look at the following diagram. You want Host A to communicate with Host B, but the e0 interface on router 3 is down. Choose the *two* events that will occur:

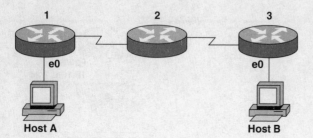

Figure 2-18

A. Router 3 will use ICMP to inform Host A that Host B cannot be reached.

B. Router 3 will use ICMP to inform Router 2 that Host B cannot be reached.

C. Router 3 will use ICMP to inform Host A, Router 1, and Router 2 that Host B cannot be reached.

D. Router 3 will send a Destination Unreachable message type.

E. Router 3 will send a Router Selection message type.

F. Router 3 will send a Source Quench message type.

47. You view the code listing below. What does the 128 refer to in the router output?

```
ROUTER# show ip route
192.168.12.0/24 is variably subnetted, 9 subnets, 3 masks
C  192.168.12.48/28 is directly connected, Loopback0
O  192.168.12.236/30 [110/128] via 192.168.12.233,00:35:36, Serial0
C  192.168.12.232/30 is directly connected, Serial0
O  192.168.12.245/32 [110/782] via 192.168.12.233,00:35:36, Serial0
O  192.168.12.240/30 [110/128] via 192.168.12.233,00:35:36, Serial0
O  192.168.12.253/32 [110/782] via 192.168.12.233,00:35:37, Serial0
O  192.168.12.249/32 [110/782] via 192.168.12.233,00:35:37, Serial0
```

Code Listing 2-6

A. OSPF cost

B. OSPF priority

C. OSPF Hop count

D. OSPF process ID

E. OSPF administrative distance

48. Choose *three* of the following options that accurately describe OSPF routing areas:

A. Each OSPF area requires a loopback interface to be configured.

B. Areas may be assigned any number from 0 to 65535.

C. Area 0 is called the backbone area.

D. Hierarchical OSPF networks do not require multiple areas.

E. Multiple OSPF areas must connect to area 0.

F. Single-area OSPF networks must be configured in area 1.

49. Choose the *three* services that use TCP:

A. DHCP

B. SMTP

C. SNMP

D. FTP

E. HTTP

F. TFTP

50. By analyzing the following diagram, you're trying to understand how the Acme Corporation works. You can see that the server in VLAN4 supplies all resources required by the user hosts in the other VLANs. Choose the *three* interfaces that are access ports:

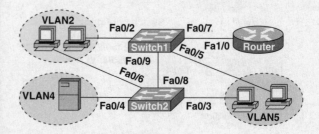

Figure 2-19

A. Switch1 – Fa0/2

B. Switch1 – Fa0/9

C. Switch2 – Fa0/3

D. Switch2 – Fa0/4

E. Switch2 – Fa0/8

F. Router – Fa1/0

51. What is the subnetwork number of a host with an IP address of 172.16.210.0/22?

- **A.** 172.16.42.0
- **B.** 172.16.107.0
- **C.** 172.16.208.0
- **D.** 172.16.252.0
- **E.** 172.16.254.0

52. When setting up Frame Relay for point-to-point subinterfaces, which of the following must not be configured?

- **A.** Frame Relay encapsulation on the physical interface
- **B.** Local DLCI on each subinterface
- **C.** IP address on the physical interface
- **D.** Subinterface type as point-to-point

53. What is the purpose of the OSPF router ID in a DR/BDR election?

- **A.** It is used with the OSPF priority values to determine which OSPF router will become the DR or BDR in a point-to-point network.
- **B.** It is used with the OSPF priority values to determine which interface will be used to form a neighbor relationship with another OSPF router.
- **C.** It is used with the OSPF priority values to determine which router will become the DR or BDR in a multi-access network.
- **D.** It is used to determine which interfaces will send Hello packets to neighboring OSPF routers.

54. Which of the following is true concerning Frame Relay multipoint subinterfaces?

- **A.** An IP address is required on the physical interface of the central router.
- **B.** All routers are required to be fully meshed.
- **C.** All routers must be in the same subnet to forward routing updates and broadcasts.
- **D.** Multipoint is the default configuration for Frame Relay subinterfaces.

55. A network administrator wants to control which user hosts can access the network based on their MAC address. What will prevent workstations with unauthorized MAC addresses from connecting to the network through a switch?

- **A.** BPDU
- **B.** Port security
- **C.** RSTP
- **D.** STP
- **E.** VTP
- **F.** Blocking mode

Answer Key for Practice Test 2

1.	A	**16.**	A	**31.**	C	**45.**	See Answer Explanation
2.	C	**17.**	B	**32.**	C	**46.**	A, D
3.	B, C, F	**18.**	A	**33.**	C, D	**47.**	A
4.	A, B, F	**19.**	A	**34.**	E	**48.**	C, D, E
5.	A	**20.**	D	**35.**	A	**49.**	B, D, E
6.	A	**21.**	D, E	**36.**	See Answer Explanation	**50.**	A, C, D
7.	C	**22.**	A, D, F	**37.**	A, C	**51.**	C
8.	C	**23.**	D	**38.**	C	**52.**	C
9.	A	**24.**	B	**39.**	C	**53.**	C
10.	B	**25.**	B	**40.**	C	**54.**	C
11.	E	**26.**	B, C, E	**41.**	A, E	**55.**	B
12.	B	**27.**	D	**42.**	C, D		
13.	D	**28.**	E	**43.**	A, C, F		
14.	D	**29.**	A	**44.**	B, C		
15.	E	**30.**	C				

Answer Explanations for Practice Test 2

1. **A.** Administrative Distance (AD) is the value a router uses to differentiate between routing information. Each routing protocol is given a value; a static route has the best AD with 1 (the lower the better; only a directly connected network is better with 0).

2. **C.** EIGRP (as well as IGRP) uses an autonomous system (AS) number in the routing configuration. As long as you use the same number on all your routers, they will exchange routing information. If they do not use the same AS number, they will not exchange information. In addition, the network statements are configured in a classful manner, which means all default host bits are off. For example, if you have a subnet of 10.10.16.0/28, the network statement under EIGRP would be 10.0.0.0.

3. **B, C, F.** The network shown in the figure has two VLANs configured; for the hosts in each VLAN to communicate, the router must be configured with subinterfaces, one for each VLAN. The block size in use is 128, so the mask is a /25 or 255.255.255.128.

4. **A, B, F.** RIPv1 is a classful routing protocols, which means all masks on every host in the network must be exactly the same. RIPv1 send broadcasts, and RIPv2 uses multicast: 224.0.0.9. RIP has many loop-avoidance mechanisms, some of which are split-horizon and hold-down timers. Others include route poison, setting infinity, and triggered updates. RIP v2 supports authentication as well; v1 does not.

5. **A.** The lines added to the ACL will be placed at the end of the access list, after the `permit ip any any` command line, which has no effect on denying packets.

6. **A.** Path cost is the first value that is used to determine which port should be blocking or forwarding. If path cost does not differentiate, then bridge id and port id can be used.

7. **C.** Port security can prevent unauthorized hosts from accessing the LAN. It can be configured with a maximum number of MAC addresses per port, or to allow only specifically configured MAC access.

8. **C.** The router is configured with the 192.168.1.158/28 address, which is the last valid host ID in the 192.168.1.144 subnet. The broadcast address for the subnet is 192.168.1.159, so the only valid host is 192.168.1.145.

9. **A.** Host1 can ping the default gateway, and traceroute does get to Router2, however, the packets cannot get past Router2, so this indicates a routing problem with Router2.

10. **B.** The cable between the switches needs to be a crossover cable, but they also need to be configured as a trunk port because multiple VLANs are configured on the switches.

11. **E.** Since you can VLSM this network, you can use one network of /25 and two /26 networks. That is 126 hosts and two 62 hosts. Add them up and that is 250 hosts.

12. **B.** The subnet mask on the TFTP is wrong. It should be 255.255.255.240, which is a /28.

13. **D.** If you have switches connected with dual links, and STP is not running, then you will have broadcast storms, multiple frame copies, and MAC table instability.

14. **D.** The `ip route` command can be used for a couple of different reasons: to set a static route to a network, and to set a default route. Here, a default route is being set. The syntax for the command includes the `ip route` command followed by the network and subnet mask being added. In this case, the fields are filled with zeros to indicate any network or default. The last field is the next hop address where the router must send packets to deliver them to the listed network.

15. **E.** Inverse ARP is the automatic process of finding a DLCI from a known IP address. If this function is not available, then the mapping of the DLCI to the IP address must be done manually through the `frame-relay map` command.

16. **A.** The bandwidth requirement and the fact that it is to be cost effective make Frame Relay the only real choice.

17. **B.** The router will not accept the IP address and mask without the `ip subnet-zero` command configured. This command allows the router to use the 0 subnet of a network that has been subnetted.

18. A. The best answer is that the MAC address was forwarded from another switch, because port Fa0/11 has many MAC addresses associated with it.

19. A. SW-A will become the root bridge because it has the lowest bridge ID, which is a combination of MAC address and priority. In this case, lowest MAC address becomes the root. Even though SW-C says it has a priority of 1; that is not possible. The lowest priority that can be set on a switch is 4096.

20. D. Although answer C is close to being correct, only answer D is correct, because you must have a space after the command `area` before listing the associated area.

21. D, E. The router output is a RIP entry in a routing table. The default administrative distance of RIP is 120, and the 120/3 means that the default AD of 120 is being used and the network in the table is three hops away.

22. A, D, F. To answer this question, you must know what a /21 is. A /21 is 255.255.248.0, which is a block size of 8, wildcard of 7, in the third octet (wildcards are always one less then the block size). Telnet uses TCP at the Transport layer and is well-known port number 23.

23. D. The `ip route` command with all zeros is a default route. Any traffic without a specific route will be sent out the interface specified at the end of the command. A next hop can also be used with the command instead of the exit interface.

24. B. Host C's address is on the wrong network. It is on the 13 network, whereas its current IP is on the 14 network.

25. B. If the revision number of the new switch is higher, the other switches will begin taking the new switch's update, which could cause connectivity problems.

26. B, C, E. A typical router can be set back to factory defaults by erasing the startup-config in NVRAM and then reloading the device. However, a switch keeps the VLAN database in Flash, and that must also be deleted on a switch to set it back to factory defaults.

27. D. A /30 or 255.255.255.252 provides only two hosts, regardless of the class of address, which is perfect for a point-to-point link.

28. E. First, you must know what a /29 is. The mask is 255.255.255.248, which means the block size is 8 in the fourth octet. A wildcard is always one less than the block size, so the answer is 0.0.0.7.

29. A. If an interface is administratively down, this means the interface is not enabled and must be enabled with the `no shutdown` command. All interfaces on a router are shut down by default.

30. C. The default configuration register is set to 0x2102. If this is changed, then the router will not boot the default setting of loading the IOS from flash and the configuration from NVRAM.

31. C. If STP is disabled on the switches, then broadcast storms, multiple frame copies, and MAC address table instability problems will occur.

32. C. The `ip route` command can be used for a couple of different reasons: to set a static route to a network, and to set a default route. The default route allows IP to send packets to remote networks that are not specifically listed in the routing table.

33. C, D. PortFast is a feature that allows a port on a switch to transition directly to forwarding. Only ports that have end stations and are not connected to other switches should be configured like this.

34. E. The steps included in a PPP session establishment are link establishment, optional authentication, and network layer protocol.

35. A. By using static routes instead of a routing protocol configured on each router, processing will be minimized. However, this can be done because the network is small. In a larger network, static routes would be difficult to maintain.

36.

Next hop 192.168.10.1	
172.44.98.1	
172.2.5.6	
Next hop 192.168.20.2	
172.16.0.33	
172.16.0.23	
Next hop 192.168.30.3	
172.16.10.10	
172.16.41.2	

Table 2-3

This is a hard question, no doubt about that. The top route is a default route, so any destination IP address that doesn't match the second and third line will be sent to 192.168.10.1. The difference between the second and third lines is the subnet mask. The second static route has a /24 mask, which makes the third octet the subnet address. Because the third static route has a /16 mask, the third octet is not part of the subnet. Once you determine that the third octet has to be a 0 to match the second static route, the rest of the answers fall into place.

37. A, C. A router running a link-state protocol uses hello packets to dynamically find neighbors and form adjacencies. Once an adjacency has been formed, it uses link state advertisement (LSA) packets to exchange topology information and updates when changes occur.

38. C. A feasible successor is stored in EIGRP's topology table, which holds all links known in the autonomous system. A successor route is copied from the topology table and placed in the routing table, which is then used by IP to route packets. The feasible successor is the backup route to the successor route.

39. C. A LAN switch uses MAC addresses to segment the network into collision domains. The switch looks at the source MAC address of each frame received on a port and places this in a forward/filter table, also called the content addressable memory (CAM) table. If a frame is received and the destination hardware (MAC) address is not found in the CAM table, the frame will be sent out all ports except the port it was received on.

40. C. The `banner motd` command means "message of the day." This is an old Unix command, but it is still useful on routers to provide messages to users logging in either via the console port or through telnet to a router or switch.

41. A, E. The ping program uses ICMP echo request and ICMP echo reply packets to find out if a host is "alive" on the network. Of course, ARP is used to resolve IP-to-hardware addresses for sending frames on a local network.

42. C, D. The wildcard in the mask is the key to the answer. 0.0.3.255 means the third octet has a wildcard of 4. The 12 in the third octet means that the access list will match 12, 13, 14, and 15, which make C and D the answers. B is wrong because the port number is wrong.

43. A, C, F. To configure a switch port to communicate with a router and share VLAN information, first choose the interface; then set the encapsulation type, in this case 802.1q; and then set the port to trunk. That is the correct order of configuration.

44. B, C. This is a pretty simple question. It ask you how to configure the interfaces, not the actual NAT commands. The interface commands are "ip nat inside" and "ip nat outside" from interface configuration mode.

crossover	switch to switch
straight-through	switch access port to router
rollover	PC COM port to switch

Table 2-4

A switch port (called an access port if it is a member of only one VLAN) directly attached to a router needs a straight-through cable. However, if you have a switch-to-switch connection, you need a crossover cable. A cable from a COM port connecting to a router or switch console port would use a rolled cable.

46. A, D. If the interface e0 of Router 3 goes down, Router 4 will send a destination unreachable message type to the transmitting host, in this cast Host A.

47. A. OSPF uses only bandwidth to determine the best path to a remote network. By calculating the entire path, OSPF determines the cost of the path, which is shown in the router output.

48. C, D, E. When configuring OSPF, you must have an area 0, which is also called the backbone area. This area may be assigned any number from 0 to 2.4 billion. You must have an area 0, according to the CCNA objectives, but you don't have to have multiple areas. All routers can be in area 0.

49. B, D, E. SMTP, FTP, and HTTP are Application layer protocols that use TCP at the Transport layer. DHCP, SNMP, and TFTP all use UDP at the Transport layer.

50. A, C, D. There are two types of ports on a switch: an access port and a trunk port. A switch port cannot be both types of ports. An access port means the switch port is part of one VLAN and is typically used for a host and/or phone. A trunk port is used to connect to other switches and to routers.

51. C. To answer this question, you must know what a /22 is. A /22 is 255.255.252.0. This is a block size of 4 in the third octet. You count in increments of 4 until you pass 210. The subnet is 208.0, and the broadcast address is 172.16.211.255.

52. C. When creating subinterfaces on a router, an IP address is not configured under the physical interface of the router. IP addresses can only be configured under the logical (subinterfaces) interfaces, or the network will not function.

53. C. When OSPF is configured on a router, a router identification (RID) is created by using the highest IP address on any active interface at the moment of OSPF startup. The RID can be changed by creating a loopback interface, also called a logical interface. This RID is used by routers to determine which router will be a designated router or backup designated router in a broadcast or nonbroadcast multi-access network.

54. C. Unlike Frame Relay point-to-point subinterfaces, multipoint subinterfaces use one subnet for all PVC connections. Point-to-point uses one subnet for each PVC.

55. B. Port security can help you manage your switched network by allowing you to filter by MAC address and controlling the number of MAC addresses allowed on each port.

Answer Sheets for Practice Test 3

Section 1
Multiple Choice Questions

CUT HERE

1 Ⓐ Ⓑ Ⓒ Ⓓ Ⓔ Ⓕ	31 Ⓐ Ⓑ Ⓒ Ⓓ Ⓔ Ⓕ
2 Ⓐ Ⓑ Ⓒ Ⓓ Ⓔ Ⓕ	32 Ⓐ Ⓑ Ⓒ Ⓓ Ⓔ Ⓕ
3 Ⓐ Ⓑ Ⓒ Ⓓ Ⓔ Ⓕ	33 Ⓐ Ⓑ Ⓒ Ⓓ Ⓔ Ⓕ
4 Ⓐ Ⓑ Ⓒ Ⓓ Ⓔ Ⓕ	34 Ⓐ Ⓑ Ⓒ Ⓓ Ⓔ Ⓕ
5 Ⓐ Ⓑ Ⓒ Ⓓ Ⓔ Ⓕ	35 Ⓐ Ⓑ Ⓒ Ⓓ Ⓔ Ⓕ
6 Ⓐ Ⓑ Ⓒ Ⓓ Ⓔ Ⓕ	36 Ⓐ Ⓑ Ⓒ Ⓓ Ⓔ Ⓕ
7 Ⓐ Ⓑ Ⓒ Ⓓ Ⓔ Ⓕ	37 Ⓐ Ⓑ Ⓒ Ⓓ Ⓔ Ⓕ
8 Ⓐ Ⓑ Ⓒ Ⓓ Ⓔ Ⓕ	38 Ⓐ Ⓑ Ⓒ Ⓓ Ⓔ Ⓕ
9 Ⓐ Ⓑ Ⓒ Ⓓ Ⓔ Ⓕ	39 Ⓐ Ⓑ Ⓒ Ⓓ Ⓔ Ⓕ
10 Ⓐ Ⓑ Ⓒ Ⓓ Ⓔ Ⓕ	40 Ⓐ Ⓑ Ⓒ Ⓓ Ⓔ Ⓕ
11 Ⓐ Ⓑ Ⓒ Ⓓ Ⓔ Ⓕ	41 Ⓐ Ⓑ Ⓒ Ⓓ Ⓔ Ⓕ
12 Ⓐ Ⓑ Ⓒ Ⓓ Ⓔ Ⓕ	42 Ⓐ Ⓑ Ⓒ Ⓓ Ⓔ Ⓕ
13 Ⓐ Ⓑ Ⓒ Ⓓ Ⓔ Ⓕ	43 Ⓐ Ⓑ Ⓒ Ⓓ Ⓔ Ⓕ
14 Ⓐ Ⓑ Ⓒ Ⓓ Ⓔ Ⓕ	44 Ⓐ Ⓑ Ⓒ Ⓓ Ⓔ Ⓕ
15 Ⓐ Ⓑ Ⓒ Ⓓ Ⓔ Ⓕ	45 Ⓐ Ⓑ Ⓒ Ⓓ Ⓔ Ⓕ
16 Ⓐ Ⓑ Ⓒ Ⓓ Ⓔ Ⓕ	46 Ⓐ Ⓑ Ⓒ Ⓓ Ⓔ Ⓕ
17 Ⓐ Ⓑ Ⓒ Ⓓ Ⓔ Ⓕ	47 Ⓐ Ⓑ Ⓒ Ⓓ Ⓔ Ⓕ
18 Ⓐ Ⓑ Ⓒ Ⓓ Ⓔ Ⓕ	48 Ⓐ Ⓑ Ⓒ Ⓓ Ⓔ Ⓕ
19 Ⓐ Ⓑ Ⓒ Ⓓ Ⓔ Ⓕ	49 Ⓐ Ⓑ Ⓒ Ⓓ Ⓔ Ⓕ
20 Ⓐ Ⓑ Ⓒ Ⓓ Ⓔ Ⓕ	50 Ⓐ Ⓑ Ⓒ Ⓓ Ⓔ Ⓕ
21 Ⓐ Ⓑ Ⓒ Ⓓ Ⓔ Ⓕ	51 Ⓐ Ⓑ Ⓒ Ⓓ Ⓔ Ⓕ
22 Ⓐ Ⓑ Ⓒ Ⓓ Ⓔ Ⓕ	52 Ⓐ Ⓑ Ⓒ Ⓓ Ⓔ Ⓕ
23 Ⓐ Ⓑ Ⓒ Ⓓ Ⓔ Ⓕ	53 Ⓐ Ⓑ Ⓒ Ⓓ Ⓔ Ⓕ
24 Ⓐ Ⓑ Ⓒ Ⓓ Ⓔ Ⓕ	54 Ⓐ Ⓑ Ⓒ Ⓓ Ⓔ Ⓕ
25 Ⓐ Ⓑ Ⓒ Ⓓ Ⓔ Ⓕ	55 Ⓐ Ⓑ Ⓒ Ⓓ Ⓔ Ⓕ
26 Ⓐ Ⓑ Ⓒ Ⓓ Ⓔ Ⓕ	
27 Ⓐ Ⓑ Ⓒ Ⓓ Ⓔ Ⓕ	
28 Ⓐ Ⓑ Ⓒ Ⓓ Ⓔ Ⓕ	
29 Ⓐ Ⓑ Ⓒ Ⓓ Ⓔ Ⓕ	
30 Ⓐ Ⓑ Ⓒ Ⓓ Ⓔ Ⓕ	

Directions: For each of the following questions, select the choice that best answers the question or completes the statement.

1. You have been asked to allow only certain MAC addresses to attach to the switch. Which of the following should you enable?

    A. BDPU Guard
    B. port security
    C. QoS
    D. STP
    E. VTP

2. Look at the following diagram. Assume that ports 1 through 3 are designated to VLAN1 and ports 4 through 6 are designated to VLAN2 on each switch. Further, assume that your switches connect via a trunk link. Pick the three events that confirm that both your VLAN and trunk are working correctly.

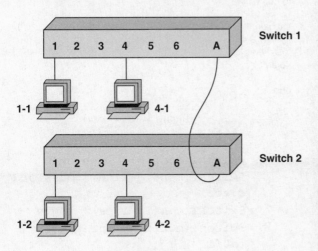

Figure 3-1

    A. Host 1-1 can ping Host 1-2.
    B. Host 1-1 can ping Host 4-2.
    C. Host 1-1 cannot ping Host 1-2.
    D. Host 4-1 cannot ping Host 1-2.
    E. Host 4-1 can ping Host 4-2.

3. Look at the following diagram. You can see the partial output from four switches. Choose the switch that acts as the spanning-tree root bridge for a network that's limited to the following four devices.

```
Vail#sh spanning-tree
VLAN0001 Spanning tree enabled protocol ieee
Root ID   Priority   32768 Address     0005.dccb.d740
Hello Time  2 sec  Max Age 20 sec  Forward Delay 15 sec

Aspen#sh spanning-tree
VLAN0001 Spanning tree enabled protocol ieee
Root ID   Priority   16384 Address     0005.dccb.d739
Hello Time  2 sec  Max Age 20 sec  Forward Delay 15 sec

Breckenridge#sh spanning-tree
VLAN0001 Spanning tree enabled protocol ieee
Root ID   Priority   8192 Address     0005.dccb.d738
Hello Time  2 sec  Max Age 20 sec  Forward Delay 15 sec

Keystone#sh spanning-tree
VLAN0001 Spanning tree enabled protocol ieee
Root ID   Priority   4096 Address     0005.dccb.d737
Hello Time  2 sec  Max Age 20 sec  Forward Delay 15 sec
```

Figure 3-2

    A. Vail
    B. Aspen
    C. Breckenridge
    D. Keystone

GO ON TO THE NEXT PAGE

4. From the following output, choose the two possible causes for status "Serial0/0 is down".

```
Corp#show interface s0/0
Serial0/0 is down, line protocol is down
  Hardware is PowerQUICC
Serial Internet address is 10.0.10.2/24
  MTU 1500 bytes, BW 1544 Kbit, DLY 20000 usec, rely
    255/255, load 4/255
  Encapsulation HDLC, loopback not set, Keepalive set
    (10 sec)
[output cut]
```

Code Listing 3-1

- **A.** Layer 1 problem
- **B.** Incorrect bandwidth setting
- **C.** Protocol mismatch
- **D.** Incorrect cable
- **E.** Incorrect IP address

5. Choose the two of the following that best describe the process identifier used to run OSPF on a router.

- **A.** It's locally significant.
- **B.** It's globally significant.
- **C.** It's needed to identify a unique instance of an OSPF database.
- **D.** It's an optional parameter required only if multiple OSPF processes are running on the router.
- **E.** All routers in the same OSPF area must have the same process ID if they are to exchange routing information.

6. Over a Telnet session, you find that you can't connect to Switch1, but you can ping the router interface Fa0/0 via the host machines attached to the switch. Both the router and Switch1 are configured properly. Looking at the following diagram, choose one set of the following commands you should use on Switch1 to solve the problem.

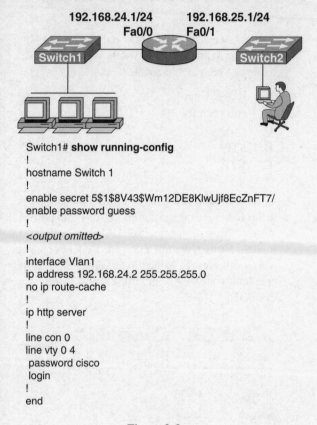

```
Switch1# show running-config
!
hostname Switch 1
!
enable secret 5$1$8V43$Wm12DE8KlwUjf8EcZnFT7/
enable password guess
!
<output omitted>
!
interface Vlan1
ip address 192.168.24.2 255.255.255.0
no ip route-cache
!
ip http server
!
line con 0
line vty 0 4
 password cisco
 login
!
end
```

Figure 3-3

- **A.** Switch1(config)# line con0
  Switch1(config-line)# password cisco
  Switch1(config-line)# login
- **B.** Switch1(config)# interface fa0/1
  Switch1(config-if)# ip address 192.168.24.3 255.255.255.0
- **C.** Switch1(config)# ip default-gateway 192.168.24.1
- **D.** Switch1(config)# interface fa0/1
  Switch1(config-if)# duplex full
  Switch1(config-if)# speed 100
- **E.** Switch1(config)# interface fa0/1
  Switch1(config-if)# switchport mode trunk

7. The Sharper Edge chain of ski shops wants to re-design its network that connects its three locations. The administrator gave the networking team 192.168.128.0 to use for addressing the entire network. After subnetting the address, the team is ready to assign the addresses. The administrator plans to configure `ip subnet-zero` and use RIP v2 as the routing protocol. As a member of the networking team, you must address the network and at the same time conserve unused addresses for future growth. With those goals in mind, match the host addresses on the left to the correct router interface.

192.168.128.184/26	Aspen 56 hosts Fa0/0
192.168.128.127/25	Breckenridge 2 hosts S0/1
192.168.128.249/29	Copper 6 hosts Fa0/0
192.168.128.241/30	Keystone 26 hosts Fa0/0
192.168.128.240/30	
192.168.128.196/27	

8. When routing a packet, which functions do routers perform? (Choose two.)

- **A.** Packet switching
- **B.** Destination host addressing
- **C.** Path selection
- **D.** VLAN membership assignment
- **E.** ARP request forwarding

9. Which of the following adds a default route to a router?

- **A.** `router(config)# ip route 0.0.0.0 10.1.1.0 10.1.1.1`
- **B.** `router(config)# ip default-route 10.1.1.0`
- **C.** `router(config)# ip default-gateway 10.1.1.0`
- **D.** `router(config)# ip route 0.0.0.0 0.0.0.0 10.1.1.1`

10. When a router is connected to a Frame Relay WAN link using a serial DTE interface, how can the interface clock rate be established?

- **A.** It is supplied by the CSU/DSU.
- **B.** It is supplied by the far-end router.
- **C.** It is determined by the `clock rate` command.
- **D.** It is supplied by layer 1 bit stream timing.

11. Your switched network is running Spanning Tree Protocol. Choose from the following statements the one that describes when it's completely converged.

- **A.** When all switches have the same BID as the root switch
- **B.** When all switches have received the MAC address of each neighboring switch
- **C.** When every enabled switch port has been assigned a unique identifier
- **D.** When every operating switch port is in either the blocking or forwarding state
- **E.** When all switches are in client, server, or transparent mode

12. Look at the following diagram. Choose the best summarization R1 can employ to display its networks to R2.

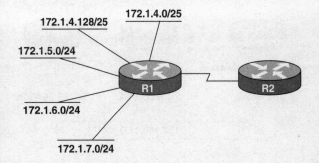

Figure 3-4

- **A.** 172.1.0.0/22
- **B.** 172.1.0.0/21
- **C.** 172.1.4.0/22
- **D.** 172.1.4.0/24
  172.1.5.0/24
  172.1.6.0/24
  172.1.7.0/24
- **E.** 172.1.4.0/25
  172.1.4.128/25
  172.1.5.0/24
  172.1.6.0/24
  172.1.7.0/24

GO ON TO THE NEXT PAGE

13. When dealing with Frame Relay multipoint subinterfaces, which statement best describes what's true about them?

    A. An IP address is required on the physical interface of the central router.

    B. All routers are required to be fully meshed.

    C. All routers must be in the same subnet to forward routing updates and broadcasts.

    D. Multipoint is the default configuration for Frame Relay subinterfaces.

14. Look at the following diagram. Which subnet address you would use for Network A?

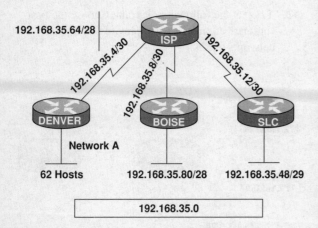

Figure 3-5

    A. 192.168.35.32/27

    B. 192.168.35.64/26

    C. 192.168.35.96/27

    D. 192.168.35.128/26

    E. 192.168.35.192/27

15. What is the default administrative distance for OSPF?

    A. 90

    B. 100

    C. 110

    D. 120

    E. 130

    F. 170

16. All of your OSPF routers in one location are configured with the same priority value. Without a loopback interface, which of the following is the value a router will use for the OSPF router ID?

    A. The IP address of the first Fast Ethernet interface

    B. The IP address of the console management interface

    C. The highest IP address among its active interfaces

    D. The lowest IP address among its active interfaces

    E. The priority value until a loopback interface is configured

17. Look at the following diagram. You need Host A to send data to Host B. Choose the three true statements that describe how Router1 will deal with a data frame it receives from Host A.

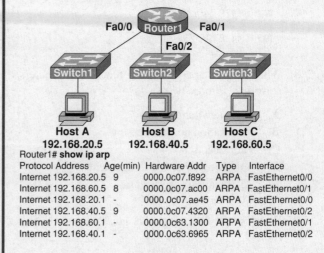

Figure 3-6

    A. Router1 will strip off the source MAC address and replace it with the MAC address on the forwarding Fast Ethernet interface.

    B. Router1 will strip off the source IP address and replace it with the IP address on the forwarding Fast Ethernet interface.

    C. Router1 will strip off the destination MAC address and replace it with the MAC address of Host B.

    D. Router1 will strip off the destination IP address and replace it with the IP address of Host B.

    E. Router1 will forward the data frame out interface Fast Ethernet 0/1.

    F. Router1 will forward the data frame out interface Fast Ethernet 0/2.

18. Which two reasons describe why you would encapsulate an ISDN link with PPP instead of HDLC?

   A. PPP is consistently implemented among different equipment vendors.

   B. PPP runs faster and more efficiently than HDLC on circuit-switched ISDN links.

   C. PPP authentication prevents unauthorized callers from establishing an ISDN circuit.

   D. PPP is easier to configure and maintain than HDLC.

   E. PPP can be routed across public facilities, whereas HDLC is not routable in circuit-switched networks.

19. You've configured a Cisco router and entered the `copy running-config startup-config` command, but when the router is power cycled, it gives you the prompt, "Would you like to enter the initial configuration dialog? [yes/no]:" Why is it doing this?

   A. There is an error in the router DRAM.

   B. The IOS image is corrupt.

   C. The configuration register is set to 0x2142.

   D. The TFTP server that contains the router configuration file is unreachable.

   E. A boot system configuration command has placed the router into setup mode.

20. Look at the following diagram. Assume that every router is configured with the `ip subnet-zero` command. Choose the two network addresses you would use for Link A and Network A.

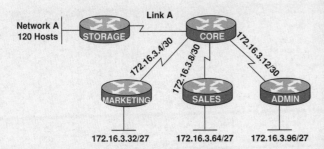

Figure 3-7

   A. Network A - 172.16.3.48/26

   B. Network A - 172.16.3.128/25

   C. Network A - 172.16.3.192/26

   D. Link A - 172.16.3.0/30

   E. Link A - 172.16.3.40/30

   F. Link A - 172.16.3.112/30

21. Which two of the following are reasons a network administrator would use access lists?

   A. To control VTY access into a router

   B. To control broadcast traffic through a router

   C. To filter traffic as it passes through a router

   D. To filter traffic that originates from a router

   E. To replace passwords as a line of defense against security incursions

22. Which of the following describes the type of physical network a default Frame Relay WAN is?

   A. Point-to-point

   B. Broadcast multi-access

   C. Nonbroadcast multi-access

   D. Nonbroadcast multipoint

   E. Broadcast point-to-multipoint

23. You can't telnet to a router at IP address 203.125.12.1 from a machine with IP address 203.125.12.23, and you think it's a problem with your protocol stack. What can you do that has the best chance of confirming your suspicion?

   A. `ping 127.0.0.0`

   B. `ping 203.125.12.1`

   C. `telnet 127.0.0.1`

   D. `ping 127.0.0.1`

   E. `tracert 203.125.12.1`

24. You've subnetted a Class C network address with a /27 mask. Choose the address that would be the broadcast address for one of your new subnets.

   A. 201.57.78.33

   B. 201.57.78.64

   C. 201.57.78.87

   D. 201.57.78.97

   E. 201.57.78.159

   F. 201.57.78.254

GO ON TO THE NEXT PAGE

25. How will spanning tree influence the functioning of your network devices if you have redundant links between switches?

    A. Spanning tree blocks client ports that suffer from excessive errors.

    B. Spanning tree learns client MAC addresses and assigns them to switch ports.

    C. Spanning tree allows these switches to load-balance across the redundant links to increase network throughput.

    D. Spanning tree learns which of the redundant links should be blocked.

    E. Spanning tree automatically configures the switches with VLAN information.

26. Choose the command you would use to view all EIGRP-feasible successor routes known to Router 1.

    A. `Router# show ip eigrp routes*`

    B. `Router# show ip eigrp summary`

    C. `Router# show ip eigrp topology`

    D. `Router# show ip eigrp adjacencies`

    E. `Router# show ip eigrp neighbors detail`

27. You have two switches, each with a VLAN configured on the switch: one with VLAN 2 and one with VLAN 3. What do you need to use to enable communication between hosts in VLAN 2 and VLAN 3?

    A. CSU/DSU connected to the switches with crossover cables

    B. Router connected to the switches with straight-through cables

    C. Router connected to the switches with crossover cables

    D. Straight-through cable only

    E. Crossover cable only

28. By looking at the following diagram, you can see that Host A and Host B are communicating. Which of the following describes how data will be addressed leaving Host A?

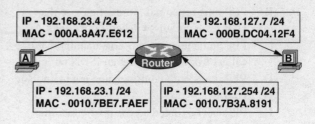

Figure 3-8

    A. Source MAC = 000A.8A47.E612
    Destination MAC = 000B.DC04.12F4
    Source IP = 192.168.23.4
    Destination IP = 192.168.23.1

    B. Source MAC = 000A.8A47.E612
    Destination MAC = 0010.7BE7.FAEF
    Source IP = 192.168.23.4
    Destination IP = 192.168.127.7

    C. Source MAC = 000A.8A47.E612
    Destination MAC = 000B.DC04.12F4
    Source IP = 192.168.23.4
    Destination IP = 192.168.127.7

    D. Source MAC = 000A.8A47.E612
    Destination MAC = 0010.7BE7.FAEF
    Source IP = 192.168.23.4
    Destination IP = 192.168.23.1

29. Match the command sequence on the left with the functions on the right that will properly configure an IP address on an Ethernet interface.

Lab# **configure terminal**	Enter privileged EXEC mode
Lab(config-if)# **ip address 192.168.3.3/24**	Enter global configuration mode
Lab(config-if)# **ip address 10.8.26.0 255.255.248.0**	Enter interface configuration mode
Lab(config)# **ip address 172.16.10.1 255.255.255.0**	Configure the interface IP address
Lab# **interface fa0/0**	Enable the interface
Lab(config)# **interface fa0/0**	
Lab(config-if)# **no shutdown**	
Lab(config-if)# **enable interface**	
Lab# **enable**	
Lab> **enable**	

30. If a host has an IP address of 172.16.211.0/22, which of the following is the subnetwork number?

- **A.** 172.16.42.0
- **B.** 172.16.107.0
- **C.** 172.16.208.0
- **D.** 172.16.252.0
- **E.** 172.16.254.0

31. Which of the following best describes what a layer 2 switch will do when it receives a frame with a destination MAC address that's not in its MAC address table?

- **A.** The frame is dropped.
- **B.** The frame is addressed with a broadcast MAC address and sent out all ports.
- **C.** The frame is sent out all ports except the receiving port.
- **D.** An ARP request is sent out all ports except the receiving port.
- **E.** A destination-unreachable message is sent back to the source address.

32. How are OSPF hello packets on a point-to-point network addressed?

- **A.** 127.0.0.1
- **B.** 172.16.0.1
- **C.** 192.168.0.5
- **D.** 223.0.0.1
- **E.** 224.0.0.5
- **F.** 254.255.255.255

33. By looking at the following diagram, choose the two access-list statements you need to permit FTP access to the HR Server from the Internet, but block all other traffic.

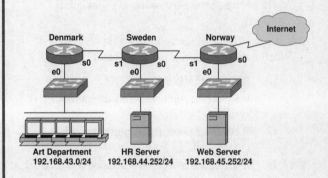

Figure 3-9

- **A.** access-list 101 permit tcp any 192.168.44.252 0.0.0.0 eq 21
- **B.** access-list 101 permit tcp any 192.168.44.252 0.0.0.0 eq 20
- **C.** access-list 101 permit tcp 192.168.44.252 0.0.0.0 any eq 20
- **D.** access-list 101 permit tcp 192.168.44.252 0.0.0.0 any eq 21
- **E.** access-list 101 deny tcp any 192.168.44.252 0.0.0.0 gt 21
- **F.** access-list 101 deny tcp 192.168.44.252 0.0.0.0 any gt 21

34. You've configured an OSPF interface with the `bandwidth 64` command. What will OSPF determine to be the cost of the link?

- **A.** 1
- **B.** 10
- **C.** 1562
- **D.** 64000
- **E.** 128000

GO ON TO THE NEXT PAGE

35. Looking at the following diagram, how can you guarantee that Switch B is elected as the root switch during the STP election process?

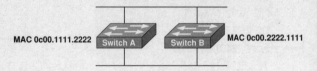

MAC 0c00.1111.2222   MAC 0c00.2222.1111

Figure 3-10

A. Clear the Switch B STP revision number.
B. Assign Switch B a low priority number.
C. Increase the Switch B priority number.
D. Change the MAC address of Switch B.

36. Choose three of the following that accurately represent the OSPF routing protocol.

A. It supports VLSM.
B. It is used to route between autonomous systems.
C. It confines network instability to one area of the network.
D. It increases routing overhead on the network.
E. It allows extensive control of routing updates.
F. It is simpler to configure than RIP v2.

37. Say you entered the `ping 192.168.5.2` command to successfully test connectivity to a recently added host machine. Choose the two protocols employed during your test.

A. ARP
B. CDP
C. DHCP
D. DNS
E. ICMP

38. Look at the following diagram. Suppose the four switches it shows are the only ones in the network, and they're connected via redundant links. Choose which one of the four switches will be elected the spanning-tree root bridge.

Switch1# **show spantree**
  VLAN1 is executing the IEEE compatible Spanning Tree Protocol
   Bridge Identifier has priority 32768, address 00d0.5868.f180
Catalyst 1900   <output omitted>
2 MB DRAM

Switch2# **show spanning-tree**
  Spanning tree 1 is executing the IEEE compatible Spanning Tree protocol
   Bridge Identifier has priority 32768, address 00d0.5868.f181
Catalyst 2900XL   <output omitted>
4 MB DRAM
2 100Base-FX ports

Switch3# **show spanning-tree**
  Spanning tree 1 is executing the IEEE compatible Spanning Tree protocol
   Bridge Identifier has priority 32768, address 00d0.5868.f182
Catalyst 2950G   <output omitted>
8 MB DRAM
2 fixed GBIC-based 1000BASE-X uplink ports

Switch4# **show spanning-tree**
  Spanning tree 1 is executing the IEEE compatible Spanning Tree protocol
   Bridge Identifier has priority 32768, address 00d0.5868.f183
Catalyst 2950G   <output omitted>
32 MB DRAM
2 10/100/1000 ports

Figure 3-11

A. Switch1
B. Switch2
C. Switch3
D. Switch4

39. Look at the following diagram. Your network's IP address is 172.31.0.0/19, and you want to configure it on the router with the partial configuration. Choose the answer that accurately identifies how many available subnets and hosts you'll have after you complete the configuration.

```
Current configuration:
!
version 12.0
service timestamps debug uptime
service timestamps log uptime
no service password-encryption
!
hostname R1
!
ip subnet-zero
!
!
ip classless
ip route 0.0.0.0 0.0.0.0 Serial0/0
no ip http server
!
<output omitted>
```

Figure 3-12

A. There are 7 useable subnets, with 30 useable host addresses.

B. There are 7 useable subnets, with 2046 useable host addresses.

C. There are 7 useable subnets, with 8190 useable host addresses.

D. There are 8 useable subnets, with 30 useable host addresses.

E. There are 8 useable subnets, with 2046 useable host addresses.

F. There are 8 useable subnets, with 8190 useable host addresses.

40. The two switches in the following diagram, Core and Core2, are both Catalyst 2950s, and you've created an addressing scheme for each site that looks like this:

Router Ethernet port—First useable address

Core—Second useable address

Core2—Third useable address

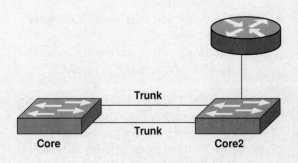

Figure 3-13

Choose the three commands you need to configure on Core2 so you can manage it remotely from any subnet located on your network.

A. `Core2(config)# interface f0/0`
`Core2(config-if)# ip address`
`192.168.1.10 255.255.255.248`

B. `Core2(config)# interface vlan 1`
`Core2(config-if)# ip address`
`192.168.1.11 255.255.255.248`

C. `Core2(config)# line con 0`
`Core2(config-line)#`
`password cisco`

D. `Core2(config)# line vty 0 4`
`Core2(config-line)# password`
`cisco`

E. `Core2(config)# ip default-`
`gateway`
`192.168.1.9`

F. `Core2(config)# ip route`
`0.0.0.0 0.0.0.0`
`192.168.1.8`

GO ON TO THE NEXT PAGE

41. Choose the two things that will happen if you enter the Switch(config)# **vtp mode client** command on a Catalyst switch.

A. The switch will ignore VTP summary advertisements.

B. The switch will forward VTP summary advertisements.

C. The switch will process VTP summary advertisements.

D. The switch will originate VTP summary advertisements.

E. The switch will create, modify, and delete VLANs for the entire VTP domain.

42. The following diagram displays a partial switch command output. Pay close attention to the topology. The internetwork has some connectivity problems indicated by the inability of Host A to ping Host B. Which of the following should you do to solve the problem?

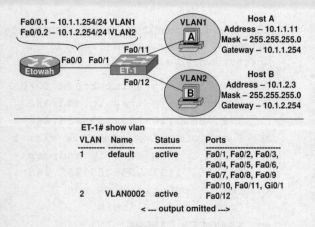

Figure 3-14

A. Change the gateway on Host A.

B. Reconfigure the IP address on Host B.

C. Name VLAN2.

D. Configure the Fa0/1 interface on the ET-1 switch as a trunk port.

E. Move switch port Fa0/1 to a different VLAN.

43. Choose the two statements that accurately describe the command ip route 172.16.3.0 255.255.255.0 192.168.2.4.

A. The command is used to establish a static route.

B. The default administrative distance is used.

C. The command is used to configure the default route.

D. The subnet mask for the source address is 255.255.255.0.

E. The command is used to establish a stub network.

44. You issue the show ip route command that allows you to view the following output. Choose the route that won't be entered into the neighboring router's routing table.

A. R 192.168.8.0/24 [120/1] via 192.168.2.2, 00:00:10, Serial0

B. R 192.168.11.0/24 [120/7] via 192.168.9.1, 00:00:03, Serial1

C. C 192.168.1.0/24 is directly connected, Ethernet0

D. R 192.168.5.0/24 [120/15] via 192.168.2.2, 00:00:10, Serial0

45. Choose two options that depict the information a router that's running a link-state protocol uses to create and sustain its topological database.

A. Hello packets

B. SAP messages sent by other routers

C. LSAs from other routers

D. Beacons received on point-to-point links

E. Routing tables received from other link-state routers

F. TTL packets from designated routers

46. Choose the three services that use TCP.

A. DHCP

B. SMTP

C. SNMP

D. FTP

E. HTTP

F. TFTP

47. EIGRP successor routes are stored where?

A. In the routing table only

B. In the neighbor table only

C. In the topology table only

D. In the routing table and neighbor table

E. In the routing table and topology table

F. In the topology table and neighbor table

48. Your Breckenridge router adds the following command to the router configuration: `ip route 192.168.12.0 255.255.255.0 172.16.12.1`. Which two things are true because of this?

A. The command establishes a static route.

B. The command invokes a dynamic routing protocol for 192.168.12.0.

C. Traffic for network 192.168.12.0 is forwarded to172.16.12.1.

D. Traffic for all networks is forwarded to 172.16.12.1.

E. The route is automatically propagated throughout the entire network.

F. Traffic for network 172.16.12.0 is forwarded to the 192.168.12.0 network.

49. Of these choices, which one is a unicast address?

A. 224.1.5.2

B. FFFF.FFFF.FFFF

C. 192.168.24.59/30

D. 255.255.255.255

E. 172.31.128.255/18

50. You want to configure a switch via a virtual terminal connection from outside your local LAN. Choose two things that you need to do to successfully gain the ability to configure your switch remotely.

A. The switch must be configured with an IP address, a subnet mask, and a default gateway.

B. The switch must be connected to a router over a VLAN trunk.

C. The switch must be reachable through a port connected to its management VLAN.

D. The switch virtual terminal must be configured with a password.

E. The switch-management VLAN must be created and have a membership of at least one switch port.

F. The switch must be fully configured as an SNMP agent.

51. If your router has both physical and logical interfaces, which of the following will establish the OSPF router ID?

A. Lowest network number of any interface

B. Lowest IP address of any logical interface

C. Lowest IP address of any physical interface

D. Highest network number of any interface

E. Highest IP address of any logical interface

F. Highest IP address of any physical interface

52. On which OSI layer does the protocol operate that imparts the information you get by using the `show cdp neighbors` command?

A. Physical

B. Data Link

C. Network

E. Transport

F. Application

53. Choose the command that configures a switch port to use the IEEE standard method of adding VLAN membership information into Ethernet frames.

A. `Switch(config)# switchport trunk encapsulation isl`

B. `Switch(config)# switchport trunk encapsulation ietf`

C. `Switch(config)# switchport trunk encapsulation dot1q`

D. `Switch(config-if)# switchport trunk encapsulation isl`

E. `Switch(config-if)# switchport trunk encapsulation dot1q`

54. You need to configure an existing serial interface so it will receive a second Frame Relay virtual circuit. Which three things do you need to do to achieve this goal?

A. Remove the IP address from the physical interface.

B. Encapsulate the physical interface with multipoint PPP.

C. Create the virtual interfaces with the `interfaces` command.

D. Configure each subinterface with its own IP address.

E. Disable split horizon to prevent routing loops between the subinterface networks.

F. Configure static Frame Relay map entries for each subinterface networks.

55. You have a Cisco router and a router from another maker that are directly connected through a serial link. What command do you need to issue on the Cisco router to create a WAN connection between the routers?

A. `Lab(config-if)# encapsulation hdlc ansi`

B. `Lab(config-if)# encapsulation ppp`

C. `Lab(config-if)# encapsulation frame-relay default`

D. `Lab(config-if)# encapsulation isdn`

Answer Key for Practice Test 3

1. B
2. A, D, E
3. D
4. A, D
5. A, C
6. C
7. See Answer Explanation
8. A, C
9. D
10. A
11. D
12. C
13. C
14. D
15. C
16. C
17. A, C, F
18. A, C
19. C
20. B, D
21. A, C
22. C
23. D
24. E
25. D
26. C
27. B
28. B
29. See Answer Explanation
30. C
31. C
32. E
33. A, B
34. C
35. B
36. A, C, E
37. A, E
38. A
39. F
40. B, D, E
41. B, C
42. D
43. A, B
44. D
45. A, C
46. B, D, E
47. E
48. A, C
49. E
50. A, D
51. E
52. B
53. E
54. A, C, D
55. B

Answer Explanations for Practice Test 3

1. B. Port Security allows you to create filters based on MAC addresses.

2. A, D, E. In this case, there is no router to route between the two VLANs, and thus your hosts should only be able to ping other hosts in the same VLAN. A and E show that hosts in one VLAN can ping hosts in the same VLAN on the other switch.

3. D. The switch with the lowest priority (4096, in this case) will become the root bridge.

4. A, D. An interface being in a down/down state indicates a layer 1 problem. That could include an incorrect cable.

5. A, C. The OSPF process ID is locally significant and identifies each individual instance of OSPF running, should multiple instances be running on a single router.

6. C. The switch does not have a default gateway defined and thus will not be able to support IP communications outside its own subnet.

7.

192.168.128.184/26	Aspen 56 hosts Fa0/0
192.168.128.241/30	Breckenridge 2 hosts S0/1
192.168.128.249/29	Copper 6 hosts Fa0/0
192.168.128.196/27	Keystone 26 hosts Fa0/0

8. A, C. Routers must switch the packets between interfaces and perform path selection based on layer 3 destination addresses. They do not assign VLAN membership, and ARP broadcasts do not cross routers.

9. D. A static route with a destination network and mask of all zeros is the default route.

10. A. In a serial connection, one device or end of the cable is the DTE (a router in most cases) and the other device or end of the cable is the DCE (CSU/DSU or ISP device). In this type of connection, the clock rate and control for the connection come from the DCE device.

11. D. Once every switch port has completed the spanning tree states and is either in blocking or forwarding state, the switched network is said to be converged.

12. C. 172.1.4.0/22 covers all addresses 172.1.4.0 through 172.1.7.255, exactly what R1 has.

13. C. Unlike Frame Relay point-to-point subinterfaces, multipoint subinterfaces use one subnet for all PVC connections. Point-to-point uses one subnet for each PVC.

14. D. You will need a /26 subnet in order to have enough address space for 62 hosts. The address space beginning at 192.168.35.64 is already in use.

15. C. The default administrative distance for OSPF is 110.

16. C. When OSPF is configured on a router, a router identification (RID) is created by using the highest IP address on any active interface at the moment of OSPF startup. The RID can be changed by creating a loopback interface, also called a logical interface. This RID is used by routers to determine which router will be a designated router or backup designated router in a broadcast or nonbroadcast multi-access network.

17. A, C, F. The layer 2 header will be rebuilt every time it passes through a router. The layer 3 header stays constant from end to end.

18. A, C. PPP is universal, whereas HDLC is vendor proprietary. Additionally, PPP can allow for authentication.

19. C. The configuration register setting can tell the router to ignore any configuration in startup-config. This is used in the password recovery sequence; however, if it is inadvertently set, it causes the behavior described.

20. B, D. You will need at least a /25 address to for Network A, and the 172.16.3.0 network is the only one available for LinkA.

21. **A, C.** When connecting two like devices together directly, you must use a crossover cable for them to communicate.

22. **C.** Frame Relay is a nonbroadcast, multi-access network.

23. **D.** Pinging the loopback address will allow you to verify proper local function of the TCP/IP stack.

24. **E.** This is the broadcast address for the 201.57.78.128 network.

25. **D.** Spanning Tree discovers redundant links and places them in blocking mode.

26. **C.** The EIGRP topology table shows feasible successors.

27. **B.** A router is required to communicate between VLANs. Router-to-switch connections use standard straight-through cables.

28. **B.** The destination MAC will be the router, which is local to Host A. The destination IP will be the ultimate destination host.

29.

`Lab> enable`	Enter privileged EXEC mode
`Lab# configure terminal`	Enter global configuration mode
`Lab(config)# interface fa0/0`	Enter interface configuration mode
`Lab(config-if)# ip address 10.8.26.0 255.255.248.0`	Configure the interface IP address
`Lab(config-if)# no shutdown`	Enable the interface

30. **C.** The subnetwork is 172.16.208.0.

31. **C.** In the case where the destination MAC is unknown, the switch will flood the frame out all ports except the receiving port.

32. **E.** OSPF uses multicast address 224.0.0.5 for hello packets.

33. **A, B.** When allowing FTP traffic, you must allow both the data and control ports. The implicit deny will deny all other traffic.

34. **C.** OSPF divides the link bandwidth into the reference bandwidth (100Mbps by default).

35. **B.** By assigning a lower priority, you can guarantee that a switch is elected root switch.

36. **A, C, E.** OSPF supports VLSM. The use of areas allows for isolation of routing instability and has extensive controls to use in influencing routing updates.

37. **A, E.** Your host will use ARP to map a destination IP to a MAC and will use ICMP to communicate with the destination host.

38. **A.** Because all priorities are equal, the switch with the lowest MAC address will become root bridge.

39. **F.** When subnetting a class B network with a /19 mask, you have 8 subnets of 8190 hosts each (assuming you are using IP subnet zero).

40. **B, D, E.** You must add the default gateway and an IP address to the VLAN1 interface. Additionally, you must add a password to the VTY so you can telnet into the switch.

41. **B, C.** The switch will forward and process VTP updates.

42. **D.** The link to the router must be configured as a trunk port in order for the hosts on the two VLANs to communicate with each other.

43. **A, B.** This is a standard static route; for a default route, the destination network and mask would be all zeros. No specific administrative distance is specified, so the default will be used.

44. **D.** This route already has a hop count of 15, which is the maximum for RIP (the routing protocol running here).

45. **A, C.** A router running a link-state protocol uses hello packets to find neighbors and form adjacencies. Once an adjacency has been formed, it uses link state advertisement (LSA) packets to exchange topology information and updates when changes occur.

46. **B, D, E.** Each of these uses TCP.

47. **E.** Successor routers are stored and found in the topology table. They are copied and placed in the routing table for IP to forward traffic with.

48. **A, C.** This is a standard static route that sends all traffic for 192.168.12.0/24 through 172.16.12.1.

49. **E.** This is a unicast address in the 172.31.128.0 subnet.

50. **A, D.** The switch must have IP communications configured, and the VTY must have a password in order for you to be able to telnet into the switch.

51. **E.** The logical address is preferred over the physical, and the highest address wins.

52. **B.** Cisco Discovery Protocol (CDP) is a Cisco proprietary protocol that works at the Data Link layer.

53. **F.** There are two trunking encapsulation methods: ISL, which is Cisco propriety, and 802.1q, which is not proprietary. Use the command `dot1q` when using 802.1q.

54. **A, C, D.** Assuming you did not already create subinterfaces, you will need to remove the IP configuration on the major (physical) interface, create multiple subinterfaces, and configure each of them.

55. **B.** PPP is always the best choice in multivendor solutions.

Answer Sheets for Practice Test 4

(Remove This Sheet and Use It to Mark Your Answers)

Section 1
Multiple Choice Questions

1 Ⓐ Ⓑ Ⓒ Ⓓ Ⓔ Ⓕ	31 Ⓐ Ⓑ Ⓒ Ⓓ Ⓔ Ⓕ
2 Ⓐ Ⓑ Ⓒ Ⓓ Ⓔ Ⓕ	32 Ⓐ Ⓑ Ⓒ Ⓓ Ⓔ Ⓕ
3 Ⓐ Ⓑ Ⓒ Ⓓ Ⓔ Ⓕ	33 Ⓐ Ⓑ Ⓒ Ⓓ Ⓔ Ⓕ
4 Ⓐ Ⓑ Ⓒ Ⓓ Ⓔ Ⓕ	34 Ⓐ Ⓑ Ⓒ Ⓓ Ⓔ Ⓕ
5 Ⓐ Ⓑ Ⓒ Ⓓ Ⓔ Ⓕ	35 Ⓐ Ⓑ Ⓒ Ⓓ Ⓔ Ⓕ
6 Ⓐ Ⓑ Ⓒ Ⓓ Ⓔ Ⓕ	36 Ⓐ Ⓑ Ⓒ Ⓓ Ⓔ Ⓕ
7 Ⓐ Ⓑ Ⓒ Ⓓ Ⓔ Ⓕ	37 Ⓐ Ⓑ Ⓒ Ⓓ Ⓔ Ⓕ
8 Ⓐ Ⓑ Ⓒ Ⓓ Ⓔ Ⓕ	38 Ⓐ Ⓑ Ⓒ Ⓓ Ⓔ Ⓕ
9 Ⓐ Ⓑ Ⓒ Ⓓ Ⓔ Ⓕ	39 Ⓐ Ⓑ Ⓒ Ⓓ Ⓔ Ⓕ
10 Ⓐ Ⓑ Ⓒ Ⓓ Ⓔ Ⓕ	40 Ⓐ Ⓑ Ⓒ Ⓓ Ⓔ Ⓕ
11 Ⓐ Ⓑ Ⓒ Ⓓ Ⓔ Ⓕ	41 Ⓐ Ⓑ Ⓒ Ⓓ Ⓔ Ⓕ
12 Ⓐ Ⓑ Ⓒ Ⓓ Ⓔ Ⓕ	42 Ⓐ Ⓑ Ⓒ Ⓓ Ⓔ Ⓕ
13 Ⓐ Ⓑ Ⓒ Ⓓ Ⓔ Ⓕ	43 Ⓐ Ⓑ Ⓒ Ⓓ Ⓔ Ⓕ
14 Ⓐ Ⓑ Ⓒ Ⓓ Ⓔ Ⓕ	44 Ⓐ Ⓑ Ⓒ Ⓓ Ⓔ Ⓕ
15 Ⓐ Ⓑ Ⓒ Ⓓ Ⓔ Ⓕ	45 Ⓐ Ⓑ Ⓒ Ⓓ Ⓔ Ⓕ
16 Ⓐ Ⓑ Ⓒ Ⓓ Ⓔ Ⓕ	46 Ⓐ Ⓑ Ⓒ Ⓓ Ⓔ Ⓕ
17 Ⓐ Ⓑ Ⓒ Ⓓ Ⓔ Ⓕ	47 Ⓐ Ⓑ Ⓒ Ⓓ Ⓔ Ⓕ
18 Ⓐ Ⓑ Ⓒ Ⓓ Ⓔ Ⓕ	48 Ⓐ Ⓑ Ⓒ Ⓓ Ⓔ Ⓕ
19 Ⓐ Ⓑ Ⓒ Ⓓ Ⓔ Ⓕ	49 Ⓐ Ⓑ Ⓒ Ⓓ Ⓔ Ⓕ
20 Ⓐ Ⓑ Ⓒ Ⓓ Ⓔ Ⓕ	50 Ⓐ Ⓑ Ⓒ Ⓓ Ⓔ Ⓕ
21 Ⓐ Ⓑ Ⓒ Ⓓ Ⓔ Ⓕ	51 Ⓐ Ⓑ Ⓒ Ⓓ Ⓔ Ⓕ
22 Ⓐ Ⓑ Ⓒ Ⓓ Ⓔ Ⓕ	52 Ⓐ Ⓑ Ⓒ Ⓓ Ⓔ Ⓕ
23 Ⓐ Ⓑ Ⓒ Ⓓ Ⓔ Ⓕ	53 Ⓐ Ⓑ Ⓒ Ⓓ Ⓔ Ⓕ
24 Ⓐ Ⓑ Ⓒ Ⓓ Ⓔ Ⓕ	54 Ⓐ Ⓑ Ⓒ Ⓓ Ⓔ Ⓕ
25 Ⓐ Ⓑ Ⓒ Ⓓ Ⓔ Ⓕ	55 Ⓐ Ⓑ Ⓒ Ⓓ Ⓔ Ⓕ
26 Ⓐ Ⓑ Ⓒ Ⓓ Ⓔ Ⓕ	
27 Ⓐ Ⓑ Ⓒ Ⓓ Ⓔ Ⓕ	
28 Ⓐ Ⓑ Ⓒ Ⓓ Ⓔ Ⓕ	
29 Ⓐ Ⓑ Ⓒ Ⓓ Ⓔ Ⓕ	
30 Ⓐ Ⓑ Ⓒ Ⓓ Ⓔ Ⓕ	

Directions: For each of the following questions, select the choice that best answers the question or completes the statement.

1. Look at the following diagram. Which route will be found in the routing table of the Main router?

```
Main#debug ip rip
RIP protocol debugging is on
Main#
*Mar  1 17:43:00.567: RIP: received v1 update from 192.168.255.21 on
Serial0/0
*Mar  1 17:43:00.571:    192.168.2.0 in 2 hops
*Mar  1 17:43:00.571:    192.168.255.16 in 1 hops
*Mar  1 17:43:41.419: RIP: received v1 update from 192.168.255.26 on
Serial0/1
*Mar  1 17:43:41.423:    192.168.2.0 in 1 hops
*Mar  1 17:43:41.427:    192.168.255.16 in 1 hops
*Mar  1 17:43:55.099: RIP: sending v1 update to 255.255.255.255 via
Serial0/0 (192.168.255.22)
*Mar  1 17:43:55.103: RIP: build update entries
*Mar  1 17:43:55.103:   network 192.168.2.0 metric 2
*Mar  1 17:43:55.107:   subnet 192.168.255.24 metric 1
*Mar  1 17:43:55.111: RIP: sending v1 update to 255.255.255.255 via
Serial0/1 (192.168.255.25)
*Mar  1 17:43:55.115: RIP: build update entries
*Mar  1 17:43:55.119: subnet 192.168.255.20 metric 1
```

Figure 4-1

A. C 192.168.2.0 is directly connected, Serial0/1

B. R 192.168.2.0/24 [120/1] via 192.168.255.26, 00:00:24, Serial0/0

C. R 192.168.255.16 [120/1] via 192.168.255.26, 00:00:24, Serial0/1

D. R 192.168.2.0/24 [120/2] via 192.168.255.21, 00:00:22, Serial0/0

2. Look at the following diagram. An access list has been designed to prevent Telnet traffic from the Graphics Department from reaching the web server attached to the Northfield router. On which router, which interface, and in what direction should the access list be placed to most efficiently implement this list? (Choose three.)

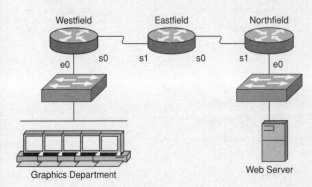

Figure 4-2

A. Westfield Router
B. Northfield Router
C. s0
D. e0
E. in
F. out

3. You're testing an ISDN circuit that uses PPP between two IP hosts. Match the indicator in the left column with the OSI layer on the right that it confirms.

	Layer 1	Layer 2	Layer 3
The line is up.			
A ping of the remote host is successful.			
A Telnet connection to the host is successful.			
A dial session to the remote host is successful.			

GO ON TO THE NEXT PAGE

4. Look at the following diagram. HostA has established a Telnet session with HostB. Which intermediate device examines the information at OSI layers 1-2 only?

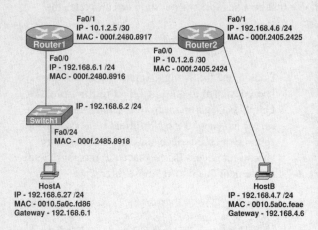

Figure 4-3

A. Switch1
B. Router1
C. Router2
D. HostB

5. You are unable to telnet to a router at address 203.125.12.1 from a workstation with the IP address 203.125.12.23. You suspect that there is a problem with your protocol stack. Which of the following actions is most likely to confirm your diagnosis?

A. `ping 127.0.0.0`
B. `ping 203.125.12.1`
C. `telnet 127.0.0.1`
D. `ping 127.0.0.1`
E. `tracert 203.125.12.1`

6. Look at the following diagram. A network technician enters the following line into the router:

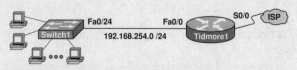

```
access-list 106 permit ip host 192.168.254.7 any
access-list 106 deny icmp 192.168.254.0 0.0.0.255 any echo
access-list 106 permit ip any any
interface Fa0/0
 ip access-group 106 in
```

Figure 4-4

Tidmore1(config)# **no access-list 106 permit ip any any**

What is the effect of this configuration?

A. The change has no effect on the packets being filtered.
B. All traffic from the 192.168.254.0 LAN to the Internet is permitted.
C. Web pages from the Internet cannot be accessed by hosts in the 192.168.254.0 LAN.
D. No hosts in the 192.168.254.0 LAN except 192.168.254.7 can access web pages from the Internet.

7. Without a loopback interface, which of the following accurately describes what an OSPF router would use for the router ID if all OSPF routers in one area were configured with the same priority value?

A. IP address of the Fast Ethernet interface
B. IP address of the console management interface
C. Highest IP address among its active interfaces
D. Lowest IP address among its active interfaces
E. Priority value until a loopback interface is configured

8. Look at the following diagram. The network has been configured with STP disabled. HostA sends an ARP request for the IP address of a site on the Internet. What will happen to this ARP request? (Choose two.)

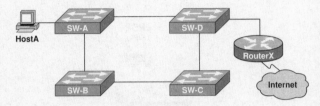

Figure 4-5

   A. Because the ARP request is a broadcast, SW-A will not forward the request.

   B. SW-A will convert the broadcast to a unicast and forward it to SW-D.

   C. The switches will propagate the broadcast, creating a broadcast storm.

   D. From a port on SW-A, HostA will receive an ARP reply containing the MAC address.

   E. From the Ethernet interface of RouterX, HostA will receive an ARP reply that contains the MAC address.

   F. The switches will propagate the broadcast until the TTL of the frame reduces to 0. Then the frame will be discarded.

9. On which OSI layer does the protocol operate that imparts the information you get by using the `show cdp neighbors` command?

   A. Physical

   B. Data Link

   C. Network

   D. Transport

   E. Application

10. Which command will configure a default route on a router?

   A. `router(config)# ip route 0.0.0.0 10.1.1.0 10.1.1.1`

   B. `router(config)# ip default-route 10.1.1.0`

   C. `router(config)# ip default-gateway 10.1.1.0`

   D. `router(config)# ip route 0.0.0.0 0.0.0.0 10.1.1.1`

11. Look at the following diagram. Computer 1 is consoled into switch A. Telnet connections and pings run from the command prompt on switch A fail. Which of the following could cause this problem?

```
A# show run
hostname A
<<output omitted>>
!interface FastEthernet0/1
switchport mode trunk
no ip address
!
<<output omitted>>
interface Vlan1
  no ip address
  no ip route-cache
!
<<output omitted>>
```

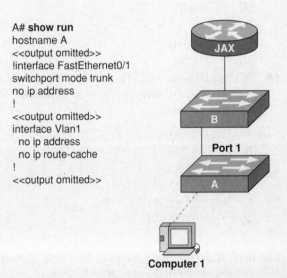

Figure 4-6

   A. Switch A is not directly connected to router JAX.

   B. Switch A does not have a default gateway assigned.

   C. Switch A does not have a CDP entry for switch B or router JAX.

   D. Switch A does not have an IP address.

   E. Port 1 on switch A should be an access port rather than a trunk port.

12. Which of the following statements are true regarding the command `ip route 172.16.3.0 255.255.255.0 192.168.2.4`? (Choose two.)

   A. The command is used to establish a static route.

   B. The default administrative distance is used.

   C. The command is used to configure the default route.

   D. The subnet mask for the source address is 255.255.255.0.

   E. The command is used to establish a stub network.

GO ON TO THE NEXT PAGE

13. What are the possible trunking modes for a switch port? (Choose three.)

 A. Transparent

 B. Auto

 C. On

 D. Desirable

 E. Client

 F. Forwarding

14. Of these choices, which three host addresses are valid members of networks that can be routed across the Internet?

 A. 10.172.13.65

 B. 172.16.223.125

 C. 172.62.12.29

 D. 192.168.23.252

 E. 198.234.12.95

 F. 212.193.48.254

15. Look at the following diagram. Assuming all hosts and servers are in the same VLAN, which statement is correct about the internetwork shown in the diagram?

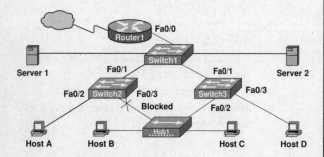

Figure 4-7

 A. Switch2 is the root bridge.

 B. Spanning Tree Protocol is not running.

 C. Host D and Server 1 are in the same network.

 D. No collisions can occur in traffic between Host B and Host C.

 E. If Fa0/0 is down on Router1, Host A cannot access Server 1.

 F. If Fa0/1 is down on Switch3, Host C cannot access Server 2.

16. Look at the following diagram. When PC1 sends an ARP request for the MAC address of PC2, network performance slows dramatically, and the switches detect an unusually high number of broadcast frames. What is the most likely cause of this?

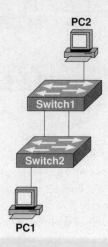

Figure 4-8

 A. The `portfast` feature is not enabled on all switch ports.

 B. The PCs are in two different VLANs.

 C. Spanning Tree Protocol is not running on the switches.

 D. PC2 is down and not able to respond to the request.

 E. The VTP versions running on the two switches do not match.

17. The command `ip route 192.168.24.64 255.255.255.192 192.168.8.2 100` was configured on a router named Corporate. No routing protocols or other static routes are configured on the Corporate router yet. Which statement is true about this command?

 A. This command sets a gateway of last resort for the Corporate router.

 B. The number 100 indicates the number of hops to the destination network.

 C. The interface with IP address 192.168.8.2 is on the Corporate router.

 D. The command creates a static route for all IP traffic with the source address 192.168.24.64.

 E. Packets destined for host 192.168.24.124 will be sent to 192.168.8.2.

18. Choose the command that will configure a switch port to use the IEEE standard method of adding VLAN membership information into Ethernet frames.

  A. `Switch(config)# switchport trunk encapsulation isl`

  B. `Switch(config)# switchport trunk encapsulation ietf`

  C. `Switch(config)# switchport trunk encapsulation dot1q`

  D. `Switch(config-if)# switchport trunk encapsulation isl`

  E. `Switch(config-if)# switchport trunk encapsulation ietf`

  F. `Switch(config-if)# switchport trunk encapsulation dot1q`

19. If you needed to permit Internet access for the hosts in your network assigned addresses in the 192.168.8.0 through 198.168.15.255 range, which wildcard mask would you employ to achieve that objective?

  A. 0.0.0.0
  B. 0.0.0.255
  C. 0.0.255.255
  D. 0.0.7.255
  E. 0.0.3.255

20. Which command displays all the EIGRP feasible successor routes known to a router?

  A. `Router# show ip eigrp routes*`
  B. `Router# show ip eigrp summary`
  C. `Router# show ip eigrp topology`
  D. `Router# show ip eigrp adjacencies`
  E. `Router# show ip eigrp neighbors detail`

21. Which sequence of actions allows telneting from a user's PC to a router using TCP/IP?

  A. Connect the PC's COM port to the router's console port using a straight-through cable.

  B. Connect the PC's COM port to the router's console port using a crossover cable.

  C. Connect the PC's COM port to the router's Ethernet port using a straight-through cable.

  D. Connect the PC's Ethernet port to the router's Ethernet port using a crossover cable.

  E. Connect the PC's Ethernet port to the router's Ethernet port using a rollover cable.

  F. Connect the PC's Ethernet port to the router's Ethernet port using a straight-through cable.

22. Which of the following are options for Frame Relay LMI types? (Choose three.)

  A. IETF
  B. Q.931
  C. Q933a
  D. IEEE
  E. Cisco
  F. ANSI

23. What is the subnetwork number of a host with an IP address of 172.16.210.0/22?

  A. 172.16.42.0
  B. 172.16.107.0
  C. 172.16.208.0
  D. 172.16.252.0
  E. 172.16.254.0

24. Look at the following diagram. What should be the IP address of the host?

Figure 4-9

  A. 192.168.5.14
  B. 192.168.5.32
  C. 192.168.5.40
  D. 192.168.5.47
  E. 192.168.5.55

GO ON TO THE NEXT PAGE

25. Look at the following diagram. The network administrator has configured the switches in the school network to use VTP. The switches are not sharing VLAN information. Which sequence of commands should be issued to correct this problem?

```
Labs# show vtp status
VTP Version                        : 2
Configuration Revision             : 1
Maximum VLANs supported locally    : 64
Number of existing VLANs           : 9
VTP Operating Mode                 : Server
VTP Domain Name                    : Labs
VTP Pruning Mode                   : Disabled
VTP V2 Mode                        : Disabled
VTP Traps Generation               : Disabled
MD5 digest                         : 0xF3 0x6D 0x21 0x7C 0x0F 0xA9 0xE9 0x60
```

```
Offices# show vtp status
VTP Version                        : 1
Configuration Revision             : 3
Maximum VLANs supported locally    : 64
Number of existing VLANs           : 9
VTP Operating Mode                 : Server
VTP Domain Name                    : Offices
VTP Pruning Mode                   : Disabled
VTP V2 Mode                        : Disabled
VTP Traps Generation               : Disabled
MD5 digest                         : 0x07 0x35 0xFA 0xD5 0xF8 0xBA 0xE5 0xD8
```

Figure 4-10

A. `Offices(config)# vtp mode client`
`Labs(config)# vtp mode client`

B. `Offices(config)# vtp domain School`
`Labs(config)# vtp domain School`

C. `Offices(config)# vtp pruning`
`Labs(config)# vtp pruning`

D. `Offices(config)# vtp version 2`
`Labs(config)# vtp version 2`

26. Which of the following IP addresses can be assigned to host devices? (Choose two.)

A. 205.7.8.32/27
B. 191.168.10.2/23
C. 127.0.0.1
D. 224.0.0.10
E. 203.123.45.47/28
F. 10.10.0.0/13

27. Look at the following diagram. Assume that ports 1 through 3 are assigned to VLAN1 and ports 4 through 6 are assigned to VLAN2 on each switch. The switches are interconnected over a trunked link. Which of the following conditions verify proper VLAN and trunk operation? (Choose three.)

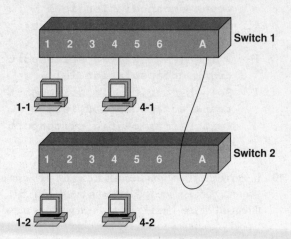

Figure 4-11

A. Host 1-1 can ping Host 1-2.
B. Host 1-1 can ping Host 4-2.
C. Host 1-1 can not ping Host 1-2.
D. Host 4-1 can not ping Host 1-2.
E. Host 4-1 can ping Host 4-2.

28. The TFR Company is implementing dialup services to enable remote office employees to connect to the local network. The company uses several different layer 3 protocols on the network. Authentication of the users connecting to the network is required for security. Additionally, some employees will be dialing long distance and will need callback support. Which protocol is the best choice for these remote access services?

A. 802.1
B. Frame Relay
C. HDLC
D. PPP
E. SLIP
F. PAP

29. Look at the following diagram. Switch1 has just been restarted and has passed the POST routine. When Host A begins communicating with Host C, what will the switch do?

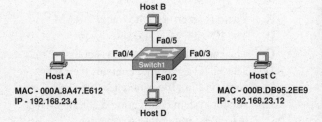

Figure 4-12

A. Switch1 will add 192.168.23.4 to the CAM table.

B. Switch1 will add 192.168.23.12 to the CAM table.

C. Switch1 will add 000A.8A47.E612 to the CAM table.

D. Switch1 will add 000B.DB95.2EE9 to the CAM table.

30. A network administrator is designing a Cisco network for a large company. The network must be able to use minimal bandwidth for routing updates; converge quickly; and support VLSM, CIDR, IP and IPX. Which routing protocol best fits the requirements of this network?

A. RIP v1

B. RIP v2

C. IGRP

D. OSPF

E. EIGRP

31. When a new trunk link is configured on an IOS-based switch, which VLANs are allowed over the link?

A. By default, all defined VLANs are allowed on the trunk.

B. Each single VLAN, or VLAN range, must be specified with the `switchport mode` command.

C. Each single VLAN, or VLAN range, must be specified with the `vtp domain` command.

D. Each single VLAN, or VLAN range, must be specified with the `vlan database` command.

32. Which command displays RIP routing updates as they are sent and received by the router?

A. `show ip protocols`

B. `show ip route rip`

C. `debug ip rip`

D. `debug ip updates`

E. `debug ip transactions`

33. In which of the following options would multiple copies of the same unicast frame be the most likely to be relayed in a switched LAN?

A. During high traffic periods

B. After broken links are re-established

C. When upper-layer protocols require high reliability

D. In an improperly implemented redundant topology

E. When a dual-ring topology is in use

34. Look at the following diagram. How can a network administrator ensure that the STP election process will result in Switch B being elected as the root switch?

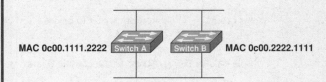

Figure 4-13

A. Clear the Switch B STP revision number.

B. Assign Switch B a low priority number.

C. Increase the Switch B priority number.

D. Change the MAC address of Switch B.

35. A network administrator issues the `ping 192.168.2.5` command and successfully tests connectivity to a host that has been newly connected to the network. Which protocols were used during the test? (Choose two.)

A. ARP

B. CDP

C. DHCP

D. DNS

E. ICMP

GO ON TO THE NEXT PAGE

36. You've just inserted a new router into an established OSPF network, but the networks attached to the recently added router aren't showing up in the routing tables of the other OSPF routers. By looking at the information in the partial configuration given below, what's causing this issue?

```
Router(config)# router ospf 1
Router(config-router)# network
   10.0.0.0 255.0.0.0 area 0
```

- **A.** The process id is configured improperly.
- **B.** The OSPF area is configured improperly.
- **C.** The network wildcard mask is configured improperly.
- **D.** The network number is configured improperly.
- **E.** The AS is configured improperly.
- **F.** The network subnet mask is configured improperly.

37. Match the security features in the column on the left to the exact security risks they help protect against in the right column. (You'll have one left over.)

Access-group	Remote access to device console
Console password	Access to the console 0 line
Enable secret	Access to connected networks or resources
CHAP authentication	Viewing of passwords
VTY password	Access to privileged mode
Service password-encryption	

38. Which command is required to apply an access list on a virtual terminal line of a router?

- **A.** `Router(config-line)# access-class 10 in`
- **B.** `Router(config-if)# ip access-class 23 out`
- **C.** `Router(config-line)# access-group 15 out`
- **D.** `Router(config-if)# ip access-group 110 in`
- **E.** `Router(config-line)# access-list 150 in`
- **F.** `Router(config-if)# ip access-list 128 out`

39. A Cisco router has been configured, and the `copy running-config startup-config` command has been issued. When the router is power cycled, the router prompts with "Would you like to enter the initial configuration dialog? [yes/no]:". Why does this happen?

- **A.** There is an error in the router DRAM.
- **B.** The IOS image is corrupt.
- **C.** The configuration register is set to 0x2142.
- **D.** The TFTP server that contains the router configuration file is unreachable.
- **E.** A boot system configuration command has placed the router into setup mode.

40. An administrator is configuring a Catalyst switch with VLAN information that must be automatically distributed to other Catalyst switches in the network. What conditions must be met in order for the VLANs configured on this switch to be automatically configured on other switches? (Choose three.)

- **A.** The switch that will share its VLAN configuration must be in VTP server mode.
- **B.** The switches must be in the same VTP domain.
- **C.** The switch that will share the VLAN information must be configured as root bridge.
- **D.** The switches must be connected over VLAN trunks.
- **E.** The switches must be configured to use the same STP version.
- **F.** The switches must have VTP pruning activated.

41. Look at the following diagram. You have been asked to diagnose a problem with the network shown. The following symptoms have been observed: None of the user hosts can access the Internet; none of the user hosts can access the server in VLAN9; host A can ping host B; host A *cannot* ping host C or host D; and host C can ping host D. What can cause these symptoms?

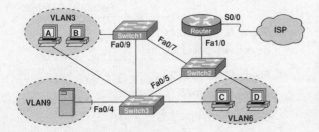

Figure 4-14

   A. Interface S0/0 on the router is down.
   B. Interface Fa1/0 on the router is down.
   C. Interface Fa0/5 on Switch3 is down.
   D. Interface Fa0/4 on Switch3 is down.
   E. Switch1 is turned off.
   F. Switch3 is turned off.

42. Your security policy dictates that only one host can be permitted to dynamically attach to each interface, and if this policy is violated, the interface should immediately shut down. Choose the two commands you need to configure on the 2950 Catalyst switch to implement your policy.

   A. `Switch1(config-if)# switchport port-security maximum 1`
   B. `Switch1(config)# mac-address-table secure`
   C. `Switch1(config)#Access-list 10 permit ip host`
   D. `Switch1(config-if)# switchport port-security violation shutdown`
   E. `Switch1(config-if)# ip access-group 10`

43. You're configuring a router to act as a hub within a Frame Relay hub-and-spoke topology. Why should you opt for using point-to-point subinterfaces instead of a multipoint interface?

   A. It avoids split-horizon issues with distance vector routing protocols.
   B. Only one IP network address needs to be used to communicate with all spoke devices.
   C. Point-to-point subinterfaces offer greater security than multipoint interface configuration.
   D. Only a single physical interface is needed with point-to-point subinterfaces, whereas a multipoint interface logically combines multiple physical interfaces.

44. Look at the following diagram. Two switches, named Top and Bottom, connect through ports configured as trunks. The trunk ports on both switches have been configured correctly, and both interfaces are up. VTP, however, is not passing VLAN information between the two switches. Based on the output of the `show vtp status` command from both switches, what is the problem?

```
Top#show vtp status
VTP Version                       : 2
Configuration Revision            : 1
Maximum VLANs supported locally   : 250
Number of existing VLANs          : 6
VTP Operating Mode                : Server
VTP Domain Name                   : cheryl
VTP Pruning Mode                  : Disabled
VTP V2 Mode                       : Disabled
VTP Traps Generation              : Disabled
MD5 digest                        : 0xBF 0x92 0x87 0xB0 0xA8 0x8F 0xDA 0x86
Configuration last modified by 0.0.0.0 at 3-1-93 00:03:32
Local updater ID is 0.0.0.0 (no valid interface found)

Bottom#show vtp status
VTP Version                       : 2
Configuration Revision            : 0
Maximum VLANs supported locally   : 250
Number of existing VLANs          : 5
VTP Operating Mode                : Server
VTP Domain Name                   : charyl
VTP Pruning Mode                  : Disabled
VTP V2 Mode                       : Disabled
VTP Traps Generation              : Disabled
MD5 digest                        : 0xF3 0x03 0x4C 0x72 0xC8 0x6B 0x29 0x62
Configuration last modified by 0.0.0.0 at 0-0-00 00:00:00
Local updater ID is 0.0.0.0 (no valid interface found)
```

Figure 4-15

   A. The domain names do not match.
   B. Only one switch can be in VTP server mode in a domain.
   C. The configuration revision numbers must match in the two switches.
   D. The VTP timer settings must match.

GO ON TO THE NEXT PAGE

45. What is the purpose of spanning tree in a switched LAN?

    A. To provide a mechanism for network monitoring in switched environments

    B. To prevent routing loops in networks with redundant switched paths

    C. To prevent switching loops in networks with redundant switched paths

    D. To manage the addition, deletion, and naming of VLANs across multiple switches

    E. To segment a network into multiple collision domains

46. Which two commands would you use to configure running OSPF, plus adding network 192.168.16.0/24 to OSPF area 0?

    A. `Router(config)# router ospf 0`

    B. `Router(config)# router ospf 1`

    C. `Router(config)# router ospf area 0`

    D. `Router(config-router)# network 192.168.16.0 0.0.0.255 0`

    E. `Router(config-router)# network 192.168.16.0 0.0.0.255 area 0`

    F. `Router(config-router)# network 192.168.16.0 255.255.255.0 area 0`

47. Which command is required for connectivity in a Frame Relay network if Inverse ARP is not operational?

    A. `frame-relay arp`

    B. `frame-relay map`

    C. `frame-relay interface-dlci`

    D. `frame-relay lmi-type`

48. Which statements describe the routing protocol OSPF? (Choose three.)

    A. It supports VLSM.

    B. It is used to route between autonomous systems.

    C. It confines network instability to one area of the network.

    D. It increases routing overhead on the network.

    E. It allows extensive control of routing updates.

    F. It is simpler to configure than RIP v2.

49. You've configured an interface with the access list shown. Based on the access list, list which information packet in the left column will be permitted and which packets will be denied?

```
Access-list 107 deny tcp
207.16.12.0 0.0.3.255 any eq
http
Access-list 107 permit ip any any
```

	Permitted	Denied
Source IP 207.16.32.14, destination application: http		
Source IP 207.16.15.9, destination port 23		
Source IP 207.16.14.7, destination port 80		
Source IP 207.16.13.14, destination application http		
Source IP 207.16.16.14, destination port 53		

50. You've configured the Ethernet 0 interface of a router with address 10.64.0.1. 255.224.0.0 and the Ethernet 1 interface with address 10.96.0.1/11. Choose the two commands you can use to configure RIP version 1 on this router so it will advertise both networks to the neighboring routers.

    A. `Router(config)# router rip`
`Router(config-router)# network 10.0.0.0 255.224.0.0`

    B. `Router(config)# router rip`
`Router(config-router)# network 10.64.0.1 255.224.0.0`
`Router(config-router)# network 10.96.0.1 255.224.0.0`

    C. `Router(config)# router rip`
`Router(config-router)# network 10.0.0.0`

    D. `Router(config)# router rip`
`Router(config-router)# network 10.64.0.0`
`Router(config-router)# network 10.96.0.0`

51. Look at the following diagram. RouterA is unable to reach RouterB. Both routers are running IOS version 12.0. After reviewing the command output and graphic, what is the most likely cause of the problem?

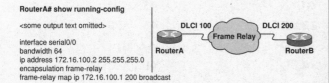

```
RouterA# show running-config

<some output text omitted>

interface serial0/0
bandwidth 64
ip address 172.16.100.2 255.255.255.0
encapsulation frame-relay
frame-relay map ip 172.16.100.1 200 broadcast
```

Figure 4-16

A. Incorrect bandwidth configuration

B. Incorrect LMI configuration

C. Incorrect map statement

D. Incorrect IP address

52. Look at the following diagram. Switches A and B have been configured with a trunked link that has been verified as working correctly. However, VTP is not propagating VLANs from one switch to the other. Based on the command output shown, what is the problem?

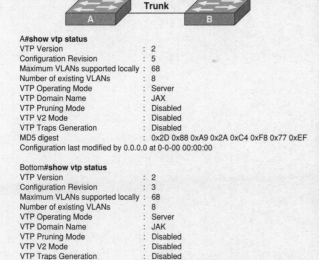

```
A#show vtp status
VTP Version                        : 2
Configuration Revision             : 5
Maximum VLANs supported locally :  68
Number of existing VLANs           : 8
VTP Operating Mode                 : Server
VTP Domain Name                    : JAX
VTP Pruning Mode                   : Disabled
VTP V2 Mode                        : Disabled
VTP Traps Generation               : Disabled
MD5 digest                         : 0x2D 0x88 0xA9 0x2A 0xC4 0xF8 0x77 0xEF
Configuration last modified by 0.0.0.0 at 0-0-00 00:00:00

Bottom#show vtp status
VTP Version                        : 2
Configuration Revision             : 3
Maximum VLANs supported locally :  68
Number of existing VLANs           : 8
VTP Operating Mode                 : Server
VTP Domain Name                    : JAK
VTP Pruning Mode                   : Disabled
VTP V2 Mode                        : Disabled
VTP Traps Generation               : Disabled
MD5 digest                         : 0xA8 0x67 0xF9 0xA8 0x92 0xE9 0x30 0x6B
Configuration last modified by 0.0.0.0 at 0-0-00 00:00:00
```

Figure 4-17

A. The revision number is not the same on both switches.

B. Only one switch can be in server mode.

C. The VTP domain name is not correctly configured.

D. VLANs have not been configured on the VTP server.

E. The VTP pruning mode is not correctly configured.

53. Which functions do routers perform when routing a packet? (Choose two.)

A. Packet switching

B. Destination host addressing

C. Path selection

D. VLAN membership assignment

E. ARP request forwarding

54. What does a layer 2 switch do if it receives a frame with a destination MAC address that is not found in its MAC address table?

A. The frame is dropped.

B. The frame is addressed with a broadcast MAC address and sent out all ports.

C. The frame is sent out all ports except the receiving port.

D. An ARP request is sent out all ports except the receiving port.

E. A destination unreachable message is sent back to the source address.

55. Which tables of EIGRP route information are held in RAM and maintained through the use of hello and update packets? (Choose two.)

A. Neighbor table

B. SPF table

C. RTP table

D. Topology table

E. Query table

F. DUAL table

Answer Key for Practice Test 4

1.	B	**15.**	C	**30.**	E	**44.**	A
2.	A, D, E	**16.**	C	**31.**	A	**45.**	C
3.	See Answer Explanation	**17.**	E	**32.**	C	**46.**	A, E
		18.	F	**33.**	D	**47.**	B
4.	A	**19.**	D	**34.**	B	**48.**	A, C, E
5.	D	**20.**	C	**35.**	A, E	**49.**	See Answer Explanation
6.	B	**21.**	D	**36.**	C		
7.	C	**22.**	C, E, F	**37.**	See Answer Explanation	**50.**	C, D
8.	C, E	**23.**	C			**51.**	C
9.	B	**24.**	C	**38.**	A	**52.**	C
10.	D	**25.**	B	**39.**	C	**53.**	A, C
11.	D	**26.**	B, F	**40.**	A, B, D	**54.**	C
12.	A, B	**27.**	A, D, E	**41.**	B	**55.**	A, D
13.	B, C, D	**28.**	D	**42.**	A, D		
14.	C, E, F	**29.**	C	**43.**	A		

Answer Explanations for Practice Test 4

1. B. The route via 192.168.255.26 has a lower metric than the route via 192.168.255.21.

2. A, D, E. Extended access lists should be placed as close to the source as possible.

3.

The line is up.	Layer 2
A ping of the remote host is successful.	Layer 3
A dial session to the remote host is successful.	Layer 1

4. A. Switches only evaluate layer 1-2 information. Routers look at layers 1-3, and the destination host examines all layers.

5. D. If you suspect an issue with the local protocol stack, pinging the loopback address will tell you if that is the problem.

6. B. Once you type in "no access-list number," the whole list is gone. And in this question, the LAN segment has no access-list effecting the connection to the Internet or anywhere else. B is the best answer. You cannot remove one line from an access-list unless you are using named access-lists.

7. C. In the election process of OSPF routers, the priority value is checked first; by default, all routers have a value of one. If a loopback interface is configured, the interface with the highest IP address is used. If there is no loopback interface, then the active interface with the highest IP address is used.

8. C, E. With STP disabled, the looped topology creates a broadcast storm. The router responds to the ARP request.

9. B. Cisco Discovery Protocol (CDP) is a Cisco proprietary protocol that works at the Data Link layer.

10. D. A default route is created by assigning a static route with the destination and mask all set to zeros.

11. D. When a switch cannot ping or telnet any other hosts, including those on its own subnet, the most likely cause is a misconfiguration of the local IP information.

12. A, B. This is a standard static route. Because no administrative distance is specified, the default will be used.

13. B, C, D. The three possible trunking modes include *on*, which means the port is configured to always be a trunk port and attempts to make the port on the far end of the segment a trunk port as well. This negotiation of trunk status is done using the Dynamic Trunking Protocol (DTP). The next mode is *desirable*, which means the port wishes to be a trunk port and sends DTP frames, but can also be an access port. The other end is not a trunk port. The third mode is *auto*, which means the port becomes a trunk port if it receives DTP frames to become one; however, it does not send DTP frames to change the other port.

14. C, E, F. To answer this question, you must know the private address ranges. There is a range in each of the classes of addresses 10.0.0.0-10.255.255.255, 172.16.0.0-172.31.255.255, and 192.168.0.0-192.168.255.255. Any of the options in these ranges will not be routed on the Internet.

15. C. The question states that all hosts and servers are in the same VLAN, which implies that the server and the host can communicate without going through a router.

16. C. If spanning tree is not running when there are loops in the topology, broadcasts will cause broadcast storms.

17. E. Because no other routing is configured on the router, this static route will be the only entry in the routing table other than connected interfaces. The 192.168.24.124 host is within the address range specified in the static route.

18. F. There are two trunking encapsulation methods: ISL, which is Cisco propriety; and 802.1q, which is not proprietary. Use the command dot1q when using 802.1q.

19. D. A wildcard is always one less than the block size. The third octet has a block size of 8, and the fourth octet has a block size of 256. This makes the mask 0.0.7.255.

20. C. Feasible successor routes are stored in the topology table. They are not shown in the routing table.

21. D. When attaching directly to a router's interface without a hub or switch in the middle, a crossover cable must be used. You cannot telnet using your PC's COM port.

22. C, E, F. The three LMI types supported by Cisco routers are Cisco, ANSI, and Q933a.

23. C. The 172.16.208.0/22 subnetwork has hosts 172.16.208.1 through 172.16.211.254.

24. C. The subnet 192.168.5.32/28 has hosts 192.168.5.33 through 192.168.5.36.

25. B. All switches that share the same VLAN information need to have the same VTP domain name configured.

26. B, F. A is a subnetwork address, C is localhost, D is a multicast address, and E is a broadcast address. Only B and F are valid host addresses (all host bits are not all ones or zeros).

27. A, D, E. In this case, there is no router to route between the two VLANs, and thus your hosts should be able to ping only other hosts in the same VLAN. A and E show that hosts in one VLAN can ping hosts in the same VLAN on the other switch.

28. D. Only PPP meets all the requirements; dialup support, authentication, multiple layer-3 protocols, and callback are all supported by PPP.

29. C. The switch will learn the source MAC address from the frames that are received on the switchport.

30. E. Of the routing protocols listed, only EIGRP supports IPX. It also supports the other items listed in the question, as do B and D.

31. A. By default, all defined VLANs are allowed on configured trunk links.

32. C. Only a `debug` command can show you updates as they are sent and received. The correct command for RIP is `debug ip rip`.

33. D. If you do not have spanning-tree enabled on your switches, and you have redundant links, you will have broadcast storms and multiple frame copies.

34. B. A lower assigned priority always results in a switch being elected the root switch.

35. A, E. In order to ping, an IP must be resolved to a MAC address to properly frame the packet. This requires an ARP request. Additionally, a ping uses ICMP to generate a request and reply.

36. C. OSPF uses an inverse mask to configure the network statement. The mask in this example should be 0.255.255.255.

37.

Access-group	Access to connected networks or resources
Console password	Access to the console 0 line
Enable secret	Access to privileged mode
VTY password	Remote access to device console
Service password-encryption	Viewing of passwords

38. A. The `access-class` command is used directly on the VTY line to apply an access list.

39. C. This configuration register setting will cause the router to boot, ignoring the startup config. It is used in password recovery; however, if this register remains set, the router will always boot without checking for a startup config.

40. A, B, D. In order for VTP to work properly, all switches must be in the same VTP domain. Additionally, the switch that will share its VLAN configuration needs to be a VTP server, and the switches must be connected using trunk links.

41. B. This router interface is required to both access the Internet and route between VLANs.

42. A, D. By using the `switchport port-security` command, you can implement a security policy on your Catalyst switches.

43. **A.** In a case where split horizon is the problem, split horizon defines the rule "it is never useful to send routing information back in the direction from which it came." With this rule in place, routing updates that come from spoke routers are never relayed from the hub router. By implementing point-to-point links and subinterfaces on the spoke router, the routing protocol looks at each of the subinterfaces as separate physical links, allowing the updates to go between each point-to-point link and update the spoke routers.

44. **A.** These two VTP domain names do not match, and thus the switches cannot exchange VTP information.

45. **C.** The Spanning Tree Protocol is used to prevent loops in the layer-2 switching topology by controlling or blocking the use of redundant links. In a layer-2 network, redundant links are not a bad thing, unless they are uncontrolled, because they provide a secondary path if the primary fails, thus eliminating single points of failure.

46. **A, E.** When configuring OSPF to route on a network, the OSPF process must be started, using the `router OSPF <process id>` command. Then, while in the router configuration mode, you can use the `network` command to add a network and enable interfaces to operate in OSPF. The `network` command in OSPF includes the network, a wildcard bit mask, and the area to which you want the network to belong.

47. **B.** If inverse ARP is not operational, you must manually map the DLCI to upper-layer addresses.

48. **A, C, E.** OSPF supports VLSM, and through the use of areas, it can confine network instability to a single portion of the network. Additionally, it gives the administrator extensive control over routing updates.

49.

Permitted	Source IP 207.16.13.14, destination application http
Permitted	Source IP 207.1614.7, destination port 80
Denied	Source IP 207.16.32.14, destination application: http
Denied	Source IP 207.16.15.9, destination port 23
Denied	Source IP 207.16.16.14, destination port 53

50. **C, D.** RIP, IGRP and EIGRP are all configured that same way: with classful addresses, which means all default host bits off. In this question, two networks are using the 10.0.0.0 classful network address. If you are studying for your CCNA exam, it would be wise to understand this type of configuration.

51. **C.** The Frame Relay map statement is incorrect on RouterA. The other information is fine.

52. **C.** The VTP domain name must be the same on both switches in order for them to share VLAN information. In this case, the two switches have different VTP domain names.

53. **A, C.** When forwarding a packet, a router must switch the packet from one interface to another. In order to know which interface to switch the packet to, the router must perform path selection. Routers do not forward ARP requests, they do not assign VLAN membership, and they do not modify the destination host address (although they do read it to make the path-selection decision).

54. **C.** When the destination address is not in the forwarding table, a switch forwards the frame out all ports except the one on which it was received. This is called flooding the frame.

55. **A, D.** EIGRP maintains a neighbor table. If a router stops sending out updates, it is removed from the neighbor table. Additionally, all routes are kept in the topology table. Only preferred routes are surfaced to the routing table.

Answer Sheets for Practice Test 5

(Remove This Sheet and Use It to Mark Your Answers)

Section 1
Multiple Choice Questions

1 Ⓐ Ⓑ Ⓒ Ⓓ Ⓔ Ⓕ	31 Ⓐ Ⓑ Ⓒ Ⓓ Ⓔ Ⓕ
2 Ⓐ Ⓑ Ⓒ Ⓓ Ⓔ Ⓕ	32 Ⓐ Ⓑ Ⓒ Ⓓ Ⓔ Ⓕ
3 Ⓐ Ⓑ Ⓒ Ⓓ Ⓔ Ⓕ	33 Ⓐ Ⓑ Ⓒ Ⓓ Ⓔ Ⓕ
4 Ⓐ Ⓑ Ⓒ Ⓓ Ⓔ Ⓕ	34 Ⓐ Ⓑ Ⓒ Ⓓ Ⓔ Ⓕ
5 Ⓐ Ⓑ Ⓒ Ⓓ Ⓔ Ⓕ	35 Ⓐ Ⓑ Ⓒ Ⓓ Ⓔ Ⓕ
6 Ⓐ Ⓑ Ⓒ Ⓓ Ⓔ Ⓕ	36 Ⓐ Ⓑ Ⓒ Ⓓ Ⓔ Ⓕ
7 Ⓐ Ⓑ Ⓒ Ⓓ Ⓔ Ⓕ	37 Ⓐ Ⓑ Ⓒ Ⓓ Ⓔ Ⓕ
8 Ⓐ Ⓑ Ⓒ Ⓓ Ⓔ Ⓕ	38 Ⓐ Ⓑ Ⓒ Ⓓ Ⓔ Ⓕ
9 Ⓐ Ⓑ Ⓒ Ⓓ Ⓔ Ⓕ	39 Ⓐ Ⓑ Ⓒ Ⓓ Ⓔ Ⓕ
10 Ⓐ Ⓑ Ⓒ Ⓓ Ⓔ Ⓕ	40 Ⓐ Ⓑ Ⓒ Ⓓ Ⓔ Ⓕ
11 Ⓐ Ⓑ Ⓒ Ⓓ Ⓔ Ⓕ	41 Ⓐ Ⓑ Ⓒ Ⓓ Ⓔ Ⓕ
12 Ⓐ Ⓑ Ⓒ Ⓓ Ⓔ Ⓕ	42 Ⓐ Ⓑ Ⓒ Ⓓ Ⓔ Ⓕ
13 Ⓐ Ⓑ Ⓒ Ⓓ Ⓔ Ⓕ	43 Ⓐ Ⓑ Ⓒ Ⓓ Ⓔ Ⓕ
14 Ⓐ Ⓑ Ⓒ Ⓓ Ⓔ Ⓕ	44 Ⓐ Ⓑ Ⓒ Ⓓ Ⓔ Ⓕ
15 Ⓐ Ⓑ Ⓒ Ⓓ Ⓔ Ⓕ	45 Ⓐ Ⓑ Ⓒ Ⓓ Ⓔ Ⓕ
16 Ⓐ Ⓑ Ⓒ Ⓓ Ⓔ Ⓕ	46 Ⓐ Ⓑ Ⓒ Ⓓ Ⓔ Ⓕ
17 Ⓐ Ⓑ Ⓒ Ⓓ Ⓔ Ⓕ	47 Ⓐ Ⓑ Ⓒ Ⓓ Ⓔ Ⓕ
18 Ⓐ Ⓑ Ⓒ Ⓓ Ⓔ Ⓕ	48 Ⓐ Ⓑ Ⓒ Ⓓ Ⓔ Ⓕ
19 Ⓐ Ⓑ Ⓒ Ⓓ Ⓔ Ⓕ	49 Ⓐ Ⓑ Ⓒ Ⓓ Ⓔ Ⓕ
20 Ⓐ Ⓑ Ⓒ Ⓓ Ⓔ Ⓕ	50 Ⓐ Ⓑ Ⓒ Ⓓ Ⓔ Ⓕ
21 Ⓐ Ⓑ Ⓒ Ⓓ Ⓔ Ⓕ	51 Ⓐ Ⓑ Ⓒ Ⓓ Ⓔ Ⓕ
22 Ⓐ Ⓑ Ⓒ Ⓓ Ⓔ Ⓕ	52 Ⓐ Ⓑ Ⓒ Ⓓ Ⓔ Ⓕ
23 Ⓐ Ⓑ Ⓒ Ⓓ Ⓔ Ⓕ	53 Ⓐ Ⓑ Ⓒ Ⓓ Ⓔ Ⓕ
24 Ⓐ Ⓑ Ⓒ Ⓓ Ⓔ Ⓕ	54 Ⓐ Ⓑ Ⓒ Ⓓ Ⓔ Ⓕ
25 Ⓐ Ⓑ Ⓒ Ⓓ Ⓔ Ⓕ	55 Ⓐ Ⓑ Ⓒ Ⓓ Ⓔ Ⓕ
26 Ⓐ Ⓑ Ⓒ Ⓓ Ⓔ Ⓕ	
27 Ⓐ Ⓑ Ⓒ Ⓓ Ⓔ Ⓕ	
28 Ⓐ Ⓑ Ⓒ Ⓓ Ⓔ Ⓕ	
29 Ⓐ Ⓑ Ⓒ Ⓓ Ⓔ Ⓕ	
30 Ⓐ Ⓑ Ⓒ Ⓓ Ⓔ Ⓕ	

CUT HERE

Directions: For each of the following questions, select the choice that best answers the question or completes the statement.

1. Look at the following diagram. A Class C address has been assigned for use in the network shown. Which subnet mask should be used to provide valid IP addresses for the number of hosts connected to router A, while wasting the fewest addresses?

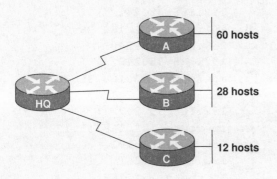

Figure 5-1

A. /24
B. /25
C. /26
D. /27
E. /28
F. /29

2. Look at the following diagram. What will be the effect of replacing the hubs with switches in the network? (Choose two.)

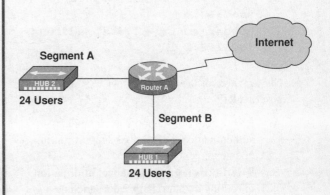

Figure 5-2

A. The number of collisions in each network will decrease.
B. The available bandwidth that each host has will increase.
C. The number of broadcasts that each host receives will decrease.
D. The hosts will need to be re-addressed to place each host in a separate subnet.
E. The gateway on each host will need to be changed to the IP address of the appropriate switch.

3. Your router discovers a remote network via a static route, EIGRP, and OSPF, and all the routing protocols are set to their default administrative distance. In this situation, which route will the router use to forward data to the newly discovered remote network?

A. The router will use the static route.
B. The router will use the OSPF route.
C. The router will use the EIGRP route.
D. The router will load-balance and use all three routes.

GO ON TO THE NEXT PAGE

4. The ISKI Corporation is configuring the serial interface of a Cisco router to connect to the router of a new ISP. After issuing the `show interfaces serial 0/0` command, it is observed that the interface is *up* and the line protocol is *down*. Which of the following commands will fix this problem?

   A. `Border# copy running-config startup-config`

   B. `Border(config-if)# no shutdown`

   C. `Border(config-if)# encapsulation ppp`

   D. `Border(config-if)# no cdp enable`

   E. `Border(config-if)# ip address 192.168.1.1`

5. Choose three of the following that accurately describe RIP.

   A. RIPv1 does not support routing update authentication. RIPv2 does support routing update authentication.

   B. RIPv1 does not include subnet information in routing updates. RIPv2 does include subnet information in routing updates.

   C. RIPv1 does not support advertising routes across WANs. RIPv2 supports advertising routes across LANs as well as WANs.

   D. RIPv1 uses hold-down timers and split horizon to prevent routing loops. RIPv2 does not require hold-down timers or split horizon to prevent routing loops.

   E. RIPv1 sends periodic routing updates over the multicast IP address 224.0.0.10. RIPv2 sends periodic routing updates over the multicast IP address 224.0.0.9.

   F. RIPv1 does not support a network-addressing scheme in which hosts within the same major network have different subnet masks. RIPv2 does allow hosts within the same major network to have different subnet masks.

6. Given a subnet mask of 255.255.255.224, which of the following addresses can be assigned to network hosts? (Chose three.)

   A. 15.234.118.63

   B. 92.11.178.93

   C. 134.178.18.56

   D. 192.168.16.87

   E. 201.45.116.159

   F. 217.63.12.192

7. Look at the following diagram. RTR-1 has been properly configured with static routing. Which set of commands will configure RTR-2 with static routing to reach the RTR-1 networks?

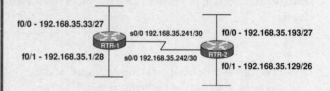

Figure 5-3

   A. `ip route 192.168.35.0 255.255.255.0 192.168.35.241`

   B. `ip route 192.168.35.0 255.255.255.240 192.168.35.242`
   `ip route 192.168.35.32 255.255.255.224 192.168.35.242`

   C. `ip route 192.168.35.128 255.255.255.192 192.168.35.241`
   `ip route 192.168.35.192 255.255.255.224 192.168.35.241`

   D. `ip route 192.168.35.0 255.255.255.240 192.168.35.241`
   `ip route 192.168.35.32 255.255.255.224 192.168.35.241`

   E. `ip route 192.168.35.128 255.255.255.192 192.168.35.242`
   `ip route 192.168.35.192 255.255.255.224 192.168.35.242`

   F. `ip route 192.168.35.1 255.255.255.240 192.168.35.241`
   `ip route 192.168.35.33 255.255.255.224 192.168.35.241`

8. Which of the following are key characteristics of PPP? (Choose three.)

   A. Can be used over analog circuits
   B. Maps a layer 2 address to layer 3 address
   C. Encapsulates several routed protocols
   D. Supports IP only
   E. Provides error correction

```
A# show run
hostname A
<<output omitted>>
!interface FastEthernet0/1
switchport mode trunk
no ip address
!
<<output omitted>>
interface Vlan1
 no ip address
 no ip route-cache
!
<<output omitted>>
```

Figure 5-4

9. Look at the following diagram. Computer 1 is consoled into switch A. Telnet connections and pings run from the command prompt on switch A fail. Which of the following could cause this problem?

   A. Switch A is not directly connected to router JAX.
   B. Switch A does not have a default gateway assigned.
   C. Switch A does not have a CDP entry for switch B or router JAX.
   D. Switch A does not have an IP address.
   E. Port 1 on switch A should be an access port rather than a trunk port.

10. What will an Ethernet switch do if it receives a unicast frame with a destination MAC that is not listed in the switch table?

    A. The switch will not forward unicast frames.
    B. The switch will forward the frame to a specific port.
    C. The switch will return a copy of the frame out the source port.
    D. The switch will remove the destination MAC from the switch table.
    E. The switch will forward the frame to all ports except the port on which it was received.

11. In a spanning-tree topology, which of the following can you use to delimit the root port on each non-root switch?

    A. Path cost
    B. Lowest port MAC address
    C. VTP revision number
    D. Highest port priority number
    E. Port priority number and MAC address

12. Which of the following is the reason you should configure port security on a switch?

    A. To prevent unauthorized Telnet access to a switch port
    B. To limit the number of layer 2 broadcasts on a particular switch port
    C. To prevent unauthorized hosts from accessing the LAN
    D. To protect the IP and MAC address of the switch and associated ports
    F. To block unauthorized access to the switch-management interfaces over common TCP ports

13. Which type of EIGRP route entry describes a feasible successor?

    A. Backup route, stored in the routing table
    B. Primary route, stored in the routing table
    C. Backup route, stored in the topology table
    D. Primary route, stored in the topology table

14. What can be done to secure the virtual terminal interface on a router? (Choose two.)

    A. Administratively shut down the interface.
    B. Physically secure the interface.
    C. Create an access list, and apply it to the virtual terminal interfaces with the `access-group` command.
    D. Configure a virtual terminal password and login process.
    E. Enter an access list, and apply it to the virtual terminal interfaces using the `access-class` command.

GO ON TO THE NEXT PAGE

15. Which characteristics are representative of a link-state routing protocol? (Choose three.)

A. Provides a common view of the entire topology
B. Exchanges routing tables with neighbors
C. Calculates shortest path
D. Utilizes event-triggered updates
E. Utilizes frequent periodic updates

16. Look at the following diagram. A network technician is asked to design a small network with redundancy. The exhibit represents this design, with all hosts configured in the same VLAN. What conclusion can be made about this design?

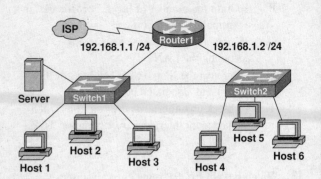

Figure 5-5

A. This design will function as intended.
B. Spanning-tree will need to be used.
C. The router will not accept the addressing scheme.
D. The connection between switches should be a trunk.
E. The router interfaces must be encapsulated with the 802.1Q protocol.

17. Look at the following diagram. A network technician has issued the command `show ip route`. The technician is trying to discover why packets are not getting to the 172.16.2.0 network. What could be the problem?

```
R1# show ip route

Codes: C-connected, S-Static, I-IGRP, R-RIP, M-mobile, B-BGP, D-EIGRP,
       EX-EIGRP external, O-OSPF, IA-OSPF inter area, E1-OSPF external type1,
       E2-OSPF external type 2, E-EGP i-IS-IS, L1-IS-IS level-1, L2-IS-IS level-2,
       *-candidate default, U-per-user static route

Gateway of last resort is not set

172.16.0.0/24 is subnetted
C 172.16.1.0 is directly connected, Ethernet0
R 10.0.0.0/8 [120/1] via 172.16.1.200, 00:00:01, Ethernet0
C 192.168.1.0/24 is directly connected, Loopback0
```

Figure 5-6

A. The Ethernet0 interface is down.
B. The hop count of RIP is incorrect.
C. The packets are being routed through the 10.0.0.0 network.
D. There is no route to the 172.16.2.0 network in the routing table.
E. The administrative distance of RIP is causing the packets to be dropped.

18. Look at the following diagram. An internetwork has been configured as shown in the diagram, with both routers using EIGRP routing for AS 44. Users on the Branch router are unable to reach any of the subnets on the HQ router. Which of the following commands is necessary to fix this problem?

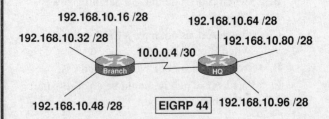

Figure 5-7

A. Branch(config-router)# **version 2**
B. Branch(config-router)# **no auto-summary**
C. Branch(config-router)# **redistribute eigrp 44**
D. Branch(config-router)# **eigrp log-neighbor-changes**
E. Branch(config-router)# **default-information originates**

19. In which of these situations will numerous copies of the same unicast frame be transmitted over a switched LAN?

A. During high traffic periods
B. After broken links are re-established
C. When upper-layer protocols require high reliability
D. In an improperly implemented redundant topology
E. When a dual ring topology is in use

20. Look at the following diagram. Which two values indicate that this router output refers to a WAN interface? (Choose two.)

```
Router# show interfaces
          is up, line protocol is up
Hardware is PowerQUICC
Internet address is 192.168.23.225/29
MTU 1500 bytes, BW 128 Kbit, DLY 20000 usec,
   reliability 255/255, txload 1/255, rxload 1/255
Encapsulation HDLC, loopback not set
Keepalive set (10 sec)
Last input 00:00:08, output 00:00:07, output hang never
Last clearing of "show interface" counters never
Input queue: 0/75/0/0 (size/max/drops/flushes); Total output drops: 0
Queueing strategy: weighted fair
Output Queue: 0/1000/64/0 (size/max total/threshold/drops)
-------- output omitted --------
24 packets output, 1512 bytes, 0 underruns
0 output errors, 0 collisions, 6 interface resets
0 output buffer failures, 0 output buffers swapped out
2 carrier transitions
-------- output omitted --------
```

Figure 5-8

A. MTU size
B. Bandwidth
C. IP address
D. Reliability
E. Encapsulation
F. Keep alive value

21. Look at the following diagram. A router interface is being configured for Frame Relay. However, as the exhibit shows, the router will not accept the command to configure the LMI type. What is the problem?

```
Router(config)# interface serial 0/0
Router(config-if)# frame-relay lmi-type cisco
                   ^

% Unrecognized command
Router(config-if)# frame-relay ?
% Unrecognized command
```

Figure 5-9

A. The interface does not support Frame Relay connections.
B. The interface does not have an IP address assigned to it yet.
C. The interface requires that the `no shutdown` command be configured first.
D. The interface requires that the `encapsulation frame-relay` command be configured first.

22. All WAN links inside the ABC Corporate network use PPP with CHAP for authentication security. Which command displays the CHAP authentication process as it occurs between two routers in the network?

A. `show CHAP authentication`
B. `show interface serial0`
C. `debug PPP authentication`
D. `debug CHAP authentication`
E. `show PPP authentication chap`

GO ON TO THE NEXT PAGE

23. Look at the following router output obtained via the `show frame-relay map` command, and choose the answer that best describes what the term `dynamic` means:

```
Vine#show frame-relay map
Serial0/0 (up): ip 192.168.10.1
dlci 16 (0x64, 0x1840), dynamic
Broadcast, status defined, active
```

A. The Serial0/0 interface is passing traffic.

B. The DLCI 16 was dynamically allocated by the router.

C. The Serial0/0 interface acquired the IP address of 192.168.10.1 from a DHCP server.

D. The DLCI 16 will be dynamically changed as required to adapt to changes in the Frame Relay cloud.

E. The mapping between DLCI 16 and the end station IP address 192.168.10.1 was learned through inverse ARP.

24. The Winery Coop has five branches throughout Napa and Sonoma, and the company wants to build a WAN to give it a completely meshed environment with a minimum of 512Kbps throughput. It also needs the most cost-effective solution. Which WAN service should the company choose?

A. Frame Relay

B. Leased lines

C. ISDN BRI

D. ATM

E. PPP

25. Based on the following switch output, how did the switch receive the MAC table entry for 0012.7f4b.6882?

```
Switch#sh mac address-table
        Mac Address Table
-------------------------------------------
Vlan    Mac Address       Type       Ports
----    -----------       --------   -----
All     0005.dccb.d740    STATIC     CPU
All     0100.0ccc.cccc    STATIC     CPU
All     0100.0ccc.cccd    STATIC     CPU
All     0100.0cdd.dddd    STATIC     CPU
  1     000a.f467.9e80    DYNAMIC    Fa0/11
  1     0010.7b7f.c2b0    DYNAMIC    Fa0/11
  1     0012.7f4b.6880    DYNAMIC    Fa0/11
  1     0012.7f4b.6881    DYNAMIC    Fa0/11
  1     0012.7f4b.6882    DYNAMIC    Fa0/11
  1     0030.80dc.460b    DYNAMIC    Fa0/11
  1     0030.9492.a5dd    DYNAMIC    Fa0/2
  1     00d0.58ad.05f4    DYNAMIC    Fa0/1
Total Mac Addresses for this criterion: 12
Switch#
```

Code Listing 5-1

A. It was forwarded from an adjacent switch.

B. It was entered from the configuration mode.

C. It was acquired by a broadcast from the switch.

D. It represents a MAC address of the switch.

26. You're adding a new router into an OSPF network, and the networks connected to your new router aren't showing up in the routing tables of the other OSPF routers. You have the subnets 10.10.10.0/24 and 10.11.11.0/24. What should your OSPF configuration be if you want to create one network entry and place both subnets into area 0?

   A. `Router(config)# router ospf 1`
      `Router(config)# network 10.0.0.0 255.0.0.0 area 0`

   B. `Router(config)# router ospf 1011`
      `Router(config)# network 10.0.0.0 255.255.255.0 area 0`

   C. `Router(config)# router ospf 1`
      `Router(config)# network 10.0.0.0 0.0.0.255 area0`

   D. `Router(config)# router ospf 1`
      `Router(config)# network 10.0.0.0 0.0.0.255 area 0`

27. Which of the following commands configures a default route to any destination network not found in the routing table?

   A. `Router(config)# ip default-route 0.0.0.0 255.255.255.255 s0`

   B. `Router(config)# ip route 0.0.0.0 255.255.255.255 s0`

   C. `Router(config)# ip default-route 0.0.0.0 s0`

   D. `Router(config)# ip route 0.0.0.0 0.0.0.0 s0`

   E. `Router(config)# ip route any any e0`

28. Look at the following diagram. After the router interfaces shown in the diagram have been configured, it is discovered that hosts in the Branch LAN cannot access the Internet. Further testing reveals additional connectivity issues. What will fix this problem?

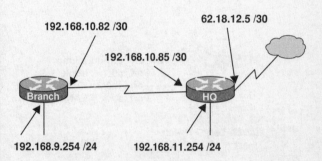

Figure 5-10

   A. Change the address of the Branch router LAN interface.

   B. Change the address of the Branch router WAN interface.

   C. Change the subnet mask of the HQ router LAN interface.

   D. Change the address of the HQ router LAN interface.

   E. Change the address of the HQ router interface to the Internet.

   F. Change the subnet mask of the HQ router interface to the Internet.

29. You need to keep the hosts with the subnet address 172.16.24.0/21 in the VLAN from accessing Telnet services. Which of the following provides the missing answers in this command?

```
access-list 110 deny protocol
172.16.24.0  mask any eq port
```

   A. Port 23

   B. Port 80

   C. Protocol IP

   D. Protocol TCP

   E. Wildcard 0.0.3.255

   F. Mask 0.0.7.255

GO ON TO THE NEXT PAGE

30. Look at the following diagram. The router has been configured to provide communication between the VLANs. Which IOS commands are required to configure switch port fa0/1 to establish a link with router R1 using the IEEE standard protocol? (Choose three.)

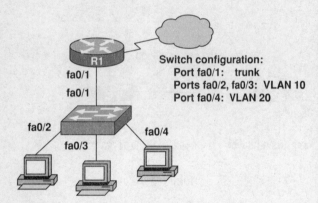

Figure 5-11

A. `Switch(config)# interface fastethernet 0/1`

B. `Switch(config)# switchport mode access`

C. `Switch(config)# switchport mode trunk`

D. `Switch(config)# switchport access vlan 1`

E. `Switch(config)# switchport trunk encapsulation isl`

F. `Switch(config)# switchport trunk encapsulation dot1q`

31. Why would you use this command?

`ip route 0.0.0.0 0.0.0.0 serial0/0`

A. It configures a router to send all packets out interface serial0/0.

B. It configures a router to block routing updates from being sent out interface serial0/0.

C. In configures a router as a firewall, blocking all unauthorized packets from exiting serial0/0.

D. It configures a router to send all packets for unknown destination networks out interface serial0/0.

E. It configures a router to drop all packets for which the destination network is unknown.

32. An inbound access list has been configured on a serial interface to deny packet entry for TCP and UDP ports 21, 23, and 25. What types of packets will be permitted by this ACL? (Choose three.)

A. FTP
B. Telnet
C. SMTP
D. DNS
E. HTTP
F. POP3

33. You're faced with reconfiguring a Catalyst 2950. Pick three steps that will guarantee the old configuration is erased.

A. Erase flash.
B. Restart the switch.
C. Delete the VLAN database.
D. Erase the running configuration.
E. Erase the startup configuration.
F. Modify the configuration register.

34. If you were implementing VLSM on a network with a single Class C IP address, which subnet mask would you use to create the most effective point-to-point serial link?

A. 255.255.255.0
B. 255.255.255.240
C. 255.255.255.248
D. 255.255.255.252
E. 255.255.255.254

35. A network administrator has installed a new router in the Lisbon office and is unable to back up the IOS image of the new router to a TFTP server located in the Gibraltar office. Given the network diagram, identify the source of the problem.

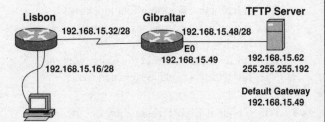

Lisbon
192.168.15.32/28
192.168.15.16/28

Gibraltar
192.168.15.48/28
E0
192.168.15.49

TFTP Server
192.168.15.62
255.255.255.192

Default Gateway
192.168.15.49

Figure 5-12

A. Incorrect default gateway of the TFTP server
B. Incorrect subnet mask of the TFTP server
C. Incorrect IP address of the TFTP server
D. Incorrect IP address on E0 of the Gibraltar router
E. Incorrect subnet mask on the Lisbon router

36. In which spanning-tree states does a switch port learn MAC addresses? (Choose two.)

A. Blocking
B. Listening
C. Forwarding
D. Learning
E. Relaying

37. You've subnetted your client's internetwork using 29 bits. You now need to configure an extended access list to control access to a whole subnetwork. To achieve this, which of the following wildcard masks should you use?

A. 255.255.255.224
B. 255.255.255.248
C. 0.0.0.224
D. 0.0.0.8
E. 0.0.0.7
F. 0.0.0.3

38. Look at the following diagram. A network technician is troubleshooting a connectivity problem on R2. The technician enters the show cdp neighbors command at the R2 console. If the network is composed only of Cisco devices, for which devices should entries be displayed?

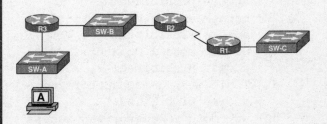

Figure 5-13

A. R1
B. SW-B and R1
C. SW-B, R1, and SW-C
D. R3, SW-B, R1, and SW-C
E. SW-A, R3, SW-B, R1, and SW-C
F. Host A, SW-A, R3, SW-B, R1, and SW-C

39. Look at the following output, and pick the option that solves the problem of why Serial0/0 won't respond to a ping from a machine on the FastEthernet0/0 LAN.

```
Napa#sh ip interface brief
Interface     IP-Address   OK? Method Status      Protocol
Ethernet0/0   192.168.10.1 YES NVRAM  up          up
Serial0/0     192.168.15.1 YES NVRAM  administratively
                                      down down
Serial0/1     192.168.16.1 YES NVRAM  up          up
Serial0/2     unassigned   YES NVRAM  administratively
                                      down down
Router#
```

Code Listing 5-2

A. Enable the Serial0/0 interface.
B. Correct the IP address for Serial0/0.
C. Correct the IP address for FastEthernet0/0.
D. Change the encapsulation type on Serial0/0.
E. Enable autoconfiguration on the Serial0/0 interface.

GO ON TO THE NEXT PAGE

40. A network administrator wants the text *"Unauthorized access prohibited!"* to be displayed before the login prompt when someone tries to initiate a Telnet session to a router. Which command can be used to configure this message?

A. `login banner x Unauthorized access prohibited! x`

B. `banner exec y Unauthorized access prohibited! y`

C. `banner motd x Unauthorized access prohibited! x`

D. `login message "Unauthorized access prohibited!"`

E. `vty motd "Unauthorized access prohibited!"`

F. `vty 0 4 banner "Unauthorized access prohibited!"`

41. Look at the following diagram. The two connected ports on the switch are not turning orange or green. What will be the most effective steps to troubleshoot this Physical layer problem? (Choose three.)

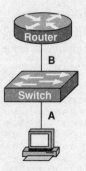

Figure 5-14

A. Ensure that the Ethernet encapsulations match on the interconnected router and switch ports.

B. Ensure that cables A and B are straight-through cables.

C. Ensure that cable A is plugged into a trunk port.

D. Ensure that the switch has power.

E. Reboot all the devices.

F. Reseat all the cables.

42. Choose two of the following options that accurately describe the tasks that the OSPF Hello protocol performs.

A. It provides dynamic neighbor discovery.

B. It detects unreachable neighbors in 90-second intervals.

C. It maintains neighbor relationships.

D. It negotiates correctness parameters between neighboring interfaces.

E. It uses timers to elect the router with the fastest links as the designated router.

43. Which type of EIGRP route entry describes a feasible successor?

A. Backup route, stored in the routing table

B. Primary route, stored in the routing table

C. Backup route, stored in the topology table

D. Primary route, stored in the topology table

44. What does a layer-2 switch do if it receives a frame with a destination MAC address that is not found in its MAC address table?

A. The frame is dropped.

B. The frame is addressed with a broadcast MAC address and sent out all ports.

C. The frame is sent out all ports except the receiving port.

D. An ARP request is sent out all ports except the receiving port.

E. A destination-unreachable message is sent back to the source address.

45. You've created the access list shown below and applied it to an interface. Which of the following are denied based on the access list?

```
access-list 107 deny tcp
  207.16.12.0 0.0.3.255 any eq
  http
access-list 107 permit ip any
  any
```

A. source IP:207.16.32.14, destination application: http

B. source IP:207.16.15.9, destination port: 23

C. source IP:207.16.14.7, destination port: 80

D. source IP:207.16.13.14, destination application: http

E. source IP:207.16.16.14, destination port: 53

46. On three different occasions, an administrator configured a router and, after testing the configuration, saved it to NVRAM by issuing the `copy running-config startup-config` command. After each successful save, the administrator issued the `reload` command. Each time, when the router restarted, the router appeared to have the default blank configuration. What could cause such results?

- **A.** The `boot system` commands were left out of the configuration.
- **B.** The NVRAM is corrupted.
- **C.** The configuration register setting is incorrect.
- **D.** The upgraded IOS just loaded is not compatible with the hardware.
- **E.** The upgraded configuration is not compatible with the hardware platform.

47. The OSPF Hello protocol performs which of the following tasks? (Choose two.)

- **A.** It provides dynamic neighbor discovery.
- **B.** It detects unreachable neighbors in 90-second intervals.
- **C.** It maintains neighbor relationships.
- **D.** It negotiates correctness parameters between neighboring interfaces.
- **E.** It uses timers to elect the router with the fastest links as the designated router.
- **F.** It broadcasts hello packets throughout the internetwork to discover all routers that are running OSPF.

48. What is the purpose of this command?

`ip route 0.0.0.0 0.0.0.0 serial0/0`

- **A.** It configures a router to send all packets out interface serial0/0.
- **B.** It configures a router to block routing updates from being sent out interface serial0/0.
- **C.** It configures a router as a firewall, blocking all unauthorized packets from exiting serial0/0.
- **D.** It configures a router to send all packets for unknown destination networks out interface serial0/0.
- **E.** It configures a router to drop all packets for which the destination network is unknown.

49. Choose the three services that use TCP.

- **A.** DHCP
- **B.** SMTP
- **C.** SNMP
- **D.** FTP
- **E.** HTTP
- **F.** TFTP

50. Look at the following diagram. How should the FastEthernet0/1 ports on the 2950 model switches that are shown in the exhibit be configured to allow connectivity between all devices?

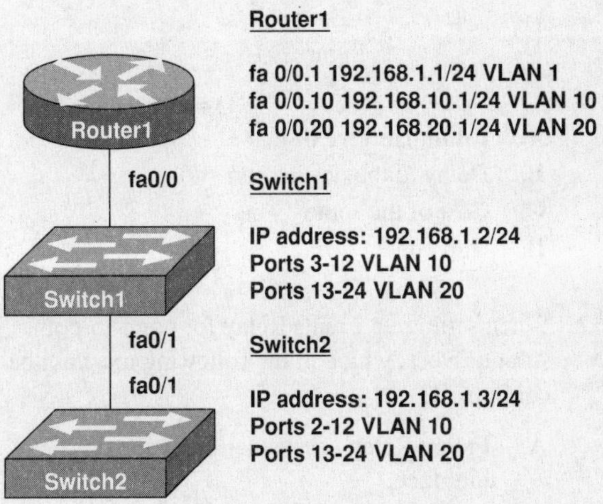

Router1

fa 0/0.1 192.168.1.1/24 VLAN 1
fa 0/0.10 192.168.10.1/24 VLAN 10
fa 0/0.20 192.168.20.1/24 VLAN 20

fa0/0

Switch1

IP address: 192.168.1.2/24
Ports 3-12 VLAN 10
Ports 13-24 VLAN 20

fa0/1

Switch2

fa0/1

IP address: 192.168.1.3/24
Ports 2-12 VLAN 10
Ports 13-24 VLAN 20

Figure 5-15

- **A.** The ports only need to be connected by a crossover cable.
- **B.** `SwitchX(config)#`
  `interface fastethernet 0/1`
  `SwitchX(config-if)#`
  `switchport mode trunk`
- **C.** `SwitchX(config)#`
  `interface fastethernet 0/1`
  `SwitchX(config-if)#`
  `switchport mode access`
  `SwitchX(config-if)#`
  `switchport access vlan 1`
- **D.** `SwitchX(config)#`
  `interface fastethernet 0/1`
  `SwitchX(config-if)#`
  `switchport mode trunk`
  `SwitchX(config-if)#`
  `switchport trunk vlan 1`
  `SwitchX(config-if)#`
  `switchport trunk vlan 10`
  `SwitchX(config-if)#`
  `switchport trunk vlan 20`

GO ON TO THE NEXT PAGE

51. Look at the following diagram. What does the number 782 represent?

```
AquaV#show ip route
--- output omitted ---
Gateway of last resort is 140.8.100.5 to network 0.0.0.0

140.8.0.0/16 is variably subnetted, 4 subnets, 4 masks
R      140.8.7.0/24 [120/3] via 150.8.12.9, 00:00:20, Serial0/1
O      140.8.5.5/32 [110/782] via 140.8.100.5, 00:38:34, Serial0/0
R      140.8.78.8/29 [120/2] via 150.8.12.9, 00:00:22, Serial0/1
C      140.8.100.0/28 is directly connected, Serial0/0
150.8.0.0/16 is variably subnetted, 2 subnets, 2 masks
C      150.8.12.0/24 is directly connected, Serial0/1
R      150.8.0.0/16 [120/4] via 150.8.12.9, 00:00:23, Serial0/1
O*   0.0.0.0/0 [110/2738] via 140.8.100.5, 00:38:34, Serial0/0
```

Figure 5-16

A. Administrative distance

B. Delay to the destination

C. Cost of the route

D. Hop count

52. When setting up Frame Relay for point-to-point subinterfaces, which of the following must not be configured?

A. Frame Relay encapsulation on the physical interface

B. Local DLCI on each subinterface

C. IP address on the physical interface

D. Subinterface type as point-to-point

53. What is the purpose of the OSPF router ID in a DR/BDR election?

A. It is used with the OSPF priority values to determine which OSPF router will become the DR or BDR in a point-to-point network.

B. It is used with the OSPF priority values to determine which interface will be used to form a neighbor relationship with another OSPF router.

C. It is used with the OSPF priority values to determine which router will become the DR or BDR in a multiaccess network.

D. It is used to determine which interfaces will send Hello packets to neighboring OSPF routers.

54. Select the statements that correctly describe full- or half-duplex Ethernet operation. (Choose two.)

A. Full-duplex Ethernet uses CSMA/CD to prevent collisions.

B. Full-duplex Ethernet uses two pairs of wires for data.

C. An Ethernet hub can operate at half or full duplex.

D. Half-duplex Ethernet uses a loopback circuit to detect collisions.

E. A 10Mbps full-duplex Ethernet card allows 20Mbps for transmitting data and 20Mbps for receiving data.

55. Of the choices below, which one is needed for connectivity in a Frame Relay network if Inverse ARP isn't operational?

A. `frame-relay arp`

B. `frame-relay map`

C. `frame-relay interface dlci`

D. `frame-relay Imi-type`

Answer Key for Practice Test 5

1. C	**15.** A, C, D	**29.** A, D, F	**43.** C
2. A, B	**16.** C	**30.** A, C, F	**44.** C
3. A	**17.** D	**31.** D	**45.** A, B, E
4. C	**18.** B	**32.** D, E, F	**46.** C
5. A, B, F	**19.** D	**33.** B, C, E	**47.** A, C
6. B, C, D	**20.** B, E	**34.** D	**48.** D
7. D	**21.** D	**35.** B	**49.** B, D, E
8. A, C, E	**22.** C	**36.** C, D	**50.** B
9. D	**23.** E	**37.** E	**51.** C
10. E	**24.** A	**38.** B	**52.** C
11. A	**25.** A	**39.** A	**53.** C
12. C	**26.** D	**40.** C	**54.** B, D
13. C	**27.** D	**41.** B, D, F	**55.** B
14. D, E	**28.** B	**42.** A, C	

Answer Explanations for Practice Test 5

1. **C.** A /26 mask allows for up to 62 hosts.

2. **A, B.** Switches decrease the number of collisions and increase the effective bandwidth each individual host has.

3. **A.** Administrative Distance (AD) is the value a router uses to differentiate between routing information. Each routing protocol is given a value; a static route has the best AD: 1 (the lower, the better; only a directly connected network is better, with an AD of 0).

4. **C.** The default encapsulation is HDLC on Cisco routers, which is proprietary. Changing to PPP encapsulation (a more universal standard) is the most likely choice to resolve the up/down issue here.

5. **A, B, F.** RIPv1 is a classful routing protocols, which means all masks on every host in the network must be exactly the same. RIPv1 sends broadcasts, and RIPv2 uses multicast: 224.0.0.9. RIP has many loop-avoidance mechanisms, some of which are split-horizon and hold-down timers. Others include route poison, setting infinity, and triggered updates. RIPv2 supports authentication as well; v1 does not.

6. **B, C, D.** With a /27 mask, you must ensure that the last 5 bits are not all ones (broadcast address) or zeros (network address). A and E are both all ones, and F is all zeros.

7. **D.** The correct routes are for the two networks (192.168.35.0 and 192.168.35.32 along with correct masks) via the RTR-1 serial interface IP address.

8. **A, C, E.** PPP can be used over analog circuits, supports multiple routed (layer 3) protocols, and uses a CRC to provide error correction.

9. **D.** Telnet and ping require that switch A has a valid IP configuration. The default gateway and CDP are not relevant here. Also, a trunk port is not required to ping or telnet.

10. **E.** When the destination MAC of a unicast frame is unknown, the switch forwards the frame on all ports except the one on which it was received.

11. **A.** Path cost is the first value that is used to determine which port should be blocking or forwarding. If path cost does not differentiate, then bridge id and port id can be used.

12. **C.** Port security can prevent unauthorized hosts from accessing the LAN. It can be configured with a maximum number of MAC addresses per port, or to allow only specifically configured MACs access.

13. **C.** A feasible successor is stored in EIGRP's topology table, which holds all links known in the autonomous system. A successor route is copied from the topology table and placed in the routing table, which is then used by IP to route packets. The feasible successor is the backup route to the successor route.

14. **D, E.** The virtual terminal can be secured with a password. Additionally, you can control source IP addresses that have access to the VTY using a standard IP access list and the `access-class` command.

15. **A, C, D.** Link-state routing protocols calculate a view of the entire topology, calculate shortest paths, and use event-triggered (not periodic) updates.

16. **C.** You cannot assign two interfaces on the same router addresses in the same subnet, or IOS will generate an error.

17. **D.** Without a route to the destination or a default route, the router will drop packets.

18. **B.** The `no auto-summary` command must be used when subnetworks are not contiguous.

19. **D.** If you have switches connected with dual links, and STP is not running, then you will have broadcast storms, multiple frame copies, and MAC table instability.

20. **B, E.** The bandwidth is below that of any LAN interface, and the encapsulation (HDLC) is not used on LAN interfaces.

21. **D.** Until the interface is configured with Frame Relay encapsulation, none of the more specific Frame Relay commands will be functional.

22. C. You must use a debug command show the authentication as it happens. In this case, the "debug ppp authentication" command.

23. E. Inverse ARP is the automatic process of finding a DLCI from a known IP address. If this function is not available, then the mapping of the DLCI to the IP address must be done manually through the frame-relay map command.

24. A. The bandwidth requirement and the fact that it is to be cost effective make Frame Relay the only real choice.

25. A. The best answer is that the MAC address was forwarded from another switch, because port Fa0/11 has many MAC addresses associated with it.

26. D. Although answer C is close, only answer D is correct because you must have a space after the command area before listing the associated area.

27. D. A default route is a static route where the destination network and mask are all zeros.

28. B. The correct address should be 192.168.10.86.

29. A, D, F. To answer this question, you must know what a /21 is. A /21 is 255.255.248.0, which is a block size of 8, wildcard of 7, in the third octet (wildcards are always one less than the block size). Telnet uses TCP at the Transport layer and is well-known port number 23.

30. A, C, F. The interface must be configured as a trunk link, and the encapsulation must be specified.

31. D. The ip route command with all zeros is a default route. Any traffic without a specific route is sent out the interface specified at the end of the command. A next hop can also be used with the command instead of the exit interface.

32. D, E, F. Ports 21, 23, and 25 are associated with FTP, Telnet, and SMTP; and because the ACL is denying these packets, these protocols will not work.

33. B, C, E. A typical router can be set back to factory defaults by erasing the startup-config in NVRAM and then reloading the device. However, a switch keeps the VLAN database in flash; so, that must also be deleted on a switch to set the switch back to factory defaults.

34. D. A /30 or 255.255.255.252 provides only two hosts, regardless of the class of address, which is perfect for a point-to-point link.

35. B. The subnet mask for a /28 network is 255.255.255.240, not 255.255.255.192.

36. C, D. In the learning and forwarding states, a switchport can learn MAC addresses.

37. E. First, you must know what a /29 is. The mask is 255.255.255.248, which means the block size is 8 in the fourth octet. A wildcard is always one less the block size, so the answer is 0.0.0.7.

38. B. The R2 router should have SW-B and R1 as CDP neighbors.

39. A. If an interface is administratively down, this means the interface is not enabled and must be enabled with the no shutdown command. All interfaces on a router are shut down by default.

40. C. The banner motd command allows you to configure a message of the day.

41. B, D, F. When the switchports fail to turn orange or green, it indicates a layer 1 problem. The wrong cable type or poorly seated cables can cause this issue, as can the switch not having power.

42. A, C. A router running a link-state protocol uses hello packets to dynamically find neighbors and form adjacencies. Once an adjacency has been formed, the router uses link state advertisement (LSA) packets to exchange topology information and updates when changes occur.

43. C. A feasible successor is stored in EIGRP's topology table, which holds all links known in the autonomous system. A successor route is copied from the topology table and placed in the routing table, which is then used by IP to route packets. The feasible successor is the backup route to the successor route.

44. C. A LAN switch uses MAC addresses to segment the network into collision domains. The switch looks at the source MAC address of each frame received on a port and places this in a forward/filter table, also called the content addressable memory (CAM) table. If a frame is received and the destination hardware (MAC) address is not found in the CAM table, the frame is sent out all ports except the port it was received on.

45. A, B, E. The wildcard in the mask is the key to the answer. 0.0.3.255 means that the third octet has a wildcard of 4. The 12 in the third octet means that the access-list will match 12, 13, 14, and 15, which make C and D permitted and A, B, E incorrect. B is wrong because the port number is wrong. A isn't in the correct block size; and E is 16, which is one more than the allowed block size.

46. C. If the configuration register setting is incorrect, it is possible that the router will boot and ignore the startup-config.

47. A, C. A router running a link-state protocol uses hello packets to dynamically find neighbors and form adjacencies. Once an adjacency has been formed, the router uses link state advertisement (LSA) packets to exchange topology information and updates when changes occur.

48. D. This is known as a default route. It configures the router to send all packets for which the router does not have a specific route out the serial0/0 interface.

49. B, D, E. SMTP, FTP, and HTTP are Application layer protocols that use TCP at the Transport layer. DHCP, SNMP, and TFTP all use UDP at the Transport layer.

50. B. Specifying that the switchports are trunk links makes them able to carry all VLAN traffic. By default, they carry all VLANs.

51. C. In this case, the 782 represents the OSPF cost of this route.

52. C. When you are creating subinterfaces on a router, an IP address is not configured under the physical interface of the router. IP addresses can be configured only under the logical (subinterfaces) interfaces, or the network will not function.

53. C. When OSPF is configured on a router, a router identification (RID) is created by using the highest IP address on any active interface at the moment of OSPF startup. The RID can be changed by creating a loopback interface, also called a logical interface. Routers use this RID to determine which router will be a designated router or backup-designated router in a broadcast or nonbroadcast multiaccess network.

54. B, D. Full-duplex Ethernet uses two pairs of wires. In full-duplex Ethernet, there is no such thing as a collision. Half-duplex Ethernet does use CSMA/CD, does have collisions, and must use a loopback circuit to detect collisions.

55. B. Inverse ARP is used to resolve an IP address to local DLCI number. If a router does not support IARP or is used on the network, a Frame Relay map must be configured for each PVC.

Answer Sheets for Practice Test 6

(Remove This Sheet and Use It to Mark Your Answers)

Section 1
Multiple Choice Questions

1 Ⓐ Ⓑ Ⓒ Ⓓ Ⓔ Ⓕ	31 Ⓐ Ⓑ Ⓒ Ⓓ Ⓔ Ⓕ
2 Ⓐ Ⓑ Ⓒ Ⓓ Ⓔ Ⓕ	32 Ⓐ Ⓑ Ⓒ Ⓓ Ⓔ Ⓕ
3 Ⓐ Ⓑ Ⓒ Ⓓ Ⓔ Ⓕ	33 Ⓐ Ⓑ Ⓒ Ⓓ Ⓔ Ⓕ
4 Ⓐ Ⓑ Ⓒ Ⓓ Ⓔ Ⓕ	34 Ⓐ Ⓑ Ⓒ Ⓓ Ⓔ Ⓕ
5 Ⓐ Ⓑ Ⓒ Ⓓ Ⓔ Ⓕ	35 Ⓐ Ⓑ Ⓒ Ⓓ Ⓔ Ⓕ
6 Ⓐ Ⓑ Ⓒ Ⓓ Ⓔ Ⓕ	36 Ⓐ Ⓑ Ⓒ Ⓓ Ⓔ Ⓕ
7 Ⓐ Ⓑ Ⓒ Ⓓ Ⓔ Ⓕ	37 Ⓐ Ⓑ Ⓒ Ⓓ Ⓔ Ⓕ
8 Ⓐ Ⓑ Ⓒ Ⓓ Ⓔ Ⓕ	38 Ⓐ Ⓑ Ⓒ Ⓓ Ⓔ Ⓕ
9 Ⓐ Ⓑ Ⓒ Ⓓ Ⓔ Ⓕ	39 Ⓐ Ⓑ Ⓒ Ⓓ Ⓔ Ⓕ
10 Ⓐ Ⓑ Ⓒ Ⓓ Ⓔ Ⓕ	40 Ⓐ Ⓑ Ⓒ Ⓓ Ⓔ Ⓕ
11 Ⓐ Ⓑ Ⓒ Ⓓ Ⓔ Ⓕ	41 Ⓐ Ⓑ Ⓒ Ⓓ Ⓔ Ⓕ
12 Ⓐ Ⓑ Ⓒ Ⓓ Ⓔ Ⓕ	42 Ⓐ Ⓑ Ⓒ Ⓓ Ⓔ Ⓕ
13 Ⓐ Ⓑ Ⓒ Ⓓ Ⓔ Ⓕ	43 Ⓐ Ⓑ Ⓒ Ⓓ Ⓔ Ⓕ
14 Ⓐ Ⓑ Ⓒ Ⓓ Ⓔ Ⓕ	44 Ⓐ Ⓑ Ⓒ Ⓓ Ⓔ Ⓕ
15 Ⓐ Ⓑ Ⓒ Ⓓ Ⓔ Ⓕ	45 Ⓐ Ⓑ Ⓒ Ⓓ Ⓔ Ⓕ
16 Ⓐ Ⓑ Ⓒ Ⓓ Ⓔ Ⓕ	46 Ⓐ Ⓑ Ⓒ Ⓓ Ⓔ Ⓕ
17 Ⓐ Ⓑ Ⓒ Ⓓ Ⓔ Ⓕ	47 Ⓐ Ⓑ Ⓒ Ⓓ Ⓔ Ⓕ
18 Ⓐ Ⓑ Ⓒ Ⓓ Ⓔ Ⓕ	48 Ⓐ Ⓑ Ⓒ Ⓓ Ⓔ Ⓕ
19 Ⓐ Ⓑ Ⓒ Ⓓ Ⓔ Ⓕ	49 Ⓐ Ⓑ Ⓒ Ⓓ Ⓔ Ⓕ
20 Ⓐ Ⓑ Ⓒ Ⓓ Ⓔ Ⓕ	50 Ⓐ Ⓑ Ⓒ Ⓓ Ⓔ Ⓕ
21 Ⓐ Ⓑ Ⓒ Ⓓ Ⓔ Ⓕ	51 Ⓐ Ⓑ Ⓒ Ⓓ Ⓔ Ⓕ
22 Ⓐ Ⓑ Ⓒ Ⓓ Ⓔ Ⓕ	52 Ⓐ Ⓑ Ⓒ Ⓓ Ⓔ Ⓕ
23 Ⓐ Ⓑ Ⓒ Ⓓ Ⓔ Ⓕ	53 Ⓐ Ⓑ Ⓒ Ⓓ Ⓔ Ⓕ
24 Ⓐ Ⓑ Ⓒ Ⓓ Ⓔ Ⓕ	54 Ⓐ Ⓑ Ⓒ Ⓓ Ⓔ Ⓕ
25 Ⓐ Ⓑ Ⓒ Ⓓ Ⓔ Ⓕ	55 Ⓐ Ⓑ Ⓒ Ⓓ Ⓔ Ⓕ
26 Ⓐ Ⓑ Ⓒ Ⓓ Ⓔ Ⓕ	
27 Ⓐ Ⓑ Ⓒ Ⓓ Ⓔ Ⓕ	
28 Ⓐ Ⓑ Ⓒ Ⓓ Ⓔ Ⓕ	
29 Ⓐ Ⓑ Ⓒ Ⓓ Ⓔ Ⓕ	
30 Ⓐ Ⓑ Ⓒ Ⓓ Ⓔ Ⓕ	

CUT HERE

Directions: For each of the following questions, select the choice that best answers the question or completes the statement.

1. Which of the following commands will display "Unauthorized access prohibited!" before the login prompt when someone initiates a Telnet session to a router?

   A. `login banner x Unauthorized access prohibited! x`

   B. `banner exec y Unauthorized access prohibited! y`

   C. `banner motd x Unauthorized access prohibited!" x`

   D. `login message "Unauthorized access prohibited!"`

2. What wildcard mask should be used with a network address that has a range of 172.16.16.0 through 172.16.31.0?

   A. 0.0.15.255
   B. 0.0.255.255
   C. 0.255.255.255
   D. 0.0.0.31

3. A router on one side of a PPP link uses the hostname RT-Denver and the password globalnet. Which command should be entered on RT-Denver to enable a connection between RT-Denver and another router named RT-Dallas?

   A. `Router#username RT-Dallas password globalnet`

   B. `Router(config)#username RT-Dallas password globalnet`

   C. `Router#username globalnet password RT-Dallas`

   D. `Router(config)#username globalnet password RT-Dallas`

GO ON TO THE NEXT PAGE

4. Look at the following diagram. Assume that the RT-Houston router has already been configured with RIP. Which of the following series of commands will enable and configure RIP routing on the RT-Dallas router?

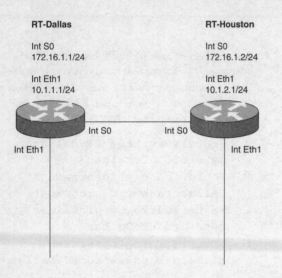

RT-Dallas

Int S0
172.16.1.1/24

Int Eth1
10.1.1.1/24

Int Eth1

Int S0

RT-Houston

Int S0
172.16.1.2/24

Int Eth1
10.1.2.1/24

Int S0

Int Eth1

Figure 6-1

A.
```
RT-Dallas(config)#router rip 100
RT-Dallas(config-router)#
network 10.0.0.0
RT-Dallas(config-router)#
network 172.16.0.0
```
B.
```
RT-Dallas(config)#router rip
RT-Dallas(config-router)#
network 10.0.0.0
RT-Dallas(config-router)#
network 172.16.0.0
```
C.
```
RT-Dallas(config)#router rip
RT-Dallas(config-router)#
interface ethernet 0
RT-Dallas(config-if)#ip address
10.1.1.1 255.255.255.0
RT-Dallas(config-if)# network
10.0.0.0
RT-Dallas(config-if)#interface
serial 1
RT-Dallas(config-if)#ip address
172.16.1.1 255.255.255.0
RT-Dallas(config-if)#network
172.16.0.0
```

D.
```
RT-Dallas(config)#router rip
RT-Dallas(config-router)#
interface ethernet 0
RT-Dallas(config-if)#ip address
172.16.1.1 255.255.255.0
RT-Dallas(config-if)#network
172.16.0.0
RT-Dallas(config-if)#interface
serial 1
RT-Dallas(config-if)#ip address
10.1.1.1 255.255.255.0
RT-Dallas(config-if)#network
10.0.0.0
```

5. Which of the following are advantages of using routers in your network? (Choose three.)

A. Limit scope of broadcast storms

B. Reduce downtime on your network

C. Route between VLANs

D. Filter traffic based on logical addresses

6. Look at the following diagram. Suppose that all routing has already been configured using EIGRP and is working properly. Additionally, suppose that the following line has been added to RT-Miami:

```
IP Route 192.168.2.0
        255.255.255.0
10.1.1.2
```

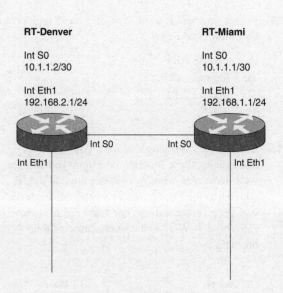

RT-Denver

Int S0
10.1.1.2/30

Int Eth1
192.168.2.1/24

Int S0

Int Eth1

RT-Miami

Int S0
10.1.1.1/30

Int Eth1
192.168.1.1/24

Int S0

Int Eth1

Figure 6-2

Which of the following will happen?

A. The Miami LAN will lose access to the Denver LAN.
B. The Denver LAN will lose access to the Miami LAN.
C. Both of the above.
D. None of the above.

7. Which of the following is a benefit of segmenting your network with switches?

A. Each port on a switch acts like a router interface.
B. Switches provide bridging functionality at wire speed.
C. Switches regenerate the digital signal at each hop.
D. Switches stop broadcast storms by default.

8. When using Frame Relay, what is the purpose of Inverse ARP?

A. Map a known IP address to a MAC address
B. Map a known IP addresses to a DLCI
C. Map a known IP addresses to Multicast addresses
D. Map a known IP address to LMI

9. You need a routing protocol that provides discontiguous network and VLSM support. It must also provide the lowest impact on router CPU and WAN utilization. Which of the following will meet these needs?

A. RIPv1
B. RIPv2
C. Static routing
D. EIGRP
E. OSPF

10. You are designing a WAN that will span seven sites. You must allow full-mesh communication of up to T1 speeds. Which of the following will most efficiently meet these requirements?

A. PPP
B. Frame Relay
C. ISDN BRI
D. OSPF
E. Point-to-point links

GO ON TO THE NEXT PAGE

11. Look at the following diagram. You have been asked to prevent the Dallas LAN from accessing web services on the Houston LAN. Which wildcard should be used to describe the entire Dallas LAN 10.1.1.1/24 in the access control list?

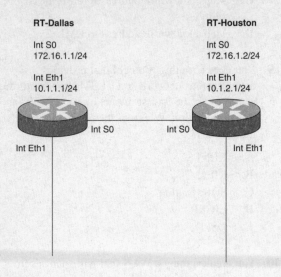

RT-Dallas

Int S0
172.16.1.1/24

Int Eth1
10.1.1.1/24

RT-Houston

Int S0
172.16.1.2/24

Int Eth1
10.1.2.1/24

Int S0   Int S0

Int Eth1   Int Eth1

Figure 6-1

- **A.** 255.255.255.0
- **B.** 255.0.0.0
- **C.** 0.0.0.254
- **D.** 0.0.0.255
- **E.** 0.0.0.8

12. Look at the following diagram. This small branch has a single /24 Internet routable network assigned, and it has been properly subnetted and assigned to the network segments. Which routing protocol is recommended to run between the branch and ISP routers?

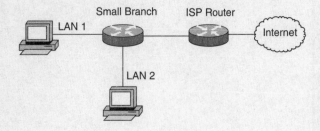

Small Branch   ISP Router

LAN 1

Internet

LAN 2

Figure 6-3

- **A.** Static routing
- **B.** EIGRP
- **C.** OSPF
- **D.** BGP
- **E.** Default routing

13. Which statement describes the switch ports in a spanning-tree network that has converged?

- **A.** All switch ports are in the forwarding state.
- **B.** All switch ports are assigned as either root or designated ports.
- **C.** All switch ports are in either the forwarding or the blocking state.
- **D.** All switch ports are either blocking or looping.

14. Which protocol is used to resolve an IP address to an Ethernet address?

- **A.** Inverse ARP
- **B.** Reverse ARP
- **C.** Interior ARP
- **D.** ARP

15. Look at the following diagram. When you are configuring these routers, the Miami router goes well. However, when you attempt to add the IP address to the Denver router's Ethernet 1 interface you get an error stating *Bad Mask /26 for address 192.168.1.1*. What is the likely cause of this problem?

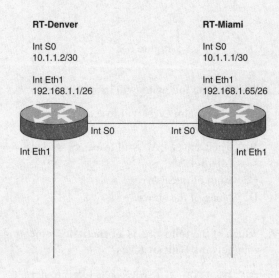

RT-Denver

Int S0
10.1.1.2/30

Int Eth1
192.168.1.1/26

RT-Miami

Int S0
10.1.1.1/30

Int Eth1
192.168.1.65/26

Int S0   Int S0

Int Eth1   Int Eth1

Figure 6-4

- **A.** You first need to add the 192.168.1.0 subnet to the routing protocol on the Miami router.
- **B.** You must add the Ethernet interface address before the serial interface address.
- **C.** You must add the `no auto-summary` command to your routing protocol on the Denver router.
- **D.** You must add the `ip subnet-zero` command to the Denver router.

16. You are at a client's site, trying to detect the source of network trouble. While using a protocol analyzer, you note the presence of BPDU frames. What is the role of BPDU frames in a network environment?

   A. BPDUs are unicast frames sent among all network connectivity devices. They contain spanning-tree algorithm information.

   B. BPDUs are multicast frames that contain the bridge ID of the source device, which is used in spanning-tree algorithm calculations.

   C. BPDUs are broadcast frames used by switches to encapsulate routing protocol information.

   D. BPDUs are multicast frames used by switches to encapsulate routing protocol information.

17. Which of these sentences are true regarding the following output? (Choose two.)

```
04:06:16: RIP: received v1 update from 192.168.40.2 on
  Serial0/1
04:06:16:     192.168.50.0 in 16 hops (inaccessible)
04:06:40: RIP: sending v1 update to 255.255.255.255
  via FastEthernet0/0 (192.168.30.1)
04:06:40: RIP: build update entries
04:06:40:      network 192.168.20.0 metric 1
04:06:40:      network 192.168.40.0 metric 1
04:06:40:      network 192.168.50.0 metric 2
04:06:40: RIP: sending v1 update to 255.255.255.255 via
Serial0/1
  (192.168.40.1)
```

Code Listing 6-1

   A. Three interfaces on the router are participating in this update.

   B. A ping to 192.168.50.1 will be successful.

   C. At least two routers are exchanging information.

   D. A ping to 192.168.40.2 will be successful.

18. Look at the following diagram. Assume all switches are running spanning tree. Which switch will be elected root bridge?

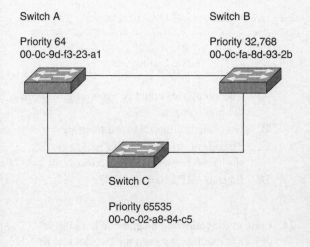

Figure 6-5

   A. Switch A

   B. Switch B

   C. Switch C

19. Look at the following diagram. You have been asked to add configuration to the RT-Denver router preventing any hosts on the 192.168.1.0/24 network from accessing web sites on the Internet. What protocol, wildcard mask, and port should you use in the following command?

```
Ip access-list 151 deny [protocol]
  192.168.1.0
  [wildcard mask] any eq [port]
```

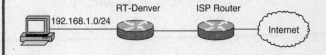

Figure 6-6

   A. ip, 255.255.255.0, 80

   B. ip, 0.0.0.255, web

   C. tcp, 0.0.0.255, 80

   D. tcp, 255.255.255.0, web

GO ON TO THE NEXT PAGE

20. What is the possible problem determined from the following output?

```
RouterA#sh int s0
Serial0 is up, line protocol is down
```

Code Listing 6-2

A. The keepalives could be set wrong between the point-to-point links.

B. No cable is attached to the interface.

C. The administrator needs to issue a no shutdown request to the interface.

D. Inverse ARP is not enabled.

21. Look at the following diagram. What kind of device is required between the two devices to allow hosts on the two VLANs to communicate with each other?

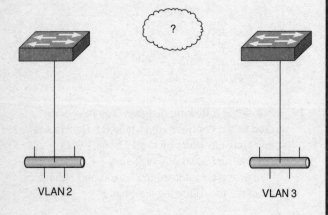

VLAN 2   VLAN 3

Figure 6-7

A. Another switch

B. Another switch, using crossover cables

C. A router

D. A bridge

22. How do you create a default route on a router?

A. Define a static route, and use all ones in place of the destination network and mask.

B. Define a static route, and use all zeros in place of the destination network and mask.

C. Define a static route, and use the keyword **default** in place of the destination network and mask.

D. Add the network statement 0.0.0.0 to the routing protocol.

23. What is the broadcast address of the subnet 192.168.99.20/30?

A. 192.168.99.127

B. 192.168.99.63

C. 192.168.99.23

D. 192.168.99.31

24. The OSPF Hello protocol performs which of the following tasks? (Choose two.)

A. It provides dynamic neighbor discovery.

B. It detects unreachable neighbors at 90-second intervals.

C. It maintains neighbor relationships.

D. It uses timers to elect the router with the fastest link as the designated router.

25. You can ping a router, but you can't telnet to it. What could the problem be?

A. IP is not configured correctly.

B. TCP is not configured correctly.

C. You didn't set the password on the router for Telnet access.

D. The default gateway on the PC is not correct.

E. The default gateway on the router is not correct.

26. Look at the following diagram. Suppose you issue a show cdp neighbor command on Switch A, and you see Switch B but not Switch C. What could be the problem? (Choose two.)

Switch A   Switch B

Priority 64   Priority 32,768
00-0c-9d-f3-23-a1   00-0c-fa-8d-93-2b

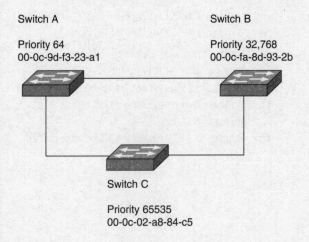

Switch C

Priority 65535
00-0c-02-a8-84-c5

Figure 6-5

A. Bad cable

B. Misconfigured IP address on Switch C

C. Bad switchport

D. All of the above

27. A routing table contains static, RIP, OSPF, and EIGRP routes for the same remote network. Which one will the router use by default?

   A. EIGRP
   B. RIP
   C. OSPF
   D. Static

28. What is the Frame Relay map command used for?

   A. To identify the hardware address of the local interface
   B. To identify the virtual circuit
   C. To map a DLCI address to an IP address
   D. To route packets in the Frame Relay PVC

29. Your supervisor has asked that you prevent Telnet traffic originating from the Internet from entering your network. You decide to create an inbound access-list filter on the interface that connects to the Internet. Which of the following is correct?

   A. `ip access-list 75 deny telnet any any`
   B. `ip access-list 101 deny ip any any eq telnet`
   C. `ip access-list 75 deny tcp any any eq telnet`
   D. `ip access-list 101 deny tcp any any eq telnet`

30. An Ethernet interface has been configured with an IP address of 184.26.29.78 and a subnet mask of 255.255.240.0. IP routing has been enabled. Which of the following entries will appear in the router's IP routing table?

   A. `C  184.26.0.0 is directly connected, Ethernet0`
   B. `C  184.26.29.16 is directly connected, Ethernet0`
   C. `C  184.26.29.78 is directly connected, Ethernet0`
   D. `C  184.26.16.0 is directly connected, Ethernet0`

31. What is the default configuration register setting for a Cisco router?

   A. 0x102
   B. 0x2102
   C. 0x1000
   D. 0x0000

32. When a switch is first powered on, the spanning-tree algorithm transitions all ports through several states. Identify the correct series of states.

   A. Learning, listening, blocking or forwarding
   B. Learning, listening, disabled or forwarding
   C. Listening, learning, blocking or forwarding
   D. Blocking, listening, learning, blocking or forwarding

33. What will the following command do when placed on a router?

   `Ip route 0.0.0.0 0.0.0.0 serial1`

   A. Override the routes learned by any routing protocol
   B. Override the routes learned by any routing protocol on interface serial1
   C. Forward all traffic out interface serial1
   D. Forward all traffic where the destination route is unknown out interface serial1

34. Your boss tells you to configure a classful routing protocol on your Cisco router. Which of the following routing protocols will provide the business solution? (Choose 3)

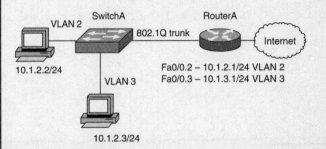

Figure 6-8

   A. RIP
   B. EIGRP
   C. IGRP
   D. OSPF
   E. RIPv2

GO ON TO THE NEXT PAGE

35. Look at the following diagram. The host on VLAN 2 is able to access the Internet but cannot ping the host on VLAN 3. Which of the following is the problem?

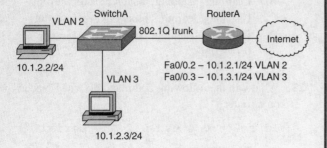

Figure 6-8

A. The router address on VLAN 2
B. The host's address on VLAN 2
C. The router address on VLAN 3
D. The host's address on VLAN 3
E. The 802.1q trunk link configuration

36. Look at the following diagram. SwitchC suffered a hardware failure; you replaced it with a spare switch that you had in inventory. You replaced the configuration but noticed that as soon as you added it to the network, SwitchA and SwitchB had some changes to their VLANs. What is the cause?

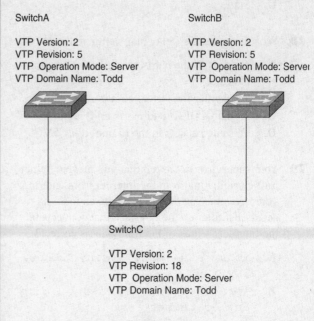

Figure 6-9

A. SwitchC should be set to transparent, not server.
B. SwitchA should be set to client, not server.
C. The revision on SwitchA needs to be increased.
D. SwitchC should be running VTP version 3.
E. The revision on SwitchC was higher than on the other switches.

37. When troubleshooting an ISDN problem, which of the following is a valid test of layer 1?

A. Ping of the remote host is successful
B. Telnet to the remote host is successful
C. Dial session to the remote host is successful
D. Line is up
E. Routing updates are working

38. When troubleshooting an ISDN problem, which of the following is a valid test of layer 2?

    A. Ping of the remote host is successful

    B. Telnet to the remote host is successful

    C. Dial session to the remote host is successful

    D. Line is up

    E. Routing updates are working

39. When troubleshooting an ISDN problem, which of the following is a valid test of layer 3?

    A. Ping of the remote host is successful

    B. Telnet to the remote host is successful

    C. Dial session to the remote host is successful

    D. Line is up

    E. Routing updates are working

40. After configuring a router, you issue a `copy running-config startup-config` command and then issue a `reload` command. After rebooting, the router comes up without a configuration. Which of the following is the most likely cause of this?

    A. A faulty router.

    B. You should have used `copy startup-config running-config` before the reload.

    C. An incorrect configuration register setting.

    D. User error.

41. Look at the following diagram. Which of the switchports can be safely configured with portfast enabled?

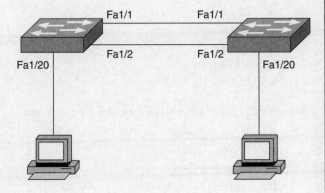

Figure 6-10

    A. Fa1/1

    B. Fa1/2

    C. Fa1/20

    D. All of the above

    E. None of the ports

42. What is the default encapsulation used on Cisco serial links?

    A. PPP

    B. IETF

    C. HDLC

    D. Frame Relay

43. With which network type will OSPF establish router adjacencies but not perform the DR/BDR election process?

    A. Point-to-point

    B. Backbone area 0

    C. Broadcast multiaccess

    D. Non-broadcast multiaccess

44. What is the default administrative distance of OSPF?

    A. 90

    B. 100

    C. 110

    D. 120

45. What will occur if two Cisco LAN switches are connected with a single crossover cable?

    A. The switch port link light will be off on both switches, indicating that the ports are not connected.

    B. The switch port link light will be off on one switch, indicating that STP has disabled the port.

    C. The switch port link lights will flash amber, indicating an error.

    D. The switch port link lights will be green, indicating normal operation.

GO ON TO THE NEXT PAGE

46. Look at the following diagram. The network has been configured, but none of the hosts can communicate with either the Internet or each other. What is the problem?

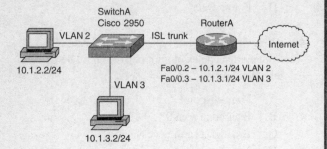

SwitchA
Cisco 2950
RouterA
VLAN 2
ISL trunk
Internet
10.1.2.2/24
Fa0/0.2 – 10.1.2.1/24 VLAN 2
Fa0/0.3 – 10.1.3.1/24 VLAN 3
VLAN 3
10.1.3.2/24

Figure 6-11

   A.   The router address on VLAN 2
   B.   The host's address on VLAN 2
   C.   The router address on VLAN 3
   D.   The host's address on VLAN 3
   E.   The ISL trunk link configuration

47. Which of the following IP addresses cannot be routed across the public Internet? (Choose two.)

   A.   127.0.0.1
   B.   204.11.17.6
   C.   172.36.2.3
   D.   192.168.78.13
   E.   1.0.0.0

48. Which wildcard mask specifies only the hosts from 192.168.34.33 through 192.168.34.62?

   A.   255.255.255.240
   B.   255.255.255.224
   C.   0.0.0.32
   D.   0.0.0.31
   E.   None of the above

49. Which of the following commands will make viewing of passwords more difficult? (Choose two.)

   A.   access-class
   B.   enable secret
   C.   enable password
   D.   VTY password
   E.   service password encryption

50. Which of the following commands will restrict access to telnet into the router? (Choose two.)

   A.   access-class
   B.   enable secret
   C.   enable password
   D.   VTY password
   E.   service password encryption

51. What are the possible trunking modes for a switchport? (Choose three.)

   A.   access
   B.   on
   C.   desirable
   D.   dot1q
   E.   auto
   F.   ISL

52. You have two routers connected with a serial link. The local router is using the default encapsulation, and the remote router is using PPP encapsulation. The serial interface output on the local router shows that the interface is up, but line protocol is down. What is the problem?

   A.   CHAP is not configured correctly.
   B.   Inverse ARP needs to be configured.
   C.   The serial interface is shut down on the remote router.
   D.   You need to change the local router encapsulation to PPP.

53. Which STP state sends and receives all data frames on the switchport?

   A.   Blocking
   B.   Listening
   C.   Learning
   D.   Forwarding
   E.   Disabled

54. Which EIGRP table lists all possible backup routes?

   A.   Topology table
   B.   Routing table
   C.   Neighbor table
   D.   ARP cache
   E.   Feasible successor

55. Which EIGRP table lists all possible routes?

   A.   Topology table
   B.   Routing table
   C.   Neighbor table
   D.   ARP cache
   E.   Feasible successor

Answer Key for Practice Test 6

1. C	15. D	29. D	43. A
2. A	16. B	30. D	44. C
3. B	17. C, D	31. B	45. D
4. B	18. B	32. D	46. E
5. A, C, D	19. C	33. D	47. A, D
6. D	20. A	34. B, D, E	48. D
7. B	21. C	35. D	49. B, E
8. B	22. B	36. E	50. A, D
9. C	23. C	37. C	51. B, C, E
10. B	24. A, C	38. D	52. D
11. D	25. C	39. A	53. D
12. E	26. A, C	40. C	54. E
13. C	27. D	41. C	55. A
14. D	28. C	42. C	

Answer Explanations for Practice Test 6

1. **C.** The "Message Of The Day" (motd) is an old Unix command that allows you to display a message when anyone connects to a router or switch device.

2. **A.** The last 4 bits of the third octet and all of the forth octet are selected. This corresponds to the subnet mask of 255.255.240.0.

3. **B.** The hostname of the router you are connecting to must be entered using the username command. The passwords entered at each router must be the same. The usernames and passwords are case sensitive.

4. **B.** When the RIP routing process is enabled on a Cisco router, parameters such as Process ID and autonomous system number are not supported. The command `router rip` cannot be used in conjunction with any additional keywords. The command `network network-number` enables the routing process to determine which of the router's interfaces will participate in the sending and receiving of routing updates. RIP is a classful routing protocol; network numbers specified must be classful. Neither subnet numbers nor interface addresses are supported when configuring RIP.

5. **A, C, D.** Routers can limit the scope of broadcast storms, create smaller inter-connected networks, and filter by logical (IP) addresses. Routers do not typically reduce downtime.

6. **D.** In this case, the static route is valid, and connectivity will remain established.

7. **B.** Switches are bridges with higher port density. They do not stop broadcast storms; they actually cause them, when improperly configured – note that "when improperly configured" means that the spanning tree protocol is disabled. *Wire speed* means with almost no latency, or delay.

8. **B.** Inverse ARP maps a known IP address to a local DLCI.

9. **C.** Although several routing protocols will meet the need, static routing minimizes router CPU and WAN utilization.

10. **B.** Frame Relay will allow the speed; BRI will not. Point-to-point links are cost prohibitive in a fully meshed environment.

11. **D.** In this case, the wildcard bits are all host bits, which in a /24 network are the last 8 bits, or the last octet.

12. **E.** In this case, static routing will provide the simplest configuration. BGP would be useful if the Internet connectivity were more complex (multiple ISPs, for example).

13. **C.** There are five different STP port states, and all ports on a switch are in blocking mode when the switch is powered up or a device is plugged into a port. After STP convergence, all ports are in either a blocking or forwarding state.

14. **D.** When a device needs to resolve a logical IP address to a physical Ethernet address (MAC), it uses the Address Resolution Protocol (ARP).

15. **D.** In this case, the 192.168.1.0/26 subnet is the first subnet in the 192.168.1.0 Class C network, and you must have subnet zero enabled to use the first and last subnets.

16. **B.** Switches running Spanning-Tree Protocol exchange Bridge Protocol Data Units (BPDUs) every two seconds. BPDUs carry bridge ID information that includes the MAC address and bridge priority of the source device.

17. **C, D.** The route to 192.168.50.0 is unreachable, and only interfaces s0/1 and FastEthernet 0/0 are participating in the RIP update. Because a route update was received, at least two routers are participating in the RIP routing process. 192.168.50.0 is inaccessible (16 hops), and network 192.168.40.2 has been received correctly with a metric of 1 (1 hop).

18. **B.** Switch A is not a valid priority number. 4096 is the lowest priority. Switch B then has the lowest "valid" priority number.

19. **C.** The protocol is TCP, the wildcard mask for a /24 network is 0.0.0.255, and the port for web traffic is 80.

20. A. If you see that the line is up but the protocol is down, you are having a clocking (keepalive) or framing issue. Check the keepalives on both ends to make sure they match; that the clock rate is set, if needed; and that the encapsulation type is the same on both ends.

21. C. Only a router can route between two VLANs. A switch may support two separate VLANs, but a layer-3 device is required for two separate VLANs to communicate.

22. B. Default routes are created by using all zeros in place of the destination network and subnet mask.

23. C. In this case, the subnet is .20, the hosts are .21 and .22, and the broadcast address is .23.

24. A, C. The Hello protocol provides dynamic neighbor discovery and maintains the neighbor relationship.

25. C. You cannot telnet into a Cisco router by default. You must set the VTY password or use the `no login` command under the VTY lines.

26. A, C. Because CDP verifies layer-2 connectivity and framing, any issues at layer 1 or 2 can cause CDP to fail.

27. D. The router will look at each route to a network and first check the administrative distance (AD) of each available route. The one with the lowest AD will be used. Static routes have an AD of 1 by default, so they will be used over the routing protocols, which all have higher ADs.

28. C. The Frame Relay `map` command tells the router which DLCI to use at layer 2, based on the destination IP address.

29. D. A standard IP access list can only deny traffic based on source IP address. To filter traffic based on a specific protocol, an extended access list must be used.

30. D. IP address 184.26.29.78 is a Class B address that has been subnetted using an additional 4 bits of mask. The network address for this IP address is 184.26.16.0.

31. B. All Cisco routers have a 16-bit software register that enables the router to select a variety of configuration options during boot. The configuration register is displayed in hexadecimal format. Each group of 4 bits (beginning with bit 15 and ending with bit 0) represents one hexadecimal digit. The factory-default configuration register for a Cisco router is 0x2102.

32. D. When a switch is first powered on, all ports are placed in the blocking state to prevent bridge loops. As ports transition from the blocked state to the listening state, they begin detecting incoming frames. As a port transitions to the learning state, it processes information contained in BPDU updates and executes the spanning-tree algorithm (STA) to calculate a loop-free topology. The STA ensures that ports on the switch are either set in the forwarding state or returned to the blocking state.

33. D. This is known as a default route. It becomes relevant only if the destination network for a packet is not known by some other means. In that case, it will forward the packet out interface serial1.

34. B, D, E. In order for your network to send subnet mask information with the route updates, you must use a classless routing protocol like RIPv2, EIGRP, or OSPF.

35. D. The host on VLAN 3 has an IP address assigned that belongs to VLAN 2.

36. E. The VTP server with the highest revision number will overwrite the VLAN database of all switches with a lower revision number.

37. C. A successful dial session up is layer 1.

38. D. The line is up is a valid layer 2 test.

39. A. Ping is a valid test of layer 3. Telnet and routing use additional protocols on top of layer 3.

40. C. If the configuration register is incorrectly set, the router can ignore the startup-config on reload and boot without any configuration.

41. C. Portfast should not be used between switches; it should be used only when hosts are connected to the switch.

42. **C.** Cisco's default encapsulation for serial links is HDLC. To use a different encapsulation, you use the `encapsulation` command at the interface level.

43. **A.** On point-to-point and point-to-multipoint networks, OSPF will not perform DR/BDR elections.

44. **C.** OSPF has a default administrative distance of 110. EIGRP is 90, and RIP (both v1 and v2) is 120.

45. **D.** To connect two switches, you need a crossover cable. When a link is working on a switch, the port link light is green, not amber.

46. **E.** The switch is a Cisco 2950, which does not support ISL trunking. It only supports IEEE 802.1q trunking.

47. **A, D.** 127.0.0.0 is reserved and not routable. 192.168.78.13 is considered private address space and thus not routable.

48. **D.** The subnet mask is 255.255.255.224 here, so you want the last 5 bits in the last octet to be wildcards. This gives 0.0.0.31.

49. **B, E.** Both B and E will encrypt the enable password. E will encrypt other passwords in the configuration as well.

50. **A, D** An access-class allows you to limit which source IP addresses have access to the router. The VTY password requires a password for access.

51. **B, C, E.** Three switchport trunking modes are on, desirable, and auto. Dot1q and ISL are not modes; they are trunking protocols. Access is not a trunking mode; it is a separate mode.

52. **D.** By default, the encapsulation on serial links is HDLC and is proprietary to each vendor. Serial links will not come up if the encapsulations do not match.

53. **D.** The forwarding port sends and receives all data frames on the bridged port.

54. **E.** Feasible successors are routes that can be surfaced to the routing table, should a primary route become unavailable.

55. **A.** All possible routes are stored in the topology table. Only the best route is surfaced to the routing table.

Answer Sheets for Practice Test 7

(Remove This Sheet and Use It to Mark Your Answers)

Section 1
Multiple Choice Questions

1 Ⓐ Ⓑ Ⓒ Ⓓ Ⓔ Ⓕ		31 Ⓐ Ⓑ Ⓒ Ⓓ Ⓔ Ⓕ
2 Ⓐ Ⓑ Ⓒ Ⓓ Ⓔ Ⓕ		32 Ⓐ Ⓑ Ⓒ Ⓓ Ⓔ Ⓕ
3 Ⓐ Ⓑ Ⓒ Ⓓ Ⓔ Ⓕ		33 Ⓐ Ⓑ Ⓒ Ⓓ Ⓔ Ⓕ
4 Ⓐ Ⓑ Ⓒ Ⓓ Ⓔ Ⓕ		34 Ⓐ Ⓑ Ⓒ Ⓓ Ⓔ Ⓕ
5 Ⓐ Ⓑ Ⓒ Ⓓ Ⓔ Ⓕ		35 Ⓐ Ⓑ Ⓒ Ⓓ Ⓔ Ⓕ
6 Ⓐ Ⓑ Ⓒ Ⓓ Ⓔ Ⓕ		36 Ⓐ Ⓑ Ⓒ Ⓓ Ⓔ Ⓕ
7 Ⓐ Ⓑ Ⓒ Ⓓ Ⓔ Ⓕ		37 Ⓐ Ⓑ Ⓒ Ⓓ Ⓔ Ⓕ
8 Ⓐ Ⓑ Ⓒ Ⓓ Ⓔ Ⓕ		38 Ⓐ Ⓑ Ⓒ Ⓓ Ⓔ Ⓕ
9 Ⓐ Ⓑ Ⓒ Ⓓ Ⓔ Ⓕ		39 Ⓐ Ⓑ Ⓒ Ⓓ Ⓔ Ⓕ
10 Ⓐ Ⓑ Ⓒ Ⓓ Ⓔ Ⓕ		40 Ⓐ Ⓑ Ⓒ Ⓓ Ⓔ Ⓕ
11 Ⓐ Ⓑ Ⓒ Ⓓ Ⓔ Ⓕ		41 Ⓐ Ⓑ Ⓒ Ⓓ Ⓔ Ⓕ
12 Ⓐ Ⓑ Ⓒ Ⓓ Ⓔ Ⓕ		42 Ⓐ Ⓑ Ⓒ Ⓓ Ⓔ Ⓕ
13 Ⓐ Ⓑ Ⓒ Ⓓ Ⓔ Ⓕ		43 Ⓐ Ⓑ Ⓒ Ⓓ Ⓔ Ⓕ
14 Ⓐ Ⓑ Ⓒ Ⓓ Ⓔ Ⓕ		44 Ⓐ Ⓑ Ⓒ Ⓓ Ⓔ Ⓕ
15 Ⓐ Ⓑ Ⓒ Ⓓ Ⓔ Ⓕ		45 Ⓐ Ⓑ Ⓒ Ⓓ Ⓔ Ⓕ
16 Ⓐ Ⓑ Ⓒ Ⓓ Ⓔ Ⓕ		46 Ⓐ Ⓑ Ⓒ Ⓓ Ⓔ Ⓕ
17 Ⓐ Ⓑ Ⓒ Ⓓ Ⓔ Ⓕ		47 Ⓐ Ⓑ Ⓒ Ⓓ Ⓔ Ⓕ
18 Ⓐ Ⓑ Ⓒ Ⓓ Ⓔ Ⓕ		48 Ⓐ Ⓑ Ⓒ Ⓓ Ⓔ Ⓕ
19 Ⓐ Ⓑ Ⓒ Ⓓ Ⓔ Ⓕ		49 Ⓐ Ⓑ Ⓒ Ⓓ Ⓔ Ⓕ
20 Ⓐ Ⓑ Ⓒ Ⓓ Ⓔ Ⓕ		50 Ⓐ Ⓑ Ⓒ Ⓓ Ⓔ Ⓕ
21 Ⓐ Ⓑ Ⓒ Ⓓ Ⓔ Ⓕ		51 Ⓐ Ⓑ Ⓒ Ⓓ Ⓔ Ⓕ
22 Ⓐ Ⓑ Ⓒ Ⓓ Ⓔ Ⓕ		52 Ⓐ Ⓑ Ⓒ Ⓓ Ⓔ Ⓕ
23 Ⓐ Ⓑ Ⓒ Ⓓ Ⓔ Ⓕ		53 Ⓐ Ⓑ Ⓒ Ⓓ Ⓔ Ⓕ
24 Ⓐ Ⓑ Ⓒ Ⓓ Ⓔ Ⓕ		54 Ⓐ Ⓑ Ⓒ Ⓓ Ⓔ Ⓕ
25 Ⓐ Ⓑ Ⓒ Ⓓ Ⓔ Ⓕ		55 Ⓐ Ⓑ Ⓒ Ⓓ Ⓔ Ⓕ
26 Ⓐ Ⓑ Ⓒ Ⓓ Ⓔ Ⓕ		
27 Ⓐ Ⓑ Ⓒ Ⓓ Ⓔ Ⓕ		
28 Ⓐ Ⓑ Ⓒ Ⓓ Ⓔ Ⓕ		
29 Ⓐ Ⓑ Ⓒ Ⓓ Ⓔ Ⓕ		
30 Ⓐ Ⓑ Ⓒ Ⓓ Ⓔ Ⓕ		

Directions: For each of the following questions, select the choice that best answers the question or completes the statement.

---

1. When entering the following command, you receive an error. What is the problem?

   ```
   access-list 110 permit ip
       any any eq 23
   ```

   A. It is a standard access list attempting to check port 23.
   B. The access list is referencing IP, but port 23 is a TCP port.
   C. It is not checking any valid host addresses.
   D. Nothing; the access list should work as written.

2. Suppose you are configuring a Frame Relay network, and Inverse ARP is not available. Which of the following must you configure to address this?

   A. `frame-relay interface dlci`
   B. `encapsulation frame-relay`
   C. `frame-relay traffic shaping`
   D. `frame-relay map`

3. Look at the following diagram. Suppose you have configured IP addressing and routing as in the diagram. When you type the **show cdp neighbor** command on RT-Denver, you see all three remaining routers. However, when you type the **show ip eigrp neighbor** command, you do not see any of the other routers as EIGRP neighbors. Which of the following is the problem?

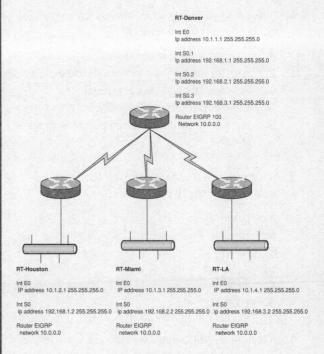

Figure 7-1

   A. The EIGRP network statements are incomplete.
   B. The IP addressing is wrong.
   C. You must add the IP `subnet zero` command.
   D. You must add the EIGRP `no auto-summary` statement.

GO ON TO THE NEXT PAGE

4. What is the signaling standard between the CPE device (usually a router) and the Frame Relay switch that is responsible for managing the connection and maintaining status between devices?

    A. ISDN BRI

    B. CIR

    C. Frame Relay LMI

    D. DLCI

5. Which STP state prevents the use of looped paths?

    A. Blocking

    B. Listening

    C. Learning

    D. Forwarding

    E. Disabled

6. When configuring a switch, what is the purpose of the `ip address` command?

    A. Assigns a name to the switch

    B. Sets the switch management IP address

    C. Sets a switchport to access mode

    D. Enables portfast on an interface

    E. Allows the switch to communicate with other subnets

7. What protocol is used to resolve a hardware address given the IP address?

    A. RARP

    B. IP

    C. ICMP

    D. ARP

    E. TCP

    F. UDP

8. Which of the following are valid reasons to use an access list? (Choose two.)

    A. To limit access to specific services, such as FTP or Web

    B. To require passwords when accessing services

    C. To limit a router's VTY access

    D. To limit all traffic to a specific bandwidth

9. Which of the following is a valid extended IP access list?

    A. `access-list 101 permit icmp 172.16.30.0 any eq 21 log`

    B. `access-list 101 permit ip 172.16.30.0 any tcp eq 21 log`

    C. `access-list 101 permit·tcp 172.16.30.0 any eq 21 log`

    D. `access-list 10 permit ip 172.16.30.0 any eq ftp`

10. When configuring OSPF on a Cisco router, the typical command looks something like this:

```
router ospf 1
```

What does the 1 represent?

    A. The number of physical networks attached to the router

    B. The autonomous system number

    C. The process ID

    D. The RID of the router

11. You have been sent the output of a `show ip interface brief` command to diagnose a problem. Which of the following outputs indicate that there is an issue with layer 1?

    A. Serial0 is up, line protocol is up

    B. Serial0 is up, line protocol is down

    C. Serial0 is down, line protocol is down

    D. Serial0 is administratively down, line protocol is up

12. Suppose you find the following static route added to a router. What does the 150 at the end of the command stand for?

```
ip route 172.16.10.0
      255.255.255.0
      172.16.20.1 150
```

    A. You want the destination to be considered 150 hops away.

    B. You are assigning the IP address of 150 to the destination.

    C. You are modifying the default administrative distance.

    D. You are assigning an administrative distance of 150 less than the default.

13. Look at the following diagram. Suppose someone else has configured IP addressing and routing as in the figure. When you type the **show cdp neighbor** command on RT-Denver, you see all three remaining routers. However, when you type the **show ip eigrp** neighbor command, you do not see the RT-Houston router as an EIGRP neighbor. Which of the following is the problem?

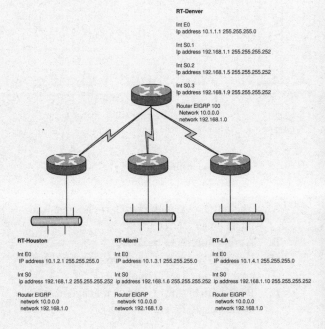

RT-Denver

Int E0
Ip address 10.1.1.1 255.255.255.0

Int S0.1
Ip address 192.168.1.1 255.255.255.252

Int S0.2
Ip address 192.168.1.5 255.255.255.252

Int S0.3
Ip address 192.168.1.9 255.255.255.252

Router EIGRP 100
Network 10.0.0.0
network 192.168.1.0

RT-Houston

Int E0
IP address 10.1.2.1 255.255.255.0

Int S0
ip address 192.168.1.2 255.255.255.252

Router EIGRP
network 10.0.0.0
network 192.168.1.0

RT-Miami

Int E0
IP address 10.1.3.1 255.255.255.0

Int S0
ip address 192.168.1.6 255.255.255.252

Router EIGRP
network 10.0.0.0
network 192.168.1.0

RT-LA

Int E0
IP address 10.1.4.1 255.255.255.0

Int S0
ip address 192.168.1.10 255.255.255.252

Router EIGRP
network 10.0.0.0
network 192.168.1.0

Figure 7-2

A. The EIGRP network statements are incomplete.

B. IP addressing is wrong.

C. You must add the IP subnet-zero command.

D. You must add the EIGRP no auto-summary statement.

14. Which one of the following are valid uses for an IP access list?

A. To filter routing updates

B. To filter administrative access to the router (VTY)

C. To filter access to specific hosts

D. To filter access to specific services

E. All of the above

15. Which protocol is used to stop network loops in a switched internetwork?

A. RIP

B. STP

C. VTP

D. ISL

16. When a switchport is set to mode access, what does that indicate?

A. A link that is part of only one VLAN

B. A link that can carry multiple VLANs

C. A switch port connected to the Internet

D. Data and voice capability on the same interface

17. You have been asked to configure a Cisco router that will have a point-to-point T1 connecting it to another brand of router. Which of the following is the best encapsulation choices for this T1?

A. Frame Relay

B. PPP

C. HDLC

D. ISDN

18. Which command displays all the EIGRP feasible successor routes known to a router?

A. show ip eigrp routes *

B. show ip eigrp summary

C. show ip eigrp topology

D. show ip eigrp adjacencies

19. When will a source host receive an ICMP unreachable message?

A. When IP is not loaded on the transmitting device

B. When a service or host is not available

C. When ARP broadcasts are not available

D. When BootP can't find a hardware address

GO ON TO THE NEXT PAGE

20. Look at the following diagram. Suppose you need to trunk multiple VLANs between SW-Denver1 and SW-Denver2. Both switches are Cisco 2950s. Which is your option when configuring Fa1/1 on these switches?

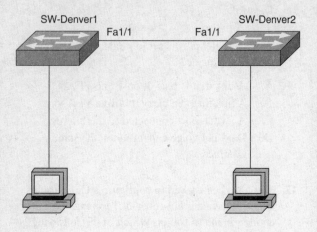

Figure 7-3

A. `switchport mode access`
B. `switchport mode trunk isl`
C. `switchport mode trunk`
D. `switchport mode etherchannel`

21. Look at the following diagram You have been asked to troubleshoot this LAN. Hosts on VLAN 45 can communicate fine with each other but not with hosts on VLAN50. What is the problem?

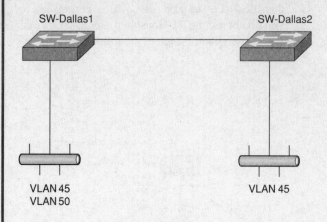

Figure 7-4

A. The link between the two switches needs to be made an 802.1q trunk.
B. A router needs to be added.
C. Switch SW-Dallas1 needs to have portfast enabled on all switchports.
D. Both switches need to have management IP addresses assigned.

22. You have been asked to create an access list that will deny the user at IP address 172.16.12.7 telnet access to the router. Which of the following lines can you use to accomplish this?

A. `access-list 10 deny`
   `172.16.12.7 any`
B. `access-list 10 deny`
   `172.16.12.7 host`
C. `access-list 10 deny`
   `172.16.12.7 0.0.0.0`
D. `access-list 10 deny`
   `172.16.12.7 255.255.255.0`

23. You have been asked to create an access list that will deny the user at IP address 172.16.12.7 telnet access to the router. Suppose you have created access-list 10 to do this. How and where do you apply the access list?

A. `int e0, ip access-group 10 in`
B. `line con 0, ip access-class 10`
C. `line vty 0, ip access-group 10`
D. `line vty 0, ip access-class 10`

24. Look at the following diagram. You have been given a single Class C network and asked to subnet it for use on the four LANs shown. Assume that no LAN needs more than 60 addresses. Which subnet mask will efficiently use the addresses and meet this requirement?

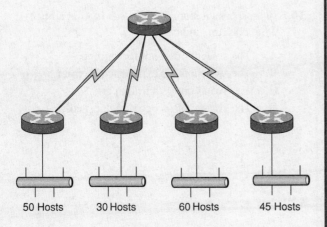

50 Hosts   30 Hosts   60 Hosts   45 Hosts

Figure 7-5

A. 255.255.255.0
B. 255.255.255.64
C. 255.255.255.128
D. 255.255.255.192

25. You want the IP addresses, retransmit interface, and queue counts for adjacent EIGRP routers. What command displays this information?

A. `show ip eigrp adjacency`
B. `show ip eigrp topology`
C. `show ip eigrp interfaces`
D. `show ip eigrp neighbors`

26. Look at the following diagram. You have been told that users in Denver are no longer able to communicate with the network. You telnet into the RT-Denver router and issue the command shown. What is the problem?

```
RT-Denver#show ip interface brief
...
Ethernet1    172.16.10.1    YES    NVRAM    administratively down    down
...
```

Int Eth1

Figure 7-6

A. Subnet mask is incorrect
B. Router needs to be reloaded
C. Can't tell from the information provided
D. LAN interface has been shut down

27. Which of the following will you find in a routing table? (Choose three.)

A. Network address
B. Routing metric
C. Exit interface for packets
D. Entering interface

28. Which one of the following commands are needed if you are running RIPv2 or EIGRP and have a discontiguous network?

A. `ip subnet-zero`
B. `ip classless`
C. `no auto-summary`
D. `support discontiguous`

GO ON TO THE NEXT PAGE

29. You connect two switches together with a crossover cable. What will be the result?

    A. The switch port link lights will be off on both switches, indicating that the ports are not connected.

    B. The switch port link light will be off on one switch, indicating that STP has disabled the port.

    C. The switch port link lights will flash amber, indicating an error.

    D. The switch port link lights will be green, indicating normal operation.

30. Which layer of the OSI model is responsible for creating packets?

    A. Data Link

    B. Network

    C. Transport

    D. Session

31. You have had a problem with users adding hubs at their desks and plugging in multiple devices. Which of the following switchport commands allows you to limit the number of MAC addresses on any port to 1 and disable the port if that number is exceeded?

    A. `switchport port-security maximum 1`

    B. `switchport maximum 1`

    C. `port-security maximum 1`

    D. `switchport port-security MAC 1`

32. Which of the following will become the RID of the router?

    A. Lowest IP address configured on the router

    B. Highest IP address configured on the router

    C. IP address of the loopback interface

    D. IP address of the BRI interface

33. Suppose you have received the following output after typing in the `show frame-relay map` command. What does `dynamic` refer to?

```
Serial 0 (up): ip
    10.1.1.1 dlci 1002
    (0xB1,0x2C10), dynamic
    broadcast,...
```

    A. The DLC was learned dynamically.

    B. LMI was detected automatically.

    C. Inverse ARP dynamically mapped L3 address to LMI.

    D. Inverse ARP dynamically mapped L3 address to DLCI.

34. How is the root bridge determined in a switched network?

    A. By the highest IP address configured on the switch

    B. By the lowest IP address configured on the switch

    C. By the lowest MAC address of all switches

    D. By the highest MAC address of all switches

35. Suppose a switchport LED is alternating between green and amber. What does this indicate?

    A. The switchport is not forwarding.

    B. The switchport is experiencing errors.

    C. The switchport is a trunk port.

    D. The switchport is operating normally.

36. Suppose a switchport status LED is solid amber. What does this indicate?

    A. The switchport is not forwarding.

    B. The switchport is experiencing errors.

    C. The switchport is a trunk port.

    D. The switchport is operating normally.

37. Look at the following diagram. You have configured the Denver and Miami routers as shown, yet the network has failed to converge. What do you suspect is the problem?

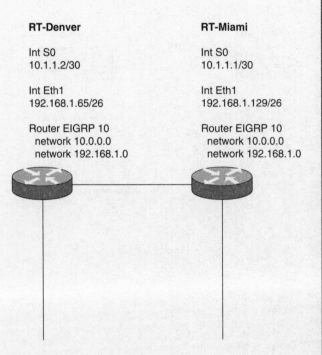

RT-Denver

Int S0
10.1.1.2/30

Int Eth1
192.168.1.65/26

Router EIGRP 10
  network 10.0.0.0
  network 192.168.1.0

RT-Miami

Int S0
10.1.1.1/30

Int Eth1
192.168.1.129/26

Router EIGRP 10
  network 10.0.0.0
  network 192.168.1.0

Figure 7-7

A. You need to add `ip subnet zero` to both routers.
B. You need to add `no auto-summary` to the EIGRP configuration of both routers.
C. You need to add network statements to the EIGRP configuration of both routers.
D. You need to modify the AS number of EIGRP on the routers.

38. Look at the following diagram. The RT-SaltLakeCity router has already been configured. You need to add OSPF to the RT-ParkCity router and add network 10.0.0.0 into area 0. Which of the following commands should you use? (Choose two.)

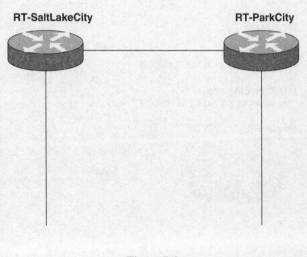

RT-SaltLakeCity   **RT-ParkCity**

Figure 7-8

A. `router ospf 1`
B. `router ospf area 0`
C. `network 10.0.0.0`
D. `network 10.0.0.0 area 0`
E. `network 10.0.0.0 0.0.0.255 area 0`

39. You are trying to connect your PC to the console port of a Cisco router. How do you connect the host to the console port?

A. Connect the PC's COM port to the router's console port using a straight-through cable.
B. Connect the PC's COM port to the router's console port using a rolled cable.
C. Connect the PC's COM port to the router's console port using a crossover cable.
D. Connect the PC's Ethernet port to the router's console port using an Ethernet cable.

GO ON TO THE NEXT PAGE

40. Look at the following diagram. You have configured the Boston router as shown in the figure. You need to add network statements to the RIP routing configuration. Which one of the following is the correct possible configuration?

RT-Boston

Interface Serial0
  ip address 10.1.0.1 255.255.0.0

Interface Ethernet0
  ip address 10.2.0.1 255.255.0.0

Router RIP
????????

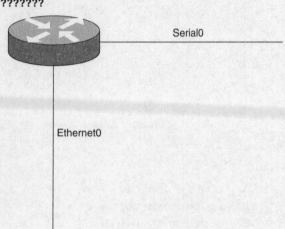

Figure 7-9

A. `network 10.0.0.0`
B. `network 10.0.0.0 255.255.0.0`
C. `network 10.1.0.0`
D. `network 10.1.0.0 255.255.0.0`
E. `network 10.2.0.0`
F. `network 10.2.0.0 255.255.0.0`

41. Which configuration task must you complete if a remote Frame Relay router does not support Inverse ARP?

A. Configure static maps.
B. Define an IP address locally.
C. Disable DHCP on the Frame Relay router.
D. Configure a static route to the remote network.

42. Look at the following diagram. HubA is plugged into port 1/15 of SwitchB. HubA has two hosts attached to it. How many MAC addresses would you expect to see on switchport 1.15?

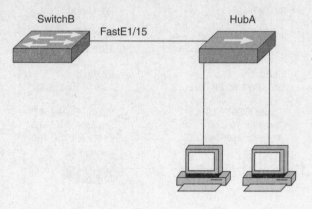

Figure 7-10

A. 1
B. 2
C. 3
D. Many

43. You're given the following criterion when connecting access from a remote site to your LAN: "Restrict access on interface e0 for Telnet and FTP." Which of the following lines should come last when you configure your access list?

A. `access-list 101 end`
B. `access-list 101 deny e0 telnet ftp`
C. `access-list 101 allow all except ftp telnet`
D. `access-list 101 permit ip 0.0.0.0 255.255.255.255 any`
E. `access-list 101 deny ip 128.12.22.55 tcp eq 20 21 23`

44. When configuring a switch, what is the purpose of the `hostname` command?

A. Assigns a name to the switch
B. Sets the switch management IP address
C. Sets a switchport to access mode
D. Enables portfast on an interface
E. Allows the switch to communicate with other subnets

45. When VLANs have been implemented within a network infrastructure, what is required for inter-VLAN communication?

    A. Nothing. VLANs operate at layer 2 and do not require a communication intermediary.

    B. A layer 2 switch that has been configured with all VLANs requiring inter-VLAN communication.

    C. A layer 2 switch that has VTP enabled.

    D. A router.

46. You have installed a new router into your network and have yet to configure access lists to filter traffic. You want to verify that routing has been successfully established and that end users will have no difficulty accessing applications across the network. Which of the following TCP/IP protocols can be used to test connectivity through all the layers of the OSI model?

    A. Telnet

    B. Ping

    C. Extended Ping

    D. Traceroute

47. You have a router running EIGRP, OSPF, and static routing. If a route to the 172.16.0.0/16 network is being learned by all three, which one will be used?

    A. EIGRP

    B. OSPF

    C. Static routing

    D. Unknown

48. What is the default administrative distance for OSPF?

    A. 1

    B. 80

    C. 90

    D. 110

49. Regarding EIGRP, which of the following are true? (Choose two.)

    A. It has a maximum hop count of 255.

    B. It can differentiate between internal and external routes.

    C. It routes IP only.

    D. All networks within an AS must use the same subnet mask.

    E. It has only one routing table.

50. Look at the following diagram. Assume that all hosts can communicate with each other. Which of the following statements must be true?

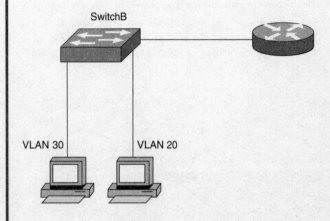

Figure 7-11

    A. The links between the hosts and the switch are trunk links.

    B. The link between the switch and the router is a trunk link.

    C. The interface on the router has a single IP address.

    D. The interface on the switch has multiple IP addresses.

    E. The interface on the router has multiple IP addresses.

GO ON TO THE NEXT PAGE

51. Look at the following diagram. Suppose someone else has configured IP addressing and routing as in the figure. When you type the `show cdp neighbor` command on RT-Denver, you see all three remaining routers. However, when you type the `show ip eigrp neighbor` command, you do not see the RT-LA router as an EIGRP neighbor. Which of the following is the problem?

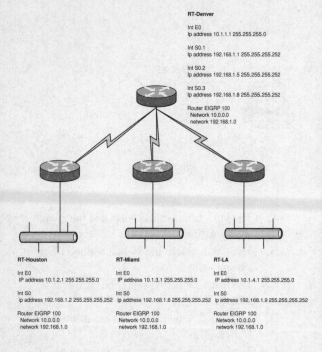

RT-Denver

Int E0
Ip address 10.1.1.1 255.255.255.0

Int S0.1
Ip address 192.168.1.1 255.255.255.252

Int S0.2
Ip address 192.168.1.5 255.255.255.252

Int S0.3
Ip address 192.168.1.8 255.255.255.252

Router EIGRP 100
Network 10.0.0.0
network 192.168.1.0

RT-Houston

Int E0
IP address 10.1.2.1 255.255.255.0

Int S0
ip address 192.168.1.2 255.255.255.252

Router EIGRP 100
Network 10.0.0.0
network 192.168.1.0

RT-Miami

Int E0
IP address 10.1.3.1 255.255.255.0

Int S0
ip address 192.168.1.6 255.255.255.252

Router EIGRP 100
Network 10.0.0.0
network 192.168.1.0

RT-LA

Int E0
IP address 10.1.4.1 255.255.255.0

Int S0
ip address 192.168.1.9 255.255.255.252

Router EIGRP 100
Network 10.0.0.0
network 192.168.1.0

Figure 7-12

A. The EIGRP network statements are incomplete.

B. IP addressing is wrong.

C. You must add the IP `subnet zero` command.

D. You must add the EIGRP `no auto-summary` statement.

52. Type the command to start IP RIP version 1 on a Cisco router.

A. `Router(config)#router rip`

B. `Router#router rip 1`

C. `Router(config)#router rip version 1`

D. `Router#router rip`

53. _____ are capable not only of dividing the collision domain into separate segments, but also of segmenting the broadcast domain.

A. Repeaters

B. Bridges

C. LAN switches

D. Routers

54. Which of the following is true regarding the Cisco 2950 switch?

A. It supports 802.1q trunk links.

B. It supports ISL trunk links.

C. It supports more than 5,000 VLANs per switch.

D. The administrative VLAN is VLAN 2 by default.

55. Look at the following diagram. You have a single Class C network address that is publicly registered. You need to address the network in the diagram. What is the most efficient subnet mask you can use to address the serial links?

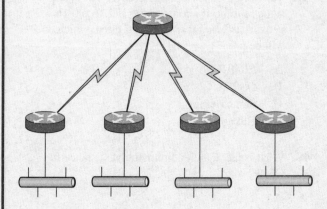

Figure 7-13

A. /24

B. /28

C. /29

D. /30

Answer Key for Practice Test 7

1. B	**15.** B	**29.** D	**43.** D
2. D	**16.** A	**30.** B	**44.** A
3. A	**17.** B	**31.** A	**45.** D
4. C	**18.** C	**32.** C	**46.** A
5. A	**19.** B	**33.** D	**47.** C
6. B	**20.** C	**34.** C	**48.** D
7. D	**21.** B	**35.** B	**49.** A, B
8. A, C	**22.** C	**36.** A	**50.** B, E
9. C	**23.** D	**37.** B	**51.** B
10. C	**24.** D	**38.** A, E	**52.** A
11. C	**25.** D	**39.** B	**53.** D
12. C	**26.** D	**40.** A	**54.** A
13. C	**27.** A, B, C	**41.** A	**55.** D
14. E	**28.** C	**42.** B	

Answer Explanations for Practice Test 7

1. **B.** An example of the correct usage when checking port values is `access-list 110 permit tcp any any eq 23`.

2. **D.** If Inverse ARP is not available, you must manually map the protocol addresses to the layer-2 addresses (DLCI).

3. **A.** In this case, the network statements for the 192.168 networks used on the serial links must be added to each of the routers' EIGRP configurations.

4. **C.** Local Management Interface (LMI) defines the signaling standard between your router and the Frame Relay switch and keeps track of virtual circuits.

5. **A.** A blocked port won't forward frames; it just listens to BPDUs. All ports are in blocking state by default when the switch is powered up. The purpose of the blocking state is to prevent the use of looped paths.

6. **B.** This command assigns an IP address to the switch, which is used to manage the switch. A switch does not need an IP address to work, but it needs one if you wish to telnet to it, for example.

7. **D.** Address Resolution Protocol (ARP) is used to find a hardware address from an IP address.

8. **A, C.** Access control lists can be used to limit access to services based on protocol and port information. Telnet access into a router is one specific service that can be limited with an access list.

9. **C.** The first option is wrong because you cannot filter by port number when specifying ICMP. The second option is wrong because it has the parameters in the wrong place. The last option is wrong because it specifies a standard access list.

10. **C.** The process ID is a number that starts the OSPF process on a router; it is locally significant to the router, meaning that it has no importance unless you start more than one process on the router, which is not typical.

11. **C.** Up/up indicates that layer 2 is down, up/down indicates that layer 1 is up but layer 2 is down, and down/down indicates a layer-1 problem. Administratively down indicates that the interface has been shut down.

12. **C.** The command `ip route network subnet-mask next-hop-address administrative-distance` is used to set a static route on that router. The administrative distance (AD) of a static route is normally 1, but you can increase it manually by entering a value at the end of the static route command. The command given in the question will set a static route to the network 172.16.10.0 by way of 172.16.20.1 (next hop) with an AD of 150.

13. **C.** In this case, everything else is correct. However, the serial connection between RT-Denver and RT-Houston is the first subnet in the 192.168.1.0 Class C network and thus the most likely cause.

14. **E.** Access control lists can do any of the things in the list.

15. **B.** Spanning-Tree Protocol (STP) is the protocol used in a layer-2 switched LAN to stop broadcast storms, multiple frame copies and other problems that can occur if a physical loop is accidentally connected into the network.

16. **A.** Access switchports connect hosts to a switch and are part of only one VLAN.

17. **B.** Frame Relay and ISDN encapsulations are not used on a p2p link. HDLC is proprietary to Cisco; therefore, PPP is the best choice.

18. **C.** EIGRP uses three different tables for routing: neighbor, topology, and route. The topology table keeps a list of every link found in the network. A feasible successor is a backup route stored in the topology table.

19. **B.** ICMP unreachable messages are returned when a service or host is not available.

20. **C.** The Cisco 2950 only supports 802.1q trunking. You cannot carry multiple VLANs on an access port. Etherchannel is used to bind multiple physical links into a single logical one.

21. B. Although switches can carry multiple VLANs, they cannot route between them. A router must be added to do this.

22. C. You can use the wildcard 0.0.0.0 to specify a specific host, or you can use the `host` parameter; however, the `host` parameter is used before the source IP address.

23. D. To control administrative access to the router, you apply the control to the VTY. In this case, an access list is referred to by the command `access-class`.

24. D. Using this mask will give you four subnets of 62 hosts each, assuming you have `ip subnet zero` enabled.

25. D. The `show ip eigrp neighbors` command shows a list of all routers with which the executing router has formed an adjacency. This command also provides the IP address of the neighbor routers and the retransmit and queue counts.

26. D. The administratively down status on the E0 interface indicates that it has been shut down.

27. A, B, C. Routing tables in a router keep track of where networks in a network are located, not hosts. They also keep track of the distance or cost to a remote network and which interface to exit to get to the remote network.

28. C. To support discontiguous networking, you first must have a routing protocol that is classless, such as RIPv2, EIGRP, or OSPF. OSPF supports discontiguous networks by default, but RIPv2 and EIGRP need to have the `no auto-summary` command enabled to support discontiguous networking.

29. D. To connect two switches together, you must have a crossover cable. The link lights will be green.

30. B. The Network layer of the OSI model is responsible for receiving segments or datagrams from the Transport layer of the OSI model. It encapsulates the segment or datagram by adding Network layer header information to create a Network layer packet. The Network layer is also responsible for receiving frames from the Data Link layer. It de-encapsulates the frame by stripping off Data Link layer protocol-encapsulation information to create Network layer packets.

31. A. This command will enable you to limit the maximum number of MAC addresses to 1. By default, the port will be disabled if this number is exceeded.

32. C. OSPF uses the highest physical-interface IP address configured on the router to choose the RID of the router. However, if loopback interfaces are created, and each has an IP address assigned, the highest IP address among the loopback interfaces is always the RID of the router.

33. D. In this case, `dynamic` refers to how the mapping was learned. The other option would be `static`.

34. C. Switches send Bridge Protocol Data Units out all interfaces every two seconds. The BPDU information includes the MAC addresses of the switches. If all switches have the default, or otherwise same, priority set, then the lowest MAC address of all the switches becomes the root bridge.

35. B. A switchport LED alternating between green and amber indicates that the switchport is experiencing excessive errors due to a link fault or another cause. If the port status is alternating green and amber, that indicates a link fault, or excessive errors.

36. A. When the port status is amber, it indicates that the switchport is not forwarding traffic (such as when STP puts a port in blocking state).

37. B. The two routers running EIGRP are, by default, both claiming to have the entire 192.168.1.0 Class C network. Disabling auto-summary will resolve this issue.

38. A, E. Proper configuration will place the area designation, along with correct network masking, in the network portion of the configuration.

39. B. Cisco console ports use a rolled cable to connect to a COM port of a PC.

40. A. Because RIP is a classful routing protocol, you only need to specify the 10.0.0.0 network. No mask is required. Selecting D and F would work, because the router would automatically change it to 10.0.0.0 in the configuration, but it is not the simplest way to configure the network statement.

41. **A.** Frame Relay can send an Inverse ARP packet to the device on the other side of the virtual circuit. If the other side does not support Inverse ARP, you must configure a static map.

42. **B.** You should see one for each host.

43. **D.** At the end of all access lists is an implicit `deny all` statement. Therefore, you must include a `permit any any` to allow traffic that does not meet your restrictions to continue. Also remember that 0.0.0.0 255.255.255.255 is the same parameter as "any."

44. **A.** This command is used to assign a name to the switch. If there is more than one switch, giving them distinct names greatly simplifies administration.

45. **D.** Devices in a VLAN are within their own broadcast domain and communicate freely among themselves. VLANs create network partitions, segmenting traffic at layer 2 of the OSI model. For inter-VLAN communication to occur, either a router, a layer 3 switch, or a route-switch module must be used.

46. **A.** Telnet is an Application layer protocol. Successfully telnetting between hosts confirms that connectivity at all layers is functioning properly.

47. **C.** By default, static routing has the lowest AD of any of the three listed routing methodologies.

48. **D.** OSPF's default administrative distance is 110.

49. **A, B.** EIGRP has a maximum hop count of 255 with a maximum hop count of 100 set by default. EIGRP can route multiple routed protocols, not just IP, and is considered a classless routing protocol, which means that networks can have different length subnet masks. EIGRP supports and can differentiate between internal and external routes.

50. **B, E.** For the host on VLAN20 to communicate with the host on VLAN 30, the router must be routing these two VLANs. Thus, the single physical interface on the router must be acting as multiple logical interfaces and therefore has multiple IP addresses. For this to work, the link between the router and switch must be a trunk link.

51. **B.** The IP addresses used on the serial link between RT-Denver and RT-LA are incorrect. They should be 192.168.1.9 and 192.168.1.10.

52. **A.** In global configuration mode, you enter **`router rip`** to start the routing process using the RIP protocol. Version 1 of RIP is the default.

53. **D.** Routers are the traditional workhorses of the corporate internetwork, segmenting both the broadcast and collision domains. Routers operate at layer 3 of the OSI model and provide substantially greater administrative control over the flow of information through a network than do devices operating at any of the lower layers.

54. **A.** The 2950 switch series only supports 802.1q trunk links. The typical number of VLANs configured on a 2950 switch is 64, but some models can support more. The administrative VLAN is VLAN 1 by default on all switches.

55. **D.** A /30 subnet mask allows two hosts per subnet, which is ideal for serial connections.

Answer Sheets for Practice Test 8

Section 1
Multiple Choice Questions

CUT HERE

1 Ⓐ Ⓑ Ⓒ Ⓓ Ⓔ Ⓕ	31 Ⓐ Ⓑ Ⓒ Ⓓ Ⓔ Ⓕ
2 Ⓐ Ⓑ Ⓒ Ⓓ Ⓔ Ⓕ	32 Ⓐ Ⓑ Ⓒ Ⓓ Ⓔ Ⓕ
3 Ⓐ Ⓑ Ⓒ Ⓓ Ⓔ Ⓕ	33 Ⓐ Ⓑ Ⓒ Ⓓ Ⓔ Ⓕ
4 Ⓐ Ⓑ Ⓒ Ⓓ Ⓔ Ⓕ	34 Ⓐ Ⓑ Ⓒ Ⓓ Ⓔ Ⓕ
5 Ⓐ Ⓑ Ⓒ Ⓓ Ⓔ Ⓕ	35 Ⓐ Ⓑ Ⓒ Ⓓ Ⓔ Ⓕ
6 Ⓐ Ⓑ Ⓒ Ⓓ Ⓔ Ⓕ	36 Ⓐ Ⓑ Ⓒ Ⓓ Ⓔ Ⓕ
7 Ⓐ Ⓑ Ⓒ Ⓓ Ⓔ Ⓕ	37 Ⓐ Ⓑ Ⓒ Ⓓ Ⓔ Ⓕ
8 Ⓐ Ⓑ Ⓒ Ⓓ Ⓔ Ⓕ	38 Ⓐ Ⓑ Ⓒ Ⓓ Ⓔ Ⓕ
9 Ⓐ Ⓑ Ⓒ Ⓓ Ⓔ Ⓕ	39 Ⓐ Ⓑ Ⓒ Ⓓ Ⓔ Ⓕ
10 Ⓐ Ⓑ Ⓒ Ⓓ Ⓔ Ⓕ	40 Ⓐ Ⓑ Ⓒ Ⓓ Ⓔ Ⓕ
11 Ⓐ Ⓑ Ⓒ Ⓓ Ⓔ Ⓕ	41 Ⓐ Ⓑ Ⓒ Ⓓ Ⓔ Ⓕ
12 Ⓐ Ⓑ Ⓒ Ⓓ Ⓔ Ⓕ	42 Ⓐ Ⓑ Ⓒ Ⓓ Ⓔ Ⓕ
13 Ⓐ Ⓑ Ⓒ Ⓓ Ⓔ Ⓕ	43 Ⓐ Ⓑ Ⓒ Ⓓ Ⓔ Ⓕ
14 Ⓐ Ⓑ Ⓒ Ⓓ Ⓔ Ⓕ	44 Ⓐ Ⓑ Ⓒ Ⓓ Ⓔ Ⓕ
15 Ⓐ Ⓑ Ⓒ Ⓓ Ⓔ Ⓕ	45 Ⓐ Ⓑ Ⓒ Ⓓ Ⓔ Ⓕ
16 Ⓐ Ⓑ Ⓒ Ⓓ Ⓔ Ⓕ	46 Ⓐ Ⓑ Ⓒ Ⓓ Ⓔ Ⓕ
17 Ⓐ Ⓑ Ⓒ Ⓓ Ⓔ Ⓕ	47 Ⓐ Ⓑ Ⓒ Ⓓ Ⓔ Ⓕ
18 Ⓐ Ⓑ Ⓒ Ⓓ Ⓔ Ⓕ	48 Ⓐ Ⓑ Ⓒ Ⓓ Ⓔ Ⓕ
19 Ⓐ Ⓑ Ⓒ Ⓓ Ⓔ Ⓕ	49 Ⓐ Ⓑ Ⓒ Ⓓ Ⓔ Ⓕ
20 Ⓐ Ⓑ Ⓒ Ⓓ Ⓔ Ⓕ	50 Ⓐ Ⓑ Ⓒ Ⓓ Ⓔ Ⓕ
21 Ⓐ Ⓑ Ⓒ Ⓓ Ⓔ Ⓕ	51 Ⓐ Ⓑ Ⓒ Ⓓ Ⓔ Ⓕ
22 Ⓐ Ⓑ Ⓒ Ⓓ Ⓔ Ⓕ	52 Ⓐ Ⓑ Ⓒ Ⓓ Ⓔ Ⓕ
23 Ⓐ Ⓑ Ⓒ Ⓓ Ⓔ Ⓕ	53 Ⓐ Ⓑ Ⓒ Ⓓ Ⓔ Ⓕ
24 Ⓐ Ⓑ Ⓒ Ⓓ Ⓔ Ⓕ	54 Ⓐ Ⓑ Ⓒ Ⓓ Ⓔ Ⓕ
25 Ⓐ Ⓑ Ⓒ Ⓓ Ⓔ Ⓕ	55 Ⓐ Ⓑ Ⓒ Ⓓ Ⓔ Ⓕ
26 Ⓐ Ⓑ Ⓒ Ⓓ Ⓔ Ⓕ	
27 Ⓐ Ⓑ Ⓒ Ⓓ Ⓔ Ⓕ	
28 Ⓐ Ⓑ Ⓒ Ⓓ Ⓔ Ⓕ	
29 Ⓐ Ⓑ Ⓒ Ⓓ Ⓔ Ⓕ	
30 Ⓐ Ⓑ Ⓒ Ⓓ Ⓔ Ⓕ	

Directions: For each of the following questions, select the choice that best answers the question or completes the statement.

---

1. What protocol sends redirects to an originating router?

   A. TCP
   B. IP
   C. ICMP
   D. UDP

2. What command shows you the IP address of your neighbor device?

   A. `show cdp`
   B. `cdp enable`
   C. `show cdp neighbors detail`
   D. `show cdp timers`

3. Look at the following diagram. You have installed the two switches SW-Seattle1 and SW-Seattle2. When you issue the `show cdp neighbor` command on them, you note that neither switch can see the other one. Which of the following is the most likely cause?

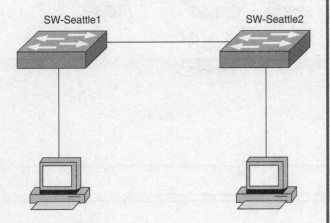

SW-Seattle1   SW-Seattle2

Figure 8-1

   A. A problem with VTP
   B. A problem with cabling
   C. A problem with trunk configuration
   D. A problem with the IP addresses on the switches

4. Which of the following will correctly add a default route to a router?

   A. `ip route any any e0`
   B. `ip route 0.0.0.0 255.255.255.255 e0`
   C. `ip route default e0`
   D. `ip route 0.0.0.0 0.0.0.0 e0`

5. How is a bridge ID assigned?

   A. It is assigned by the administrator who sets the MAC address.
   B. It is assigned the highest IP address and priority.
   C. It is assigned using the priority and the MAC address.
   D. Bridge IDs are not assigned.

6. What does the `config mem` command do?

   A. Configures the router using the running-config contents
   B. Configures the router using the startup-config contents
   C. Configures the router using the contents of a file from a TFTP server
   D. None of the above

GO ON TO THE NEXT PAGE

7. Look at the following diagram. You have configured the network as shown, yet it has failed to converge. Which of the following is the likely reason?

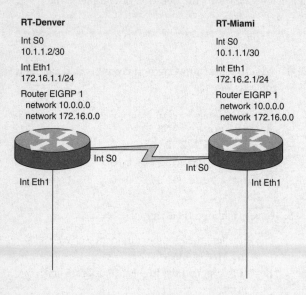

RT-Denver

Int S0
10.1.1.2/30

Int Eth1
172.16.1.1/24

Router EIGRP 1
  network 10.0.0.0
  network 172.16.0.0

RT-Miami

Int S0
10.1.1.1/30

Int Eth1
172.16.2.1/24

Router EIGRP 1
  network 10.0.0.0
  network 172.16.0.0

Figure 8-2

A. You need to configure default routes on the two routers.

B. The EIGRP AS numbers need to be added.

C. The EIGRP network statements are incorrect.

D. You need to add the `no auto-summary` command to EIGRP.

8. You have been asked to recommend a WAN service for a small rural network. It has 11 offices and needs fully meshed connectivity and at least 768Kbps of throughput. Which of the following is the best option?

A. HDLC
B. PPP
C. Frame Relay
D. Point-to-point links
E. ISDN

9. What does the `config net` command do?

A. Configures the router using the running-config contents
B. Configures the router using the startup-config contents
C. Configures the router using the contents of a file from a TFTP server
D. None of the above

10. What are the valid hosts for the subnet on which the address 172.16.4.14 255.255.252.0 resides?

A. 5.1 to 7.1
B. 4.1 to 8.254
C. 4.1 to 4.255
D. 4.1 to 7.254

11. Look at the following diagram. Suppose you have been given the 192.168.74.0/24 network to use at this site. You need to create subnets for each of the three VLANs. Assuming that you have VLSM available, what is the largest number of host addresses you can have?

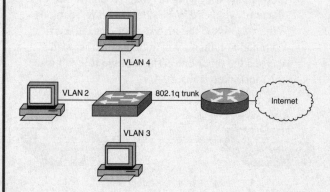

Figure 8-3

A. 128
B. 186
C. 250
D. 256

12. Look at the following diagram. Suppose you have been given the 192.168.74.0/24 network to use at this site. You need to create subnets for each of the three VLANs. In this case, you cannot use VLSM. What is the largest number of host addresses you can have?

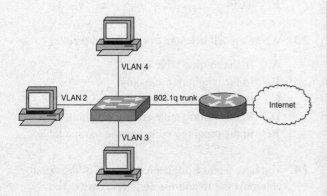

Figure 8-3

A. 128
B. 186
C. 250
D. 256

13. What is wrong with the following command?

```
access-list 10 permit tcp
    any any eq
    23
```

A. It is an extended access list that does not check the source and destination addresses.
B. It is a standard access list that does not check the source and destination addresses.
C. It is a standard access list attempting to check TCP ports.
D. Nothing; it will work as written.

14. Which of the following pieces of information will you not find in a routing table?

A. Route metrics
B. Default network
C. Default gateway
D. Directly connected active networks

15. Look at the following diagram. You have been asked to troubleshoot a network problem. What is the most likely cause of network connectivity issues here?

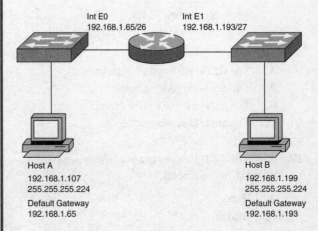

Figure 8-4

A. Host A configuration
B. Host B configuration
C. Int E0 configuration
D. Int E1 configuration

16. What will stop network loops from occurring in distance-vector networks in which a downed link is set to infinity?

A. RTMP
B. Poisoned updates
C. Route poisoning
D. Poison reverse

17. Which one of the following are valid ways for a switch to learn a MAC address?

A. Static configuration
B. Dynamic learning
C. VTP
D. STP

GO ON TO THE NEXT PAGE

18. The following commands have been added to a router to allow it to communicate with an existing OSPF network, but it is not working. What is the likely cause?

```
Router ospf 10
Network 172.16.0.0
        255.255.0.0
        area 0
```

   A. The OSPF AS number is incorrect.
   B. The network address is incorrect.
   C. The network mask is incorrect.
   D. The area ID is incorrect.

19. Which of the following can you use to segment a LAN? (Choose three.)

   A. Hub
   B. Bridge
   C. Switch
   D. Router

20. Consider the following entry from a routing table. What does the 110 stand for?

```
O  10.0.0.0/8  [110/20]
        via
        192.168.10.1, 00:06:37,
        Ethernet
        0
```

   A. The administrative distance
   B. The distance metric
   C. The OSPF area
   D. OSPF
   E. EIGRP

21. Consider the following entry from a routing table. What does the 20 stand for?

```
O  10.0.0.0/8  [110/20]
        via
        192.168.10.1, 00:06:37,
        Ethernet
        0
```

   A. The administrative distance
   B. The distance metric
   C. The OSPF area
   D. OSPF
   E. EIGRP

22. Which of the following protocols provides logical addressing and routing through an internetwork?

   A. IP
   B. ARP
   C. BootP
   D. ICMP
   E. TCP

23. Where are EIGRP successor routes stored?

   A. In the routing table only
   B. In the neighbor table only
   C. In the topology table only
   D. In the routing table and the neighbor table
   E. In the topology table and the routing table

24. You have a single registered Class C address that you must use to address an internetwork. You cannot use NAT, but you can use VLSM. What is the most efficient choice to use for point-to-point serial links?

   A. /24
   B. /28
   C. /29
   D. /30
   E. /31

25. Which of the following subnet masks corresponds with a /18 network?

   A. 255.255.255.0
   B. 255.255.192.0
   C. 255.255.255.128
   D. 255.255.224.0
   E. 255.255.0.0

26. Which of the following wildcard masks corresponds with a /18 network?

   A. 0.0.192.255
   B. 0.0.63.255
   C. 0.0.128.255
   D. 0.0.17.255
   E. 0.0.0.255

27. Look at the following diagram. You have a router with routing configured as illustrated. Suppose a packet destined for 10.0.23.253 enters the router. Which interface will the router send it out?

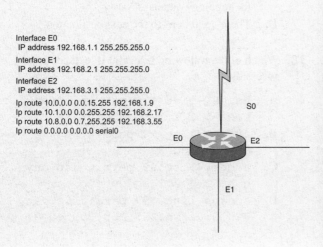

```
Interface E0
  IP address 192.168.1.1 255.255.255.0
Interface E1
  IP address 192.168.2.1 255.255.255.0
Interface E2
  IP address 192.168.3.1 255.255.255.0
Ip route 10.0.0.0 0.0.15.255 192.168.1.9
Ip route 10.1.0.0 0.0.255.255 192.168.2.17
Ip route 10.8.0.0 0.7.255.255 192.168.3.55
Ip route 0.0.0.0 0.0.0.0 serial0
```

Figure 8-5

A. E0
B. E1
C. E2
D. S0

28. Which of the following routing protocols combines characteristics of both the distance-vector and link-state routing protocols?

A. RTMP
B. NLSP
C. EIGRP
D. NLSP

29. Which of the following commands allows you to support discontiguous networking with RIPv2 and EIGRP?

A. `ip subnet-zero`
B. `cut-through`
C. `VLSM continue`
D. `no auto-summary`
E. `auto-summary`
F. `auto-contiguous`

30. What is the last available host address for the IP subnet on which 172.20.7.150 255.255.255.192 resides?

A. 172.20.7.255
B. 172.20.7.190
C. 172.20.7.191
D. 172.20.7.129
E. 172.20.255.255

31. Look at the following diagram. You have a router with routing configured as illustrated. Suppose a packet destined for 10.0.12.157 enters the router. Which interface will the router send it out?

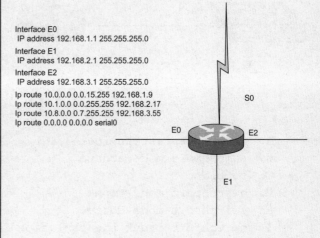

```
Interface E0
  IP address 192.168.1.1 255.255.255.0
Interface E1
  IP address 192.168.2.1 255.255.255.0
Interface E2
  IP address 192.168.3.1 255.255.255.0
Ip route 10.0.0.0 0.0.15.255 192.168.1.9
Ip route 10.1.0.0 0.0.255.255 192.168.2.17
Ip route 10.8.0.0 0.7.255.255 192.168.3.55
Ip route 0.0.0.0 0.0.0.0 serial0
```

Figure 8-5

A. E0
B. E1
C. E2
D. S0

32. What is the host range of the subnet in which the following IP address resides?

```
172.16.10.33
255.255.255.224
```

A. 172.16.10.32 - 10.63
B. 172.16.10.33 - 10.63
C. 172.16.10.32 - 10.64
D. 172.16.10.33 - 10.62

GO ON TO THE NEXT PAGE

33. What does EIGRP use to find redundant paths in the internetwork?

    A. Hop count

    B. OSPF

    C. DUAL

    D. Bandwidth and delay of the line

34. Look at the following diagram. Suppose you are asked to configure the switch with an IEEE standard trunk link to the router. Which of the following commands should you use? (Choose three.)

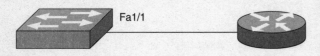

Figure 8-6

    A. `interface fastethernet 1/1`

    B. `switchport mode access`

    C. `portfast`

    D. `switchport mode trunk`

    E. `switchport mode dot1q`

    F. `switchport trunk encapsulation dot1q`

35. Where would a router boot from if a configuration register was set to 0x0101?

    A. Flash

    B. ROM

    C. Boot ROM

    D. NVRAM

36. Which of the following are spanning-tree port states? (Choose three.)

    A. Learning

    B. Spanning

    C. Listening

    D. Forwarding

    E. Filtering

37. Suppose a route has an administrative distance of 0. What does this mean?

    A. It is a static route.

    B. The route is directly connected.

    C. This route is not in the routing table but is in the topology database.

    D. There are 0 hops to the next destination.

38. Which of the following is a valid IP extended access list?

    A. `access-list 110 permit ip any host 1.1.1.1 eq ftp`

    B. `access-list 10 permit tcp ip any any eq 21`

    C. `access-list 99 permit udp any host 2.2.2.2 eq ip`

    D. `access-list 199 permit tcp any 0.0.0.0 255.255.255.255 eq 21`

39. Which of the following cables should you use to attach a PC COM port to a router to configure it?

    A. Straight-through

    B. Crossover

    C. Rollover

    D. Null modem

40. What is the default administrative distance of RIP?

    A. 1

    B. 100

    C. 120

    D. 150

41. You have a Cisco router and a non-Cisco router connected through a point-to-point serial link. Both routers are configured for HDLC encapsulation, yet they are not able to communicate. What is the likely problem?

    A. Cisco is proprietary, and you must have two Cisco routers.

    B. You are using a proprietary HDLC encapsulation.

    C. You are using the PPP encapsulation.

    D. It does work by default.

42. Look at the following diagram. Which one of the following are possible properties of the link between the two switches, assuming that it is configured correctly?

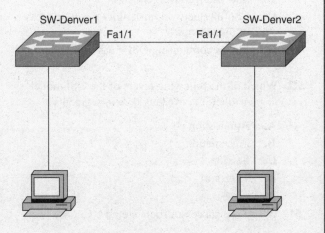

Figure 8-7

A. Portfast enabled
B. Trunk link
C. Sraight-through cable
D. Crossover cable

43. Look at the following diagram. You have a router with routing configured as illustrated. Suppose a packet destined for 192.168.3.171 enters the router. Which interface will the router send it out?

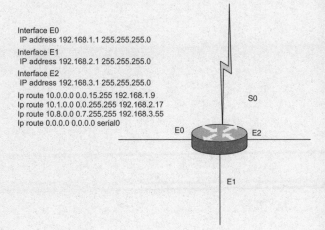

Figure 8-5

A. E0
B. E1
C. E2
D. S0

44. What is the purpose of the Spanning Tree Protocol?

A. Creates link-state routing tables
B. Stops switched loops in bridged networks
C. Works with LSA to create a route table
D. Stops electromagnetic Ethernet storms

45. Which of the following statements regarding EIGRP successor routes are valid? (Choose two.)

A. A successor route is used by EIGRP to forward traffic to a destination.
B. Successor routes are saved in the topology table to be used if the primary route fails.
C. Successor routes are flagged as active in the routing table.
D. A successor route may be backed up by a feasible successor route.
E. Successor routes are stored in the neighbor table following the discovery process.

46. Which type of Ethernet cable is used to connect a router to an Ethernet switch?

A. Rolled
B. Crossover
C. Straight-through
D. Fooled

GO ON TO THE NEXT PAGE

47. Look at the following diagram. Suppose you wish to permit hosts at LA and Chicago to access web sites on the Internet, but not hosts in Miami. Also, you do not want anyone not in Miami to access web sites hosted in Miami. Which of the following lines might you use in an ACL to complete this, assuming the last line of the access list is `access-list 110 permit ip any any`?

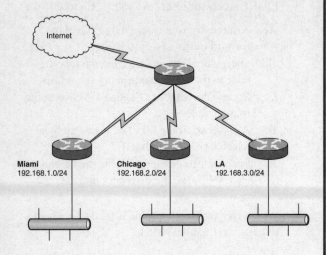

Figure 8-8

A. `access-list 110 deny tcp 192.168.0.0 0.0.0.255 any eq 80`

B. `access-list 110 permit tcp 192.168.0.0 0.0.0.255 any eq 80`

C. `access-list 110 deny tcp any 192.168.0.0 0.0.0.255 eq 80`

D. `access-list 110 permit tcp any 192.168.0.0 0.0.0.255 eq 80`

48. Which of the following is a valid standard IP access-list command?

A. `access-list 110 permit 172.16.0.0 0.0.255.255`

B. `access-list 10 permit ip any`

C. `access-list 10 deny any any eq ftp log`

D. `access list 100 permit ip any any`

49. Which of the following are benefits of designing OSPF in a hierarchical fashion? (Choose three.)

A. Decreases routing overhead

B. Speeds up convergence

C. Confines network instability to single areas of the network

D. Makes configuring OSPF easier

50. Which of the following layers of the OSI model is responsible for converting data to segments?

A. Application

B. Presentation

C. Session

D. Transport

51. Where is a successor route stored? (Choose two.)

A. In the topology table

B. In the neighbor table

C. In the routing table

D. In the ARP cache

52. Look at the following diagram. Suppose you do not want anyone not in Miami to access web sites hosted in Miami. You have created the following access list; where should you best apply it and in what direction?

```
access-list 110 deny tcp
    any 192.168.0.0
    0.0.0.255 eq 80
access-list 110 permit ip
    any any
```

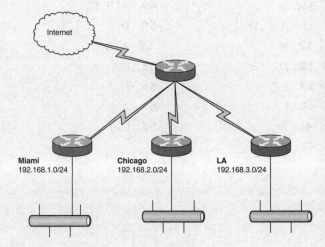

Figure 8-8

A. LA and Chicago, outbound on a serial interface
B. LA and Chicago, inbound on a serial interface
C. Miami, outbound on a serial interface
D. Miami, inbound on a serial interface

53. Which of the following will be the RID of a router?

A. The lowest IP address of an interface
B. The highest IP address of an interface
C. The lowest IP address of a logical interface
D. The highest IP address of a logical interface

54. Which statement is true regarding what VTP transparent mode accomplishes?

A. Transparent mode only forwards messages and advertisements; it does not add them to their own database.
B. Transparent mode both forwards messages and advertisements and adds them to their own database.
C. Transparent mode does not forward messages and advertisements.
D. Transparent mode makes a switch dynamically secure.

55. What command should follow this command?

```
access-list 110 deny tcp
    any host
    1.1.1.1 eq ftp
```

A. `access-list 110 deny host
    1.1.1.1 any eq ftp`
B. `access-list 110 permit any any
    ip 255.255.255.255 ftp`
C. `access-list 110 permit ip any
    0.0.0.0 255.255.255.255`
D. None; it is fine as is.

Answer Key for Practice Test 8

1. C	**15.** A	**29.** D	**43.** C
2. C	**16.** C	**30.** B	**44.** B
3. B	**17.** A, B	**31.** A	**45.** A, D
4. D	**18.** C	**32.** D	**46.** C
5. C	**19.** B, C, D	**33.** C	**47.** A, C
6. B	**20.** A	**34.** A, D, F	**48.** B
7. D	**21.** B	**35.** B	**49.** A, B, C
8. C	**22.** A	**36.** A, C, D	**50.** D
9. C	**23.** E	**37.** B	**51.** A, B
10. D	**24.** D	**38.** D	**52.** D
11. C	**25.** B	**39.** C	**53.** D
12. B	**26.** B	**40.** C	**54.** A
13. C	**27.** D	**41.** B	**55.** C
14. C	**28.** C	**42.** B, D	

Answer Explanations for Practice Test 8

1. **C.** Internet Control Message Protocol (ICMP) redirect messages are used by routers to notify the hosts on the data link that a better route is available for a particular destination.

2. **C.** The show CDP neighbors detail command gives you detailed information concerning neighboring devices.

3. **B.** In this case, the most likely cause is a cabling problem. Not seeing a CDP neighbor usually indicates a layer 1 or 2 problem (like not using a crossover cable between two switches).

4. **D.** The correct syntax for a default route is to create a static route with the destination network and mask as all zeros.

5. **C.** The priority and the MAC address are combined to build the bridge ID.

6. **B.** The config command can use the keyword terminal (t), memory (mem), or network (net). The difference is where the information originates (terminal from RAM, memory from NVRAM, and network from a TFTP server).

7. **D.** The 172.16.0.0 Class B network has been correctly subnetted, and the subnets are used on discontiguous networks. In this case, the automatic summarization must be disabled.

8. **C.** HDLC and PPP are encapsulations, not WAN technologies per se. P2P and ISDN links would be cost-prohibitive in a fully meshed topology. Because Frame Relay can provide multiple PVCs on a single physical link, it is the best recommendation.

9. **C.** The config command can use the keyword terminal (t), memory (mem), or network (net). The difference is where the information originates (terminal from RAM, memory from NVRAM, and network from a TFTP server).

10. **D.** The Class B subnet mask of 255.255.252.0 gives you 64 subnets, each with 1,022 hosts. The host specified in the question is in the second subnet: 256 − 252 = 4. The valid hosts for the 4.0 subnet are the numbers between the subnets, or 4.1 to 7.254. The broadcast address for the 4.0 subnet is 7.255.

11. **C.** With VLSM, you can create one /25 subnet and two /26 subnets. The /25 subnet yields 126 hosts, and each /26 subnet yields 62 hosts.

12. **B.** Because you cannot use VLSM, you must create three /26 subnets. Each /26 subnet yields 62 hosts.

13. **C.** This access list is a standard access list (number values 1 through 99). Standard access lists can check only the source address.

14. **C.** The purpose of a default gateway is to provide an access point that is external to the Cisco router and capable of routing packets destined for remote networks. The command ip default-gateway is used when the router is not routing IP.

15. **A.** Host A has a subnet mask of 255.255.255.224 applied to a /26 network. The correct mask would be 255.255.255.192 for a /26. If you answered C, you were close; but if you changed the configuration of E0 to /27, you would still need to change either the IP address or the default gateway on Host A, because with a /27 mask those two addresses would be in separate subnets.

16. **C.** The router that has the link fail sends a route poisoning, setting the metric to an unreachable level. In the case of RIP, the router sets the hop count to 16.

17. **A, B.** Switches can learn MAC addresses through either static configuration or dynamic learning. VTP carries VLAN information, not MAC addresses.

18. **C.** The mask is incorrect here; it should be 0.0.255.255.

19. **B, C, D.** Hubs do not segment the network but rather extend the distance a LAN can run. Bridge, switches, and routers are used to segment networks (although at different layers).

20. A. The 110 is the administrative distance for this route.

21. B. The 20 is the distance metric for this route.

22. A. Internet Protocol (IP) is a routed protocol that provides logical addressing and routing through an internetwork. .

23. E. The topology table keeps a list of every link in the network. The best links are placed in the routing table and are considered successor routes. Other links to the same remote networks are considered backup routes and called feasible successors.

24. D. The /30 subnet mask will give you two hosts per subnet, which is perfect for addressing serial links where only two addresses are required.

25. B. A /18network indicates that the first two octets, and the first two bits of the third octet, are part of the network address.

26. B. In a /18 network, the last six bits in the third octet, and all bits in the forth octet, are host bits. Setting these bits to ones (wildcard bits) yields the correct wildcard mask.

27. D. Because this IP address does not fall into any of the ranges specified by the static routes, it will follow the default route and be sent out S0.

28. C. Enhanced Interior Gateway Routing Protocol (EIGRP) is classified as a hybrid routing protocol. It uses distance-vector-based routing metrics to determine the best path to remote networks. It can converge faster than a traditional distance-vector routing protocol, however, because of the way it employs characteristics of link-state routing protocols. EIGRP maintains a topology table of the network and sends topology change updates when topology changes occur.

29. D. To allow the use of discontiguous networks, you need to supply the command `no auto-summary` under the routing protocol configuration on the classful-network boundary router.

30. B. The subnet mask is 255.255.255.192, so the block size is 64. Based on that block size, the network addresses are 172.20.7.64 and 172.20.7.128. This device is on the 128 network, and that network has a broadcast of 191, so the last host is 190.

31. A. The static route to 10.0.0.0 0.0.15.255 includes this host. The target IP address is connected on interface E0.

32. D. The network block size is 256 minus 224, or 32; therefore, the networks start every 32 addresses. The first network is 172.16.10.0, the second is 172.16.10.32, the third is 172.16.10.64, and so on. This host is on the 172.16.10.32 network, and the range is .33 through .62 with the broadcast at .63.

33. C. You probably chose D, bandwidth and delay of the line, but that option is incorrect. To find redundant paths, EIGRP uses Diffusing Update Algorithm (DUAL). Bandwidth and delay of the line are used to find the best path to a route after DUAL finds all the paths.

34. A, D, F. A will be used to select the appropriate interface; you must then specify the mode as trunk and the encapsulation as dot1q (the IEEE standard; ISL is Cisco proprietary).

35. B. The configuration register is used to tell the router how to load the IOS and configuration. The value 0x0101 tells the router to boot from ROM.

36. A, C, D. The five port states are blocking, listening, learning, forwarding, and disabled.

37. B. Directly connected networks have the highest administrative distance, or trustworthiness rating, which is 0.

38. D. Extended access lists use the numbers 100 through 199, which eliminates options B and C. To filter on an upper-layer protocol, you must use UDP or TCP in the protocol field, so option A is wrong.

39. C. A rollover cable is used to attach to the console port of a router to configure it.

40. C. Routing Information Protocol (RIP) has an AD of 120 by default.

41. **B.** Cisco routers run a proprietary High-Level Data Link Control (HDLC) encapsulation on all serial links by default. To get a Cisco router to connect to a non-Cisco router, you need to change that encapsulation to PPP.

42. **B, D.** Portfast should not be enabled between switches, only between hosts and switches. The link could be a trunk link if it is carrying multiple VLANs. A crossover cable is used to connect two switches.

43. **C.** This host is connected on interface E2.

44. **B.** Bridges use the spanning-tree algorithm, enabling a learning bridge to dynamically work around loops in a network topology by creating a spanning tree.

45. **A, D.** Successor routes are routes that are considered the best route (think successful!). Feasible successor routes are backup routes stored in the topology table.

46. **C.** A straight-through Ethernet cable is used to connect a host or router to a switch.

47. **A, C.** A will block access from hosts on the Miami subnet to external web sites, and C will block anyone, regardless of source, from accessing web sites in Miami.

48. **B.** Options A and D use access-list numbers that are reserved for extended IP access lists. Option C filters by protocol, which a standard IP access list cannot do.

49. **A, B, C.** OSPF hierarchical design, if done correctly, can help decrease routing protocol overhead as well as speed up convergence time of the network. If a problem occurs, the whole network isn't flooded with information; only routers within the troublesome area are affected. However, a multi-area design is a much more difficult configuration.

50. **D.** The Transport layer of the OSI model receives raw data from the Session layer to create segments. The Transport layer divides the data stream into units and encapsulates the information with Transport layer header-specific information.

51. **A, B.** The successor routes are stored in both the topology table and the neighbor table. Feasible successors are stored in the topology table and are considered backup routes.

52. **D.** Although A would work, D is the best place for an access list of this type.

53. **D.** By default, the highest IP address of any active interface at the moment of OSPF startup is the RID of the router. However, if a logical interface is configured, then the IP address of the logical interface is the RID of the router.

54. **A.** The transparent switch is a stand-alone switch that can be connected to your network for management. It does not add VLAN information to its VLAN database, nor does it share its configured VLAN information. It passes VLAN information received from one trunked port out a different trunked port if configured.

55. **C.** You cannot create a deny list without at least one permit. The command `access-list 110 permit ip any any` (0.0.0.0 255.255.255.255 is the same as the `any` command) is a wildcard that permits everything not eliminated from a deny test statement.

Answer Sheets for Practice Test 9

(Remove This Sheet and Use It to Mark Your Answers)

Section 1
Multiple Choice Questions

1 Ⓐ Ⓑ Ⓒ Ⓓ Ⓔ Ⓕ	31 Ⓐ Ⓑ Ⓒ Ⓓ Ⓔ Ⓕ
2 Ⓐ Ⓑ Ⓒ Ⓓ Ⓔ Ⓕ	32 Ⓐ Ⓑ Ⓒ Ⓓ Ⓔ Ⓕ
3 Ⓐ Ⓑ Ⓒ Ⓓ Ⓔ Ⓕ	33 Ⓐ Ⓑ Ⓒ Ⓓ Ⓔ Ⓕ
4 Ⓐ Ⓑ Ⓒ Ⓓ Ⓔ Ⓕ	34 Ⓐ Ⓑ Ⓒ Ⓓ Ⓔ Ⓕ
5 Ⓐ Ⓑ Ⓒ Ⓓ Ⓔ Ⓕ	35 Ⓐ Ⓑ Ⓒ Ⓓ Ⓔ Ⓕ
6 Ⓐ Ⓑ Ⓒ Ⓓ Ⓔ Ⓕ	36 Ⓐ Ⓑ Ⓒ Ⓓ Ⓔ Ⓕ
7 Ⓐ Ⓑ Ⓒ Ⓓ Ⓔ Ⓕ	37 Ⓐ Ⓑ Ⓒ Ⓓ Ⓔ Ⓕ
8 Ⓐ Ⓑ Ⓒ Ⓓ Ⓔ Ⓕ	38 Ⓐ Ⓑ Ⓒ Ⓓ Ⓔ Ⓕ
9 Ⓐ Ⓑ Ⓒ Ⓓ Ⓔ Ⓕ	39 Ⓐ Ⓑ Ⓒ Ⓓ Ⓔ Ⓕ
10 Ⓐ Ⓑ Ⓒ Ⓓ Ⓔ Ⓕ	40 Ⓐ Ⓑ Ⓒ Ⓓ Ⓔ Ⓕ
11 Ⓐ Ⓑ Ⓒ Ⓓ Ⓔ Ⓕ	41 Ⓐ Ⓑ Ⓒ Ⓓ Ⓔ Ⓕ
12 Ⓐ Ⓑ Ⓒ Ⓓ Ⓔ Ⓕ	42 Ⓐ Ⓑ Ⓒ Ⓓ Ⓔ Ⓕ
13 Ⓐ Ⓑ Ⓒ Ⓓ Ⓔ Ⓕ	43 Ⓐ Ⓑ Ⓒ Ⓓ Ⓔ Ⓕ
14 Ⓐ Ⓑ Ⓒ Ⓓ Ⓔ Ⓕ	44 Ⓐ Ⓑ Ⓒ Ⓓ Ⓔ Ⓕ
15 Ⓐ Ⓑ Ⓒ Ⓓ Ⓔ Ⓕ	45 Ⓐ Ⓑ Ⓒ Ⓓ Ⓔ Ⓕ
16 Ⓐ Ⓑ Ⓒ Ⓓ Ⓔ Ⓕ	46 Ⓐ Ⓑ Ⓒ Ⓓ Ⓔ Ⓕ
17 Ⓐ Ⓑ Ⓒ Ⓓ Ⓔ Ⓕ	47 Ⓐ Ⓑ Ⓒ Ⓓ Ⓔ Ⓕ
18 Ⓐ Ⓑ Ⓒ Ⓓ Ⓔ Ⓕ	48 Ⓐ Ⓑ Ⓒ Ⓓ Ⓔ Ⓕ
19 Ⓐ Ⓑ Ⓒ Ⓓ Ⓔ Ⓕ	49 Ⓐ Ⓑ Ⓒ Ⓓ Ⓔ Ⓕ
20 Ⓐ Ⓑ Ⓒ Ⓓ Ⓔ Ⓕ	50 Ⓐ Ⓑ Ⓒ Ⓓ Ⓔ Ⓕ
21 Ⓐ Ⓑ Ⓒ Ⓓ Ⓔ Ⓕ	51 Ⓐ Ⓑ Ⓒ Ⓓ Ⓔ Ⓕ
22 Ⓐ Ⓑ Ⓒ Ⓓ Ⓔ Ⓕ	52 Ⓐ Ⓑ Ⓒ Ⓓ Ⓔ Ⓕ
23 Ⓐ Ⓑ Ⓒ Ⓓ Ⓔ Ⓕ	53 Ⓐ Ⓑ Ⓒ Ⓓ Ⓔ Ⓕ
24 Ⓐ Ⓑ Ⓒ Ⓓ Ⓔ Ⓕ	54 Ⓐ Ⓑ Ⓒ Ⓓ Ⓔ Ⓕ
25 Ⓐ Ⓑ Ⓒ Ⓓ Ⓔ Ⓕ	55 Ⓐ Ⓑ Ⓒ Ⓓ Ⓔ Ⓕ
26 Ⓐ Ⓑ Ⓒ Ⓓ Ⓔ Ⓕ	
27 Ⓐ Ⓑ Ⓒ Ⓓ Ⓔ Ⓕ	
28 Ⓐ Ⓑ Ⓒ Ⓓ Ⓔ Ⓕ	
29 Ⓐ Ⓑ Ⓒ Ⓓ Ⓔ Ⓕ	
30 Ⓐ Ⓑ Ⓒ Ⓓ Ⓔ Ⓕ	

CUT HERE

Directions: For each of the following questions, select the choice that best answers the question or completes the statement.

1. Which of the following will allow "Unauthorized access prohibited!" to be displayed before the login prompt when someone tries to initiate a Telnet session to a router?

   A. `login banner x Unauthorized access prohibited! x`

   B. `banner exec y Unauthorized access prohibited! y`

   C. `banner motd x "Unauthorized access prohibited!" x`

   D. `login message "Unauthorized access prohibited!"`

2. Look at the following diagram. Switch SW-Seattle01 has recently been added to the network but has yet to get appropriate VLAN information from the VTP domain. What is causing this problem? (Choose two.)

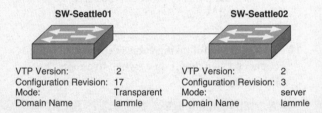

SW-Seattle01

VTP Version: 2
Configuration Revision: 17
Mode: Transparent
Domain Name: lammle

SW-Seattle02

VTP Version: 2
Configuration Revision: 3
Mode: server
Domain Name: lammle

Figure 9-1

   A. VTP domain name
   B. VTP configuration revision number
   C. VTP mode
   D. VTP version

3. Which of the following information will you not find in a routing table?

   A. Route metrics
   B. Default network
   C. Default gateway
   D. Directly connected active networks

4. Which of the following is a correct subinterface used in Frame Relay networks?

   A. `interface ethernet0/0.10 point-to-point`

   B. `interface serial0/0.11 point-to-point`

   C. `subinterface serial0.1`

   D. `subinterface fasterthernet0.1 multipoint`

5. Look at the following diagram. The following line appears in the routing table of the RT-Denver router:

   ```
   ??  192.168.1.0/26 is
       directly connected,
       Ethernet 0
   ```

   What would you expect the first character to be?

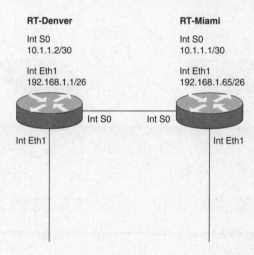

RT-Denver

Int S0
10.1.1.2/30

Int Eth1
192.168.1.1/26

Int S0   Int S0

Int Eth1

RT-Miami

Int S0
10.1.1.1/30

Int Eth1
192.168.1.65/26

Int Eth1

Figure 9-2

   A. O
   B. R
   C. D
   D. C

GO ON TO THE NEXT PAGE

6. What are the valid hosts for the subnet on which 192.168.10.40 255.255.255.224 resides?

    A. 192.168.10.32–63

    B. 192.168.10.33–64

    C. 192.168.10.33–62

    D. 192.168.10.34–65

7. Which of the following are benefits of segmenting your network with routers? (Choose three.)

    A. They provide Application layer security.

    B. They filter by logical address.

    C. They create internetworks.

    D. They stop broadcast storms.

8. What is the purpose of the Spanning Tree Protocol (STP)?

    A. Create link-state routing tables

    B. Stop switching loops in bridged networks

    C. Work with LSA to create a route table

    D. Stop broadcast storms

9. Look at the following diagram. You have been asked to connect these two switches. What type of device do you need to install to provide full communication?

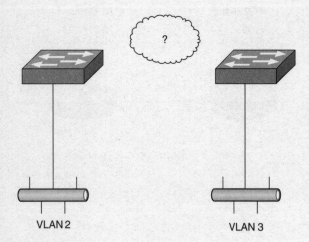

Figure 9-3

    A. Crossover cable

    B. Router

    C. Switch with 802.1q trunks

    D. Server

10. Which of the following messages displays the code image running in router memory?

    A. System Bootstrap, Version 12.1(3r)T2, RELEASE SOFTWARE (fc1) Copyright (c) 2000 by cisco Systems, Inc. C2600 platform with 32768 Kbytes of main memory

    B. program load complete, entry point: 0x80008000, size: 0x43b7fc. Self decompressing the image: #################################### #################################### #################################### ########################[OK]

    C. Cisco Internetwork Operating System Software IOS (tm) C2600 Software (C2600-I-M), Version 12.1(8), RELEASE SOFTWARE (fc1) Copyright (c) 1986-2001 by cisco Systems, Inc. Compiled Tue 17-Apr-01 04:55 by kellythw Image text-base: 0x80008088, data-base: 0x8080853C

    D. cisco 2621 (MPC860) processor (revision 0x101) with 26624K/6144K bytes of memory. Processor board ID JAD050697JB (146699779)M860 processor: part number 0, mask 49 Bridging software. X.25 software, Version 3.0.0.2 FastEthernet/IEEE 802.3 interface(s) 1 Serial network interface(s) 32K bytes of non-volatile configuration memory. 8192K bytes of processor board System flash (Read/Write)

11. Which of the following cables do you use to connect a switchport on a switch to a router's Ethernet interface?

    A. Straight through

    B. Crossover

    C. Rollover

    D. Null modem

12. You have a Class C network address and need eight subnets using the 255.255.255.224 mask. What command must be in effect to allow the use of eight subnets with this mask?

    A. `no auto-summary`

    B. `ip subnet-zero`

    C. `ip unnumbered`

    D. `ip classless`

13. Look at the following diagram. You have been asked to troubleshoot a problem. Users in LA and Miami are having issues sharing files with each other. What is the likely cause of the problem?

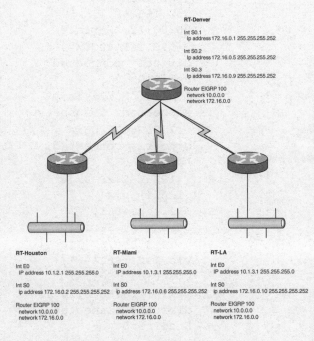

RT-Denver

Int S0.1
Ip address 172.16.0.1 255.255.255.252

Int S0.2
Ip address 172.16.0.5 255.255.255.252

Int S0.3
Ip address 172.16.0.9 255.255.255.252

Router EIGRP 100
network 10.0.0.0
network 172.16.0.0

RT-Houston

Int E0
IP address 10.1.2.1 255.255.255.0

Int S0
ip address 172.16.0.2 255.255.255.252

Router EIGRP 100
network 10.0.0.0
network 172.16.0.0

RT-Miami

Int E0
IP address 10.1.3.1 255.255.255.0

Int S0
ip address 172.16.0.6 255.255.255.252

Router EIGRP 100
network 10.0.0.0
network 172.16.0.0

RT-LA

Int E0
IP address 10.1.3.1 255.255.255.0

Int S0
ip address 172.16.0.10 255.255.255.252

Router EIGRP 100
network 10.0.0.0
network 172.16.0.0

Figure 9-4

A. EIGRP autosummary
B. IP subnet zero
C. IP addressing
D. EIGRP network statements

14. What are the valid hosts for the subnet on which 192.168.10.5 255.255.255.252 resides?

A. 4–7
B. 5–6
C. 4–10
D. 4–8

15. Look at the following diagram. You have an administrator at 10.1.1.65 who manages several servers on the 10.1.2.0/24 subnet using SSL. No other users should be accessing that subnet. You have created the access list shown. Which interface and direction should you apply it on to achieve the desired result?

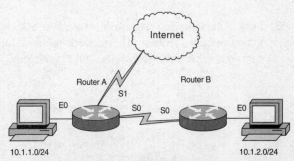

Internet

Router A   Router B

E0   S1   S0   S0   E0

10.1.1.0/24   10.1.2.0/24

Access-list 101 permit tcp 10.1.1.65 255.255.255.255 any eq 443
Access-list 101 deny ip any 10.1.2.0 0.255.255.255
Access-list 101 permit ip any any

Figure 9-5

A. RouterA, E0, in
B. RouterA, E0, out
C. RouterA, S0, in
D. RouterA, S0, out
E. RouterB, E0, in
F. RouterB, E0, out

16. Which of the following series of commands restricts Telnet access to the router?

A. `RouterA(config)#access-list 10 permit 172.16.1.1`
   `RouterA(config)#line con 0`
   `RouterA(config-line)#ip access-group 10 in`

B. `RouterA(config)#access-list 10 permit 172.16.1.1`
   `RouterA(config)#line vty 0 4`
   `RouterA(config-line)#access-class 10 out`

C. `RouterA(config)#access-list 10 permit 172.16.1.1`
   `RouterA(config)#line vty 0 4`
   `RouterA(config-line)#access-class 10 in`

D. `RouterA(config)#access-list 10 permit 172.16.1.1`
   `RouterA(config)#line vty 0 4`
   `RouterA(config-line)#ip access-group 10 in`

GO ON TO THE NEXT PAGE

17. If you want to deny ping traffic entering your network, which protocol should you filter?

    A. ICMP

    B. IGRP

    C. TCP

    D. UDP

18. Look at the following diagram. You have been asked to troubleshoot a problem. This network has failed to converge. What is the likely cause of the problem?

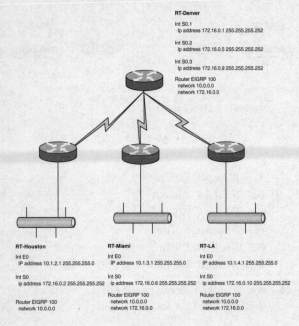

RT-Denver

Int S0.1
  Ip address 172.16.0.1 255.255.255.252

Int S0.2
  Ip address 172.16.0.5 255.255.255.252

Int S0.3
  Ip address 172.16.0.9 255.255.255.252

Router EIGRP 100
  network 10.0.0.0
  network 172.16.0.0

RT-Houston

Int E0
  IP address 10.1.2.1 255.255.255.0

Int S0
  ip address 172.16.0.2 255.255.255.252

Router EIGRP 100
  network 10.0.0.0

RT-Miami

Int E0
  IP address 10.1.3.1 255.255.255.0

Int S0
  ip address 172.16.0.6 255.255.255.252

Router EIGRP 100
  network 10.0.0.0
  network 172.16.0.0

RT-LA

Int E0
  IP address 10.1.4.1 255.255.255.0

Int S0
  ip address 172.16.0.10 255.255.255.252

Router EIGRP 100
  network 10.0.0.0
  network 172.16.0.0

Figure 9-6

    A. EIGRP auto-summary

    B. IP subnet zero

    C. IP addressing

    D. EIGRP network statements

19. What does a router do with a received packet that is destined for an unknown network?

    A. Forwards the packet

    B. Drops the packet

    C. Holds the packet until the next route update

    D. Sends a broadcast for the unknown network

20. You have the following routing table. Which of the following networks will not be placed in the neighbor's routing table?

```
R    192.168.30.0/24
     [120/15] via
     192.168.40.1,
     00:00:12, Serial0
C    192.168.40.0/24 is
     directly connected,
     Serial0
     172.16.0.0/24 is
     subnetted, 1 subnets
C    172.16.30.0 is
     directly connected,
     Loopback0
R    192.168.20.0/24
     [120/1] via
     192.168.40.1,
     00:00:12, Serial0
R    10.0.0.0/8 [120/5]
     via 192.168.40.1,
     00:00:07, Serial0
C    192.168.50.0/24 is
     directly connected,
     Ethernet0
```

    A. 172.16.30.0

    B. 192.168.30.0

    C. 10.0.0.0

    D. All of them will be placed in the neighbor's routing table.

21. Look at the following diagram. You have been asked to install the router shown in the diagram. What kind of cable and connection do you need to configure between the router and the switch?

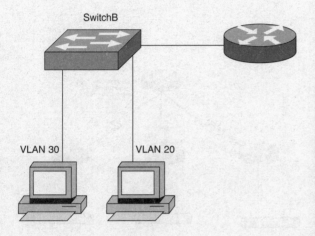

Figure 9-7

    A. Straight-through cable, 100/half connection

    B. Crossover cable, 100/half connection

    C. Straight-through cable, 802.1q connection

    D. Crossover cable, 802.1q connection

22. What happens if you do not set the VTY password?

    A. You can't log on from the console port.

    B. You can't log on from the aux port.

    C. You can't telnet into the router.

    D. Nothing.

23. What does the following command mean?

```
access-list 110 permit ip
    any 0.0.0.0
    255.255.255.255
```

    A. It is a standard IP access list that permits network 0.0.0.0 only.

    B. It is an extended IP access list that permits network 0.0.0.0 only.

    C. It is an extended list that permits any host or network.

    D. It is invalid.

24. What is the default encapsulation used on Cisco serial links?

    A. PPP

    B. IETF

    C. HDLC

    D. Frame Relay

25. Look at the following diagram. You have a router with routing configured as illustrated. Suppose that a packet destined for 10.1.174.254 enters the router. Which interface will the router send it out?

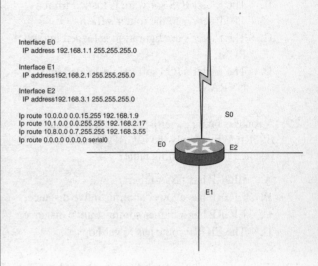

Figure 9-8

    A. E0

    B. E1

    C. E2

    D. S0

26. A port in the STP _____ state populates the MAC address table but doesn't forward data frames.

    A. Blocking

    B. Listening

    C. Learning

    D. Forwarding

27. What configuration commands configure a router for fallback? (Choose three.)

    A. `copy tftp flash`

    B. `boot system flash`

    C. `boot system rom`

    D. `boot system tftp`

    E. `boot system host`

GO ON TO THE NEXT PAGE

28. The command `copy tftp flash` initiates what event?

  A. The router configuration is copied from a TFTP server to the router.

  B. The router IOS software is loaded from a TFTP server to the router's flash.

  C. The router's configuration is loaded into boot ROM.

  D. The router's IOS software is loaded into NVRAM.

29. A route is being advertised by both RIP and EIGRP. Why is only the EIGRP-learned route injected into the routing table?

  A. EIGRP has faster timers.

  B. EIGRP has a lower administrative distance.

  C. EIGRP has a higher administrative distance.

  D. The EIGRP route has fewer hops.

30. Which configuration task must you complete if a remote Frame Relay router does not support Inverse ARP?

  A. Configure static maps.

  B. Define an IP address locally.

  C. Disable DHCP on the Frame Relay router.

  D. Configure a static route to the remote network.

31. Look at the following diagram. You have been asked to troubleshoot a problem. This network has failed to converge. What is the likely cause of the problem?

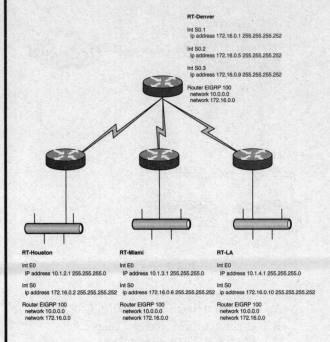

Figure 9-9

  A. EIGRP auto-summary

  B. IP subnet zero

  C. IP addressing

  D. EIGRP network statements

32. You're given the following criterion when connecting access from a remote site to your LAN: "Restrict access on interface e0 for Telnet and FTP." Which of the following lines should come last when you configure your access list?

  A. `access-list 101 end`

  B. `access-list 101 deny e0 telnet ftp`

  C. `access-list 101 allow all except ftp telnet`

  D. `access-list 101 permit ip 0.0.0.0 255.255.255.255 any`

  E. `access-list 101 deny ip 128.12.22.55 tcp eq 20 21 23`

33. Which of the following are true regarding Frame Relay? (Choose two.)

   A. Subinterface configuration is provided by multipoint and point-to-point interfaces.

   B. Frame Relay uses an SVC at layer 2.

   C. Frame Relay uses two Bearer channels.

   D. Frame Relay point-to-point subinterfaces must be configured with their own subnet.

34. What is the suggested mask used with VLSM that provides the most efficient use of addressing on a point-to-point serial link?

   A. /24

   B. /25

   C. /27

   D. /28

   E. /29

   F. /30

35. Which of the following is a valid IP extended access list?

   A. `access-list 10 permit ip any host 172.16.10.1 eq www log`

   B. `access-list 110 permit ip any 172.16.10.1 0.0.0.0 eq smtp log`

   C. `access-list 99 permit tcp any host eq ftp log`

   D. `access-list 101 deny tcp 172.16.1.1 0.0.0.0 host 1.1.1.1 eq ftp`

36. What does a bridge use to filter traffic on a network?

   A. IP addresses

   B. Broadcasts

   C. Application data

   D. Media Access Control addresses

37. You have a Frame Relay network. What type of encapsulation is necessary if the routers are from different vendors?

   A. IETF

   B. Cisco

   C. ANSI

   D. IEEE

38. Look at the following diagram. In the network pictured, how many host addresses will be in the MAC forwarding table on each switch? Assume that the network and hosts have been running for some time.

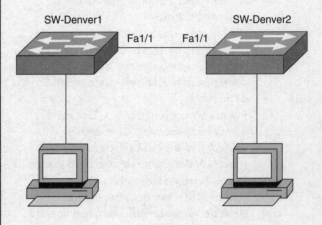

Figure 9-10

   A. None

   B. Two

   C. Four

   D. More

39. Which of the following describes a full-duplex transmission?

   A. Uses a single cable

   B. Uses a point-to-point connection when only two hosts are present

   C. Transmits data in both directions, but only one way at a time

   D. Transmits data in only one direction

GO ON TO THE NEXT PAGE

40. Which of the following describes the steps of data encapsulation?

    A. User information is converted to data, data is converted to segments, segments are converted to packets or datagrams, packets are converted to frames, and frames are converted to bits.

    B. Data is converted to frames, segments are converted to packets or datagrams, packets are converted to segments, frames are converted to bits, and bits are converted to data.

    C. Frames are converted to bits, bits are converted to segments, segments are converted to packets or datagrams, and packets or datagrams are converted to data.

    D. Data is converted to packets, packets are converted to segments, segments are converted to datagrams, and datagrams are converted to frames. Frames are then converted to bits.

41. Look at the following diagram. You have a router with routing configured as illustrated. Suppose that a packet destined for 10.11.128.255 enters the router. Which interface will the router send it out?

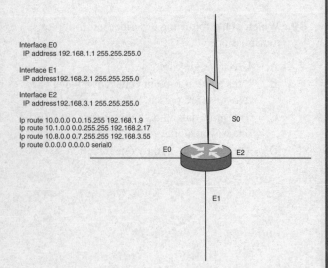

Interface E0
  IP address 192.168.1.1 255.255.255.0

Interface E1
  IP address192.168.2.1 255.255.255.0

Interface E2
  IP address192.168.3.1 255.255.255.0

Ip route 10.0.0.0 0.0.15.255 192.168.1.9
Ip route 10.1.0.0 0.0.255.255 192.168.2.17
Ip route 10.8.0.0 0.7.255.255 192.168.3.55
Ip route 0.0.0.0 0.0.0.0 serial0

Figure 9-8

    A. E0

    B. E1

    C. E2

    D. S0

42. What is the IEEE version of spanning tree?

    A. 802.5

    B. 802.3E

    C. 802.2B

    D. 802.1D

43. You want to back up the IOS on your router to a network server. Which three things should be done prior to performing this task?

    A. Make sure the network server can be accessed.

    B. Check that the authentication for access is set.

    C. Make sure the administrator workstation and the router's LAN connection are in the same subnet.

    D. Verify any file-naming and path requirements.

    E. Make sure the server can load and run the bootstrap code.

44. You connect a new host into the Sales VLAN; however, this new host cannot see the Sales server. What could be the problem?

    A. The host is not using the correct version of Windows.

    B. The switch needs to be reloaded after a configuration takes place.

    C. The port on the switch is not in the correct VLAN.

    D. The host needs to update its MAC address to one that works on the type of segment it is connected to.

45. Which statements are true regarding classless routing protocols? (Choose two.)

    A. The use of discontiguous subnets is not allowed.

    B. The use of variable-length subnet masks is permitted.

    C. RIPv1 is a classless routing protocol.

    D. RIPv2 supports classless routing.

46. What command do you type at a CLI prompt to see the configuration register setting?

    A. `show router boot`

    B. `show flash`

    C. `show nvram`

    D. `show version`

    E. `show config-register`

47. What command shows the Frame Relay protocol statistics?

   A. `sh frame stat`
   B. `sh frame-relay traffic`
   C. `sh ip frame-relay stat`
   D. `sh frame-relay ip`

48. Which of the following use ICMP to test IP connectivity? (Choose two.)

   A. Ping
   B. ARP
   C. Traceroute
   D. Telnet

49. What is the default encapsulation for Cisco routers running Frame Relay?

   A. HDLC
   B. Cisco
   C. PPP
   D. Frame Relay

50. You type `show interface serial 0` and see this:

```
Serial 0 is up, line
   protocol is down
```

In which layer of the OSI could the problem be?

   A. Physical
   B. Data Link
   C. Network
   D. Transport

51. Look at the following diagram. You have been asked to create an access list that will allow access to a web server at the 192.168.1.27 subnet but will not allow any other communication with the Internet. Which of the following should you choose?

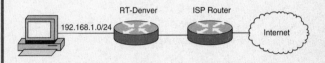

Figure 9-11

   A. `access-list 10 permit ip any host 192.168.1.27 eq 80`
   B. `access-list 101 permit tcp any host 192.168.1.27 eq 80`
   C. `access-list 10 permit ip host 192.168.1.27  any eq 80`
   D. `access-list 101 permit ip host 192.168.1.27 any eq 80`

52. What does a switch do with a multicast frame received on an interface?

   A. Forwards the switch to the first available link
   B. Drops the frame
   C. Floods the network with the frame
   D. Sends back a message to the originating station asking for a name resolution

GO ON TO THE NEXT PAGE

53. Look at the following diagram. You have been asked to create an access list on the RT-Denver router that will block telnet access from the Internet to a server at 192.168.1.198 and allow any other communications with the Internet.

```
access-list 101 deny tcp
     any host 192.168.1.198
     eq telnet
access-list 101 permit ip
     any any
```

Which interface, and in which direction, should you apply this access list?

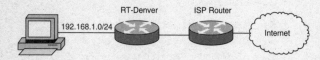

Figure 9-11

A. Interface facing the ISP, in
B. Interface facing the ISP, out
C. Interface facing the LAN, in
D. Interface facing the LAN, out

54. You need a routing protocol that supports both discontiguous networks and VLSM. It must also provide the lowest impact on router CPU and WAN utilization. Which of the following will provide this?

A. RIPv1
B. RIPv2
C. Static routing
D. EIGRP
E. OSPF

55. Look at the following diagram. You have a router with routing configured as illustrated. Suppose that a packet destined for 10.16.112.17 enters the router. Which interface will the router send it out?

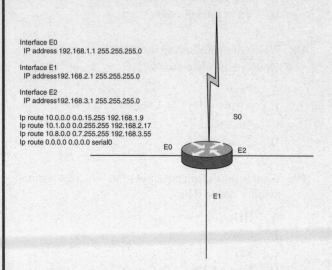

Figure 9-8

A. E0
B. E1
C. E2
D. S0

Answer Key for Practice Test 9

1. C	**15.** A	**29.** B	**43.** A, C, D
2. B, C	**16.** C	**30.** A	**44.** C
3. C	**17.** A	**31.** A	**45.** B, D
4. B	**18.** D	**32.** D	**46.** D
5. D	**19.** B	**33.** A, D	**47.** B
6. C	**20.** B	**34.** F	**48.** A, C
7. B, C, D	**21.** C	**35.** D	**49.** B
8. B	**22.** C	**36.** D	**50.** B
9. B	**23.** C	**37.** A	**51.** B
10. C	**24.** C	**38.** B	**52.** C
11. A	**25.** B	**39.** B	**53.** A
12. B	**26.** C	**40.** A	**54.** C
13. C	**27.** B, C, D	**41.** C	**55.** D
14. B	**28.** B	**42.** D	

Answer Explanations for Practice Test 9

1. **C.** The "Message Of The Day" (motd) is an old Unix command that allows you to display a message when anyone connects to a router or switch device.

2. **B, C.** VTP is not updating because the switch is in transparent mode, not server or client mode. If the switch is placed in an incorrect mode, the wrong mode will prevent it from receiving updates.

3. **C.** The purpose of a default gateway is to provide an access point that is external to the Cisco router and capable of routing packets destined for remote networks. The command `ip default-gateway` is used when the router is not routing IP; the default gateway does not appear in the routing table.

4. **B.** Frame Relay runs on serial interfaces and creates a subinterface using the `interface` *type number.subinterface* command.

5. **D.** The identifier for directly connected routes in a routing table is C.

6. **C.** The 224 mask is 3 bits for subnets and 5 bits for host addressing. That means you have 8 subnets, each with 30 hosts. The valid subnets increment by 256 − 224 = 32: 0, 32, 64, 96, 128, 160, 192, 224. The valid hosts are the numbers between the subnets, except for the all-zeros and all-ones hosts. The valid hosts in the 32 subnet are 33 through 62, and 63 is the broadcast address.

7. **B, C, D.** Routers filter by logical address, create internetworks, and stop broadcast storms.

8. **B.** Bridges use the spanning-tree algorithm, enabling a learning bridge to dynamically work around loops in a network topology by creating a spanning tree.

9. **B.** Only a router can route between separate VLANs. Although switches can carry multiple VLANs, they cannot route between them.

10. **C.** Although a lot of information is displayed during startup, only option C has the code image name.

11. **A.** A standard Ethernet cable is all you need to connect a router to a switch. If you had two switchports, you would need a crossover cable.

12. **B.** To allow the use of eight subnets with a /27 Class C mask, you must have implemented the `ip subnet-zero` command, which is on by default on all Cisco routers using the 12.*x* IOS.

13. **C.** The LA and Miami LANs have the same address assigned.

14. **B.** A 252 mask gives you 6 bits for subnets and 2 bits for hosts. This gives you 64 subnets, each with 2 hosts. The host specified in the question is in the second subnet, 0 being the first (the increment is 256 − 252 = 4). The valid hosts are 5 and 6. 7 is the broadcast for the 4 subnet.

15. **A.** This ACL can only be placed on RouterA, E0, in to achieve only the desired result. Placing the ACL on any other interface would either do nothing or impact more than is stated in the policy.

16. **C.** Telnet access to the router is restricted by using either a standard or extended IP access list on the VTY lines on the router. The command `access-class` is used to apply the access list to the VTY lines.

17. **A.** The ping (Packet Internet Groper) utility uses Internet Control Message Protocol (ICMP) echo messages to test network connectivity.

18. **D.** The Houston router is missing the 172.16.0.0 network statement. Without this, it will not enable EIGRP on the serial interface and thus will not form a neighbor relationship with Denver.

19. **B.** If a router receives a packet that is looking for a destination network that is not in the routing table, the router drops the packet.

20. **B.** The network 192.168.30.0 cannot be placed in the next router's routing table because it is already at 15 hops. One more hop will make the route 16 hops, and that is not valid.

21. **C.** You need a straight-through cable between the router and switch. Because there are multiple VLANs, you must have a trunk link (802.1q) configured.

22. C. If you do not set the VTY password, you will be denied access when trying to telnet into the router, due to the default presence of the `login` command and its requirement that a password be set. You can set the password during setup or at any time after you finish the initial configuration of your router.

23. C. The command `access-list 110 permit ip any any` (0.0.0.0 255.255.255.255 is the same as the `any` command) is a wildcard allowing any host or network access to any other host or network.

24. C. Cisco's default encapsulation for serial links is High-Level Data Link Control (HDLC). To use a different encapsulation, you use the `encapsulation` command in interface configuration mode.

25. B. This IP address falls into the range 10.1.0.0 0.0.255.255 and thus will be routed out interface E1.

26. C. A switch port in STP learning state listens to BPDUs and learns all the paths in the switched network.

27. B, C, D. If you configure your router using the commands `boot system flash`, `boot system tftp`, and `boot system rom`, in that order, the router first tries to boot from flash. If that is unsuccessful, it tries to boot from a TFTP host; if that is unsuccessful, it boots into ROM mode.

28. B. By typing `copy tftp flash`, you tell the router to go to a TFTP host and download the IOS software to the router's flash memory.

29. B. Routers always look at the administrative distance of a route before using metrics. EIGRP has an administrative distance of 90, and RIP has an administrative distance of 120.

30. A. Frame Relay can send an Inverse ARP packet to the device on the other side of the virtual circuit. If the other side does not support Inverse ARP, you must configure a static map.

31. A. The 10.0.0.0 network is discontiguous across the Ethernet interfaces of the branch routers. In this case, EIGRP auto-summarization must be disabled.

32. D. At the end of all access lists is an implicit `deny all` statement. Therefore, you must include a `permit any any` to allow traffic that does not meet your restrictions to continue. Also remember that 0.0.0.0 255.255.255.255 is the same parameter as `any`.

33. A, D. Frame Relay subinterface configuration is provided by either point-to-point or multipoint subinterfaces. Even though Frame Relay can use an SVC, it is not widely supported or implemented and so is not the best answer to this question. Also, point-to-point interfaces have their own subnet addresses.

34. F. A /30 provides two hosts, which is the most efficient for point-to-point links.

35. D. Extended IP access lists use access list numbers 100–199 or 2000–2699 and can filter on the protocol field in the Network layer header as well as on port numbers in the Transport layer header. Of course, source and destination IP addresses can be used as well. To filter on an upper-layer protocol, such as WWW, SMTP, or FTP, you cannot use IP in the protocol field; instead, you must use either UDP or TCP, depending on the Application layer protocol.

36. D. Bridges can read frames and filter only by MAC (hardware) address.

37. A. The default Frame Relay encapsulation is Cisco's proprietary encapsulation, and that can be used only if you have Cisco routers on both sides of the Frame Relay link. If you have multiple vendors, you need to use Internet Engineering Task Force (IETF) encapsulation.

38. B. Each switch should learn the MAC address of the hosts on the network. Because this diagram shows only two hosts, the correct answer is B.

39. B. Full-duplex transmission uses a point-to-point connection from the transmitter of the transmitting station to the receiver of the receiving station. Host-to-host means dedicated transmission to the receiving pair as well as dedicated receiving from the transmitting pair.

40. A. Encapsulation describes the conversion of data for use at each layer. The order of conversion is as follows: user information is converted to data, data to segments, segments to packets or datagrams, packets to frames, and frames to bits.

41. C. This IP address falls into the range 10.8.0.0 0.7.255.255 and thus will be routed out interface E2.

42. D. IEEE 802.1D is the Spanning Tree Protocol specification.

43. A, C, D. Before you try to back up the IOS on your router to a network server, ping the server from the router to make sure you have connectivity. Also, verify that you have the Trivial FTP (TFTP) server software running, that the default path is set, and that the host running the TFTP software is in the same subnet as the router's LAN connection to the TFTP host.

44. C. There could be many answers for this problem, but the best answer is that the port has not been assigned to the correct VLAN.

45. B, D. Classless routing protocols send subnet mask information with each route update. This means they support VLSM, CIDR, and discontiguous networking. EIGRP, OSPF, and RIPv2 are considered classless routing protocols.

46. D. You can see the current setting of the configuration register by using the `show version` command.

47. B. The `show frame-relay traffic` command shows the Frame Relay protocol statistics.

48. A, C. Both ping and traceroute use ICMP to test IP connectivity in an internetwork. Ping uses ICMP echo requests and responses, and traceroute uses destination-unreachable and IP TTL time-exceeded messages.

49. B. Cisco routers run High-Level Data Link Control (HDLC) over serial interfaces by default; however, if you are running Frame Relay, they will run the Cisco Frame Relay encapsulation by default.

50. B. The first up in the line is the Physical layer, and the second up is the Data Link layer.

51. B. The correct range for an extended access list is 100-199, the correct protocol and port is TCP 80, and the source address is *any*, but the destination is host 192.168.1.27.

52. C. If a switch receives a broadcast or multicast frame on a switchport, it is flooded out all ports except for the port it was received on.

53. A. This ACL will work on either A or D; however, A is a better choice.

54. C. B, D, and E all meet the minimum requirements of supporting VLSM and discontiguous subnets. However, only static routing minimizes router CPU and WAN utilization.

55. D. This IP address does not fall into any of the specified ranges and thus will follow the default route out interface serial 0.

Answer Sheets for Practice Test 10

(Remove This Sheet and Use It to Mark Your Answers)

Section 1
Multiple Choice Questions

CUT HERE

1 Ⓐ Ⓑ Ⓒ Ⓓ Ⓔ Ⓕ		31 Ⓐ Ⓑ Ⓒ Ⓓ Ⓔ Ⓕ
2 Ⓐ Ⓑ Ⓒ Ⓓ Ⓔ Ⓕ		32 Ⓐ Ⓑ Ⓒ Ⓓ Ⓔ Ⓕ
3 Ⓐ Ⓑ Ⓒ Ⓓ Ⓔ Ⓕ		33 Ⓐ Ⓑ Ⓒ Ⓓ Ⓔ Ⓕ
4 Ⓐ Ⓑ Ⓒ Ⓓ Ⓔ Ⓕ		34 Ⓐ Ⓑ Ⓒ Ⓓ Ⓔ Ⓕ
5 Ⓐ Ⓑ Ⓒ Ⓓ Ⓔ Ⓕ		35 Ⓐ Ⓑ Ⓒ Ⓓ Ⓔ Ⓕ
6 Ⓐ Ⓑ Ⓒ Ⓓ Ⓔ Ⓕ		36 Ⓐ Ⓑ Ⓒ Ⓓ Ⓔ Ⓕ
7 Ⓐ Ⓑ Ⓒ Ⓓ Ⓔ Ⓕ		37 Ⓐ Ⓑ Ⓒ Ⓓ Ⓔ Ⓕ
8 Ⓐ Ⓑ Ⓒ Ⓓ Ⓔ Ⓕ		38 Ⓐ Ⓑ Ⓒ Ⓓ Ⓔ Ⓕ
9 Ⓐ Ⓑ Ⓒ Ⓓ Ⓔ Ⓕ		39 Ⓐ Ⓑ Ⓒ Ⓓ Ⓔ Ⓕ
10 Ⓐ Ⓑ Ⓒ Ⓓ Ⓔ Ⓕ		40 Ⓐ Ⓑ Ⓒ Ⓓ Ⓔ Ⓕ
11 Ⓐ Ⓑ Ⓒ Ⓓ Ⓔ Ⓕ		41 Ⓐ Ⓑ Ⓒ Ⓓ Ⓔ Ⓕ
12 Ⓐ Ⓑ Ⓒ Ⓓ Ⓔ Ⓕ		42 Ⓐ Ⓑ Ⓒ Ⓓ Ⓔ Ⓕ
13 Ⓐ Ⓑ Ⓒ Ⓓ Ⓔ Ⓕ		43 Ⓐ Ⓑ Ⓒ Ⓓ Ⓔ Ⓕ
14 Ⓐ Ⓑ Ⓒ Ⓓ Ⓔ Ⓕ		44 Ⓐ Ⓑ Ⓒ Ⓓ Ⓔ Ⓕ
15 Ⓐ Ⓑ Ⓒ Ⓓ Ⓔ Ⓕ		45 Ⓐ Ⓑ Ⓒ Ⓓ Ⓔ Ⓕ
16 Ⓐ Ⓑ Ⓒ Ⓓ Ⓔ Ⓕ		46 Ⓐ Ⓑ Ⓒ Ⓓ Ⓔ Ⓕ
17 Ⓐ Ⓑ Ⓒ Ⓓ Ⓔ Ⓕ		47 Ⓐ Ⓑ Ⓒ Ⓓ Ⓔ Ⓕ
18 Ⓐ Ⓑ Ⓒ Ⓓ Ⓔ Ⓕ		48 Ⓐ Ⓑ Ⓒ Ⓓ Ⓔ Ⓕ
19 Ⓐ Ⓑ Ⓒ Ⓓ Ⓔ Ⓕ		49 Ⓐ Ⓑ Ⓒ Ⓓ Ⓔ Ⓕ
20 Ⓐ Ⓑ Ⓒ Ⓓ Ⓔ Ⓕ		50 Ⓐ Ⓑ Ⓒ Ⓓ Ⓔ Ⓕ
21 Ⓐ Ⓑ Ⓒ Ⓓ Ⓔ Ⓕ		51 Ⓐ Ⓑ Ⓒ Ⓓ Ⓔ Ⓕ
22 Ⓐ Ⓑ Ⓒ Ⓓ Ⓔ Ⓕ		52 Ⓐ Ⓑ Ⓒ Ⓓ Ⓔ Ⓕ
23 Ⓐ Ⓑ Ⓒ Ⓓ Ⓔ Ⓕ		53 Ⓐ Ⓑ Ⓒ Ⓓ Ⓔ Ⓕ
24 Ⓐ Ⓑ Ⓒ Ⓓ Ⓔ Ⓕ		54 Ⓐ Ⓑ Ⓒ Ⓓ Ⓔ Ⓕ
25 Ⓐ Ⓑ Ⓒ Ⓓ Ⓔ Ⓕ		55 Ⓐ Ⓑ Ⓒ Ⓓ Ⓔ Ⓕ
26 Ⓐ Ⓑ Ⓒ Ⓓ Ⓔ Ⓕ		
27 Ⓐ Ⓑ Ⓒ Ⓓ Ⓔ Ⓕ		
28 Ⓐ Ⓑ Ⓒ Ⓓ Ⓔ Ⓕ		
29 Ⓐ Ⓑ Ⓒ Ⓓ Ⓔ Ⓕ		
30 Ⓐ Ⓑ Ⓒ Ⓓ Ⓔ Ⓕ		

Directions: For each of the following questions, select the choice that best answers the question or completes the statement.

1. You need to connect a company's new remote offices together. Three of their networks have at least 50 hosts each, and one network has only 10 hosts. They have multivendor routers connected by serial links and use separate subnets at each location. The company has one Class C address to use. Which of the following protocols is most appropriate for this scenario?

   A. TCP/IP
   B. RIPv2
   C. RIPv1
   D. EIGRP

2. Which of the following statements is true regarding RIP routing?

   A. You must specify all directly connected subnets.
   B. You must specify all directly connected networks.
   C. RIP can be used in networks with 16 hops.
   D. RIP is great in large networks.

3. Look at the following diagram. You have been asked to prevent users in Houston from telnetting into hosts at LA. You have configured the Houston router as shown but have been informed that the users in Houston still have telnet access to LA. What is the most likely cause of the problem?

   A. Access list applied in the wrong direction
   B. Access list is misconfigured
   C. Access list is on the wrong router
   D. Access list is on the wrong interface

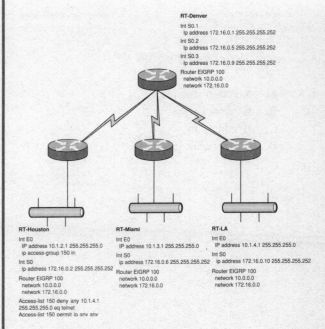

Figure 10-1

GO ON TO THE NEXT PAGE

4. Look at the following diagram. You have been asked to troubleshoot a problem. This network has failed to converge. What is the likely cause of the problem?

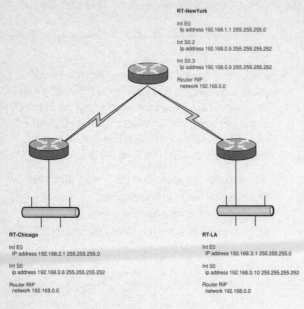

RT-NewYork

Int E0
Ip address 192.168.1.1 255.255.255.0

Int S0.2
Ip address 192.168.0.5 255.255.255.252

Int S0.3
Ip address 192.168.0.9 255.255.255.252

Router RIP
network 192.168.0.0

RT-Chicago

Int E0
IP address 192.168.2.1 255.255.255.0

Int S0
ip address 192.168.0.6 255.255.255.252

Router RIP
network 192.168.0.0

RT-LA

Int E0
IP address 192.168.3.1 255.255.255.0

Int S0
ip address 192.168.0.10 255.255.255.252

Router RIP
network 192.168.0.0

Figure 10-2

A. RIP auto-summary
B. IP subnet zero
C. IP addressing
D. RIP network statements

5. What will occur if two Cisco LAN switches are connected with a single crossover cable?

A. The switchport link light will be off on both switches, indicating that the ports are not connected.
B. The switchport link light will be off on one switch, indicating that STP has disabled the port.
C. The switchport link lights will flash amber, indicating an error.
D. The switchport link lights will be green, indicating normal operation.

6. What wildcard mask should you apply to mask networks 172.16.8.0/21?

A. 0.0.8.255
B. 0.0.255.255
C. 0.255.255.255
D. 0.0.7.255

7. Look at the following diagram. The network has been configured using static routing and has been working fine. As configured, can a user in Miami ping the serial 0 interface in RT-LA?

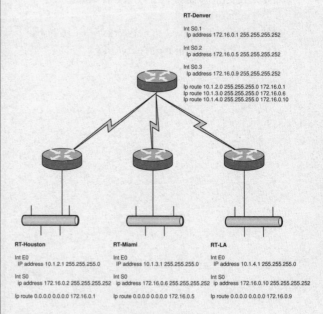

RT-Denver

Int S0.1
Ip address 172.16.0.1 255.255.255.252

Int S0.2
Ip address 172.16.0.5 255.255.255.252

Int S0.3
Ip address 172.16.0.9 255.255.255.252

Ip route 10.1.2.0 255.255.255.0 172.16.0.1
Ip route 10.1.3.0 255.255.255.0 172.16.0.6
Ip route 10.1.4.0 255.255.255.0 172.16.0.10

RT-Houston

Int E0
IP address 10.1.2.1 255.255.255.0

Int S0
ip address 172.16.0.2 255.255.255.252

Ip route 0.0.0.0 0.0.0.0 172.16.0.1

RT-Miami

Int E0
IP address 10.1.3.1 255.255.255.0

Int S0
ip address 172.16.0.6 255.255.255.252

Ip route 0.0.0.0 0.0.0.0 172.16.0.5

RT-LA

Int E0
IP address 10.1.4.1 255.255.255.0

Int S0
ip address 172.16.0.10 255.255.255.252

Ip route 0.0.0.0 0.0.0.0 172.16.0.9

Figure 10-3

A. Yes
B. No

8. You are reviewing the configuration files on a Cisco router that is configured to support PPP authentication. You notice the following command: `ppp authentication chap callin`. How does the router interpret this command?

    A. Only incoming calls that initiate a PPP connection are authenticated using CHAP.

    B. The router responds to a CHAP challenge only when acting as the calling party.

    C. The router expects the authenticating peer to supply the password `callin`.

    D. The router only authenticates a peer that has been configured with the hostname `callin`.

9. _____ are commonly used to divide a single collision domain by creating multiple smaller collision domains and are capable of supporting full-duplex transmission operation.

    A. Repeaters

    B. Hubs

    C. LAN switches

    D. Routers

10. What is a disadvantage of using switches in your network?

    A. Filter by MAC address

    B. Stop broadcast storms

    C. Don't stop broadcast storms

    D. Can only use up to four bridges in any LAN

11. Look at the following diagram. VTP does not seem to be working in this switched LAN. What is the most likely problem?

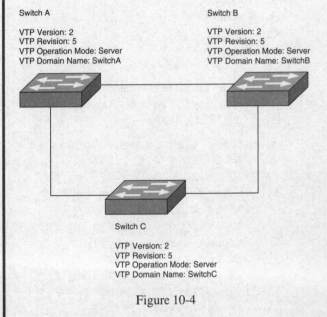

Switch A

VTP Version: 2
VTP Revision: 5
VTP Operation Mode: Server
VTP Domain Name: SwitchA

Switch B

VTP Version: 2
VTP Revision: 5
VTP Operation Mode: Server
VTP Domain Name: SwitchB

Switch C

VTP Version: 2
VTP Revision: 5
VTP Operation Mode: Server
VTP Domain Name: SwitchC

Figure 10-4

    A. VTP version

    B. VTP revision numbers

    C. VTP mode

    D. VTP domain name

12. While reviewing your running configuration, you notice an access list line that reads `access-list 10 deny 192.168.5.19`. The wildcard mask field is notably absent. How is this access list line interpreted by the router?

    A. A wildcard mask of 0.0.0.0 is assumed.

    B. A wildcard mask of 255.255.255.0 is assumed.

    C. A wildcard mask of 0.0.0.255 is used as the default for a Class C address.

    D. A wildcard mask of 255.255.255.255 is assumed.

13. What OSPF term refers to a network or router interface?

    A. Link

    B. Area

    C. LSA

    D. STP

GO ON TO THE NEXT PAGE

14. In which STP state does a port prepare to forward data frames without populating the MAC address table?

    A. Blocking

    B. Listening

    C. Learning

    D. Forwarding

15. Which of the following commands is correct if you want to deny FTP from network 172.16.10.0 to network 172.16.20.0?

    A. `access-list 10 deny tcp`
       `172.16.10.0 0.0.0.255`
       `172.16.20.0 0.0.0.255 eq ftp`

    B. `access-list 110 deny tcp`
       `172.16.10.0 0.0.0.255`
       `172.16.20.0 0.0.0.255 eq ftp`

    C. `access-list 10 deny ip`
       `172.16.10.0 0.0.0.255`
       `172.16.20.0 0.0.0.255 eq ftp`

    D. `access-list 110 deny ip`
       `172.16.10.0 0.0.0.255`
       `172.16.20.0 0.0.0.255 eq ftp`

16. Which configuration register setting tells the router to look in NVRAM for the boot sequence?

    A. 0x142

    B. 0x101

    C. 0x2101

    D. 0x2102

17. Given the routing table entry below, which of the following options are used by default to calculate the number 32300? (Choose two.)

```
E  192.168.10.0
   [90/32300] via
   192.168.26.17,00:00:35
   Ethernet 0
```

    A. MTU

    B. Bandwidth

    C. Administrative distance

    D. Hop count

    E. Metric

    F. Delay

18. Which of the following describe the process identifier that is used to run OSPF on a router? (Choose two.)

    A. It is locally significant.

    B. It is globally significant.

    C. It is needed to identify a unique instance of an OSPF database.

    D. It is an optional parameter required only if multiple OSPF processes are running on the router.

    E. All routers in the same OSPF area must have the same process ID if they are to exchange routing information.

19. Which types of OSPF network elect a backup designated router (BDR)? (Choose two.)

    A. Broadcast

    B. Non-broadcast multi-access

    C. Point-to-point

    D. Broadcast multipoint

20. Which command sequence can you use to enable IP RIP version 1 on a router?

    A. `router rip`
       `network 172.16.1.0`
       `network 10.1.0.0`

    B. `router rip`
       `network 172.16.0.0`
       `network 10.0.0.0`

    C. `router rip`
       `network 172.16.1.0 172.16.1.1`
       `network 10.1.0.0 10.1.1.1`

    D. `router rip`
       `network 172.16.1.0`
       `255.255.255.0`
       `network 10.1.0.0`
       `255.255.0.0`

21. Which command sequence assigns the login password `cisco` on the console terminal line?

    A. `line vty 0`
       `login password cisco`

    B. `line console`
       `login password cisco`

    C. `line login terminal`
       `password Cisco`

    D. `line console 0`
       `login password CISCO`

    E. `line console 0`
       `login password cisco`

22. Describe the first step in data encapsulation.

    A. Headers are applied to a frame.

    B. Frame types are used in Cisco interfaces.

    C. Change user data into a usable format to transmit on a network.

    D. Change bits into packets.

23. You have purchased a layer 2 switch. Which of the following are true regarding switches? (Choose two.)

    A. A switch is a hub with more ports.

    B. A switch is a multiport bridge.

    C. Switches learn IP addresses from each frame and filter the network using these addresses.

    D. Switches learn MAC addresses by examining the source address of each frame.

24. What is the IEEE version of spanning tree?

    A. 802.5

    B. 802.3E

    C. 802.2B

    D. 802.1D

25. What are the ways that you can enter setup mode on a router? (Choose two.)

    A. By typing the `clear flash` command

    B. By typing the `erase start` command and rebooting the router

    C. By typing the `setup` command

    D. By typing the `setup mode` command

26. Look at the following diagram. You have been asked to prevent the LA users from accessing external web sites. You have configured the RT-LA router as shown but have been informed that users at LA still have access to external web sites. What is the problem?

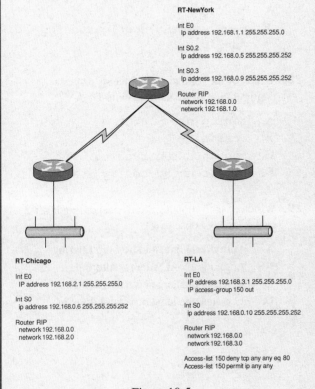

Figure 10-5

    A. Access list applied in the wrong direction

    B. Access list is misconfigured

    C. Access list is on the wrong router

    D. Access list is on the wrong interface

GO ON TO THE NEXT PAGE

27. Which of these commands are used to configure information into RAM on a router? (Choose three.)

   A. `configure memory`

   B. `configure terminal`

   C. `copy tftp flash`

   D. `copy flash startup-config`

   E. `copy running-config startup-config`

   F. `copy startup-config running-config`

28. Which of the following commands places a configuration from NVRAM into DRAM?

   A. `config net`

   B. `config t`

   C. `copy startup running`

   D. `copy running-config startup`

29. Which of the following are true regarding layer 2 switching? (Choose two.)

   A. It provides logical-addressing filtering.

   B. It provides MAC address filtering.

   C. It creates one large collision domain.

   D. It creates one large broadcast domain.

30. Look at the following diagram. You have been asked to troubleshoot a problem. This network has failed to converge. What is the likely cause of the problem?

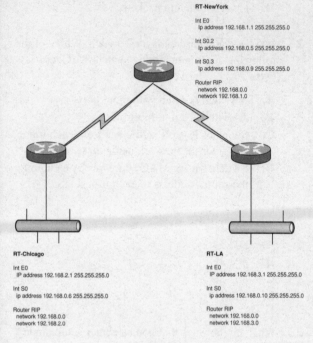

Figure 10-6

   A. RIP auto-summary

   B. IP subnet zero

   C. IP addressing

   D. RIP network statements

31. If you have a layer-2 switch with 12 ports, and only 10 are in use, how many collision domains and broadcast domains do you have?

   A. 12 collision domains and 12 broadcast domains

   B. 10 collision domains and 1 broadcast domain

   C. 1 collision domain and 12 broadcast domains

   D. 1 collision domain and 1 broadcast domain

32. What is the subnet broadcast address that the host 192.168.10.17 with a mask of 255.255.255.240 uses?

   A. 192.168.10.16

   B. 192.168.10.19

   C. 192.168.10.23

   D. 192.168.10.31

33. What is the subnet broadcast address that the host 172.16.10.12 with a mask of 255.255.255.128 uses?

A. 172.16.10.127
B. 172.16.10.255
C. 172.16.255.255
D. 172.16.10.128

34. What is the valid host range of the IP subnet on which the address 172.16.10.61 255.255.255.224 resides?

A. 172.16.10.48-63
B. 172.16.10.33-62
C. 172.16.10.0-254
D. 172.16.10.60-94

35. What does the following command do?

```
RouterA#config net
```

A. Configures DRAM parameters on the router
B. Configures NVRAM parameters on the router
C. Merges a router configuration stored on a TFTP host into running-config
D. Merges a router configuration from NVRAM into running-config

36. What does the following command do?

```
RouterA#config mem
```

A. Configures DRAM parameters on the router
B. Configures NVRAM parameters on the router
C. Merges a router configuration stored on a TFTP host into running-config
D. Merges a router configuration from NVRAM into running-config

37. Look at the following diagram. You notice that someone has placed an administrative distance of 150 on the static route on RT-Denver used to reach the RT-LA LAN. What will the impact of this be?

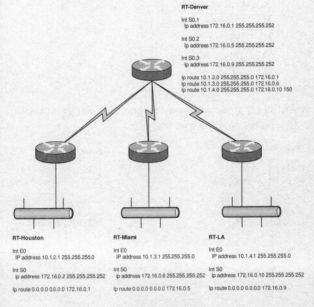

Figure 10-7

A. Traffic will be sent to Houston and Miami before being sent to LA.
B. The LA LAN will be unreachable.
C. The static route will be effective only if another route is withdrawn from the routing table.
D. None of the above.

38. If you want to change the default administrative distance for a static route to 150, what should you do?

A. Set the global command for static-routing to 150.
B. Change the network to a different router interface that runs Fast Ethernet or Gigabit Ethernet.
C. Add an administrative distance parameter to the end of a static route entry.
D. Add the permanent parameter to the end of a static route entry.

39. Which command can you use to see the configuration register setting on a Cisco router?

A. `show terminal`
B. `show version`
C. `show flash`
D. `show config-register`

GO ON TO THE NEXT PAGE

181

40. You have large files that you need to transfer from your home to your remote corporate office. You need to do this periodically and quickly. What technology is best suited for your situation?

A. Frame Relay
B. Ethernet
C. ISDN
D. Token Ring
E. ATM

41. Look at the following diagram. Which switch will be become the root bridge?

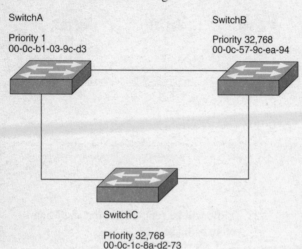

SwitchA

Priority 1
00-0c-b1-03-9c-d3

SwitchB

Priority 32,768
00-0c-57-9c-ea-94

SwitchC

Priority 32,768
00-0c-1c-8a-d2-73

Figure 10-8

A. SwitchA
B. SwitchB
C. SwitchC
D. There is not enough information provided.

42. If you want to see the DLCI number used by LMI for your router's management PVC, which command should you use?

A. `show frame-relay`
B. `show frame pvc`
C. `show interface`
D. `show ip interface`
E. `show frame-relay lmi`

43. When configuring a switch, what is the purpose of the `ip address` command?

A. Assigns a name to the switch
B. Sets the switch-management IP address
C. Sets a switchport to access mode
D. Enables portfast on an interface
E. Allows the switch to communicate with other subnets

44. What does a Frame Relay switch use to distinguish between each Permanent Virtual Circuit (PVC) connection?

A. DLCIs
B. BECNs
C. FECNs
D. LMIs

45. Which OSPF network type establishes router adjacencies but does not perform the DR/BDR election process?

A. Point-to-point
B. Broadcast multi-access
C. Non-broadcast multi-access
D. Backbone area 0

46. Which of the following solutions are used to reduce the chance of distance-vector routing loops? (Choose two.)

A. Split horizon
B. Route poisoning
C. Area hierarchies
D. Link-state algorithms

47. Look at the following diagram. You need to connect these two switches so that all hosts will be able to communicate with all other hosts on the same VLAN. Which of the following do you need?

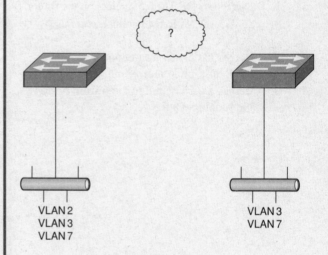

VLAN 2
VLAN 3
VLAN 7

VLAN 3
VLAN 7

Figure 10-9

A. A router
B. Another switch
C. A crossover cable
D. A straight-through cable

48. When you enter router passwords during the setup dialog, what is the difference between the enable password and the enable secret password?

- **A.** The enable password is encrypted.
- **B.** The enable secret password uses IPSec password authentication.
- **C.** The enable secret password cannot be seen as cleartext when the configuration is viewed.
- **D.** The enable secret password acts as a backup in case the enable password is compromised.

49. Look at the following diagram. You have been asked to configure the switch. Which of the following connections can you configure with portfast? (Choose three.)

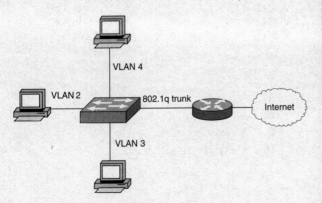

Figure 10-10

- **A.** The host on VLAN2
- **B.** The host on VLAN3
- **C.** The host on VLAN4
- **D.** The 802.1Q trunk link

50. You have just issued the `erase startup-config` command and reloaded your router. Which mode will your router be in when you reboot?

- **A.** Setup
- **B.** Startup
- **C.** User EXEC
- **D.** User privileged
- **E.** Global configuration

51. Look at the following diagram. You have been asked to troubleshoot a problem. This network has failed to converge. What is the likely cause of the problem?

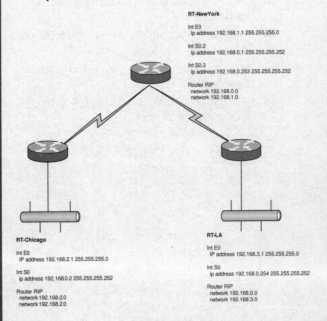

Figure 10-11

- **A.** RIP auto-summary
- **B.** IP subnet zero
- **C.** IP addressing
- **D.** RIP network statements

52. You just entered the following command:

```
Router(config)#line console 0
```

Which operation is most likely to follow?

- **A.** Configure the terminal type.
- **B.** Enter protocol parameters for a serial line.
- **C.** Create a password on the console terminal line.
- **D.** Establish a terminal type 4 connection to a remote host.
- **E.** Change from configuration mode to console privileged mode.

53. As data passes downward through the layers of the OSI model, it is encapsulated into various formats. Which of the following is the correct order of encapsulation?

- **A.** Bit, packet, frame, segment
- **B.** Bit, frame, packet, segment
- **C.** Segment, packet, frame, bit
- **D.** Segment, frame, packet, bit

GO ON TO THE NEXT PAGE

54. The configuration register on your router is set to the factory default. What are the settings for the console port?

    A. 19,200bps, 8 data bits, no parity, 1 stop bit, no flow control

    B. 9600bps, 7 data bits, no parity, 1 stop bit, no flow control

    C. 9600bps, 8 data bits, no parity, 1 stop bit, no flow control

    D. 2400bps, 8 data bits, no parity, 1 stop bit, hardware flow control

55. Look at the following diagram. You need to connect these two switches so that all hosts will be able to communicate with all other hosts. Which of the following do you need?

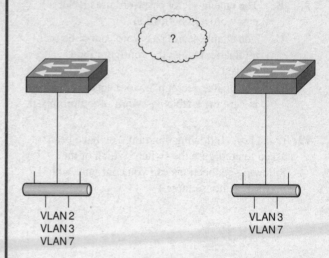

VLAN 2
VLAN 3
VLAN 7

VLAN 3
VLAN 7

Figure 10-9

    A. A router

    B. Another switch

    C. A crossover cable

    D. A straight-through cable

Answer Key for Practice Test 10

1.	B	**15.**	B	**29.**	B, D	**43.**	B
2.	B	**16.**	D	**30.**	C	**44.**	A
3.	B	**17.**	B, F	**31.**	B	**45.**	A
4.	D	**18.**	A, C	**32.**	D	**46.**	A, B
5.	D	**19.**	A, B	**33.**	A	**47.**	C
6.	D	**20.**	B	**34.**	B	**48.**	C
7.	B	**21.**	E	**35.**	C	**49.**	A, B, C
8.	A	**22.**	C	**36.**	D	**50.**	A
9.	C	**23.**	B, D	**37.**	D	**51.**	B
10.	C	**24.**	D	**38.**	C	**52.**	C
11.	D	**25.**	B, C	**39.**	B	**53.**	C
12.	A	**26.**	A	**40.**	C	**54.**	C
13.	A	**27.**	A, B, F	**41.**	A	**55.**	A
14.	B	**28.**	C	**42.**	C		

Answer Explanations for Practice Test 10

1. B. EIGRP should always seem like a good answer on a Cisco exam, but remember that it is proprietary, and the scenario given in the question involves multiple vendors. Also, the question states that the business requirements dictate (you have to read between the lines) that you need Variable Length Subnet Masks (VLSMs), so RIPv1 will not work.

2. B. Routing Information Protocol (RIP) is not good in large networks. When you configure RIP, you need to specify all directly connected networks you wish to route for in a classful manner.

3. B. The access list has an incorrect wildcard mask. It should be 0.0.0.255, not 255.255.255.0.

4. D. Although each of the three routers has the 192.168.0.0 network for the WAN segments, each router is missing the 192.168 network statement for the LAN segment.

5. D. To connect two switches together, you need a crossover cable. When a link is working on a switch, the port will be green.

6. D. The 0.0.7.255 wildcard mask corresponds to the /21 mask.

7. B. The Miami and LA routers both have default routes, and the Denver router knows about all subnets in the network (some connected, some through static routes).

8. A. When the command `ppp authentication` has been issued using the `callin` keyword, the router will authenticate a remote peer only if the remote peer initiated the call.

9. C. Only switches divide collision domains. Routers divide broadcast domains.

10. C. Because a switch does not create separate networks like a router does, if a broadcast storm takes place, a switch forwards the frames.

11. D. All switches that are participating in the same VTP domain must be configured with the same VTP domain name. In this diagram, each switch is configured to be part of a different VTP domain and thus will not share VTP information with the other switches in the figure.

12. A. The wildcard mask is optional when you are configuring a standard access list. If a wildcard mask is not specified, the router interprets the statement to be that the list is to match all bits of the source address.

13. A. Within OSPF, *link* is synonymous with *interface*.

14. B. An STP listening port listens to BPDUs to make sure no loops occur on the network before passing data frames. A port in the listening state prepares to forward data frames without populating the MAC address table.

15. B. When you are trying to find the correct answer from an access-list command string, always start by checking the access-list number. For extended lists that filter by upper-layer protocol, the number must be 100–199; this makes options A and C wrong. The next thing you need to check is the upper-layer protocol, which in this example is `ftp`. If you are filtering by FTP, the protocol field must be `tcp`. Only option B has the correct syntax.

16. D. The configuration register setting of 0x2102 tells the router to look in NVRAM for the boot sequence, which by default is to boot the IOS from flash and the configuration from NVRAM (startup-config).

17. B, F. 32300 is the composite metric for the route. EIGRP uses bandwidth and delay of the line, by default, to create the composite metric.

18. A, C. The process ID on a router doesn't do much; it just starts the OSPF routing protocol on your router. It is locally significant, which means that all routers can use the same number, or all different numbers—it doesn't matter. The only time this number matters is if you have an autonomous system boundary router (ASBR), which participates in two separate autonomous systems, and this is rare.

19. A, B. No DR is assigned on any type of point-to-point link. No DR/BDR is assigned on the NBMA point-to-multipoint due to the hub/spoke topology.

20. B. When you are configuring RIP, the networks are entered using classful notation (10.0.0.0, 172.16.0.0).

21. **E.** Option A sets the password for the virtual terminals (Telnet). Options B and C are invalid commands due to syntax errors. Option D has the correct command syntax, but it sets the password to CISCO. Passwords are case sensitive, so only the last sequence (option E) is correct.

22. **C.** The five encapsulation steps are as follows:
    1. User information is converted to data.
    2. Data is converted to segments.
    3. Segments are converted to packets or datagrams.
    4. Packets or datagrams are converted to frames.
    5. Frames are converted to bits.

23. **B, D.** Switches are considered multiple-port bridges by Cisco, and they filter by MAC address, not IP address.

24. **D.** IEEE 802.1D is the Spanning Tree Protocol specification.

25. **B, C.** Not that you would want to enter setup mode, but if you did, you could erase the contents of NVRAM by using the `erase startup-config` command and then rebooting the router. You can also type `setup` from privileged mode at any time.

26. **A.** This access list needs to be applied inbound on the Ethernet interface. When a user is attempting to communicate with a web server, their initial packet (which the router sees as inbound on the Ethernet interface) is destined for TCP port 80 on the web server. This access list, as applied, prevents users not in LA from connecting to any web sites hosted in LA.

27. **A, B, F.** The commands `configure memory`, `configure terminal`, and `configure network` are all used to configure information into RAM. However, `copy startup-config running-config` is the same as the older `configure memory` command.

28. **C.** The `copy startup-config running-config` command copies the contents of NVRAM into DRAM.

29. **B, D.** Layer 2 devices (switches) filter a network by using hardware addressing and create one large broadcast domain by default. Layer 2 devices also break up collision domains.

30. **C.** The WAN segments are part of the same Class C network, 192.168.0.0. This configuration will generate an error when applied to the RT-NewYork router regarding a duplicate IP address. A better solution would be to subnet the Class C. Further inspection of the addressing on the WAN links would show that the likely intention was to use a /30 mask.

31. **B.** Each switchport is its own collision domain; and, by default, each switch is one broadcast domain.

32. **D.** 255.255.255.240. $256 - 240 = 16$; $16 + 16 = 32$. Therefore, the subnet broadcast must be 192.168.10.31.

33. **A.** The subnet is 172.16.10.0, and the broadcast address is 172.16.10.127. This is determined by looking at the host ID, which is 12 in this case. Because it is less than 128, the subnet must be 0 in the fourth octet.

34. **B.** $256 - 224 = 32$. $32 + 32 = 64$. The subnet is 172.16.10.32, and the broadcast address is the number right before the next subnet (63 in this question). The valid hosts are the numbers between the subnet address and the broadcast address: 33 through 62.

35. **C.** `config net` is used to take a configuration stored on a TFTP host and merge it into running-config.

36. **D.** The `config mem` command is used to merge or restore a configuration from startup-config to running-config.

37. **D.** In this case, where no other dynamic routing protocols are running, modifying the AD on the static route will have no effect. If the router were running RIP or OSPF, for example, the static route would be effective only if that routing process lost the route.

38. **C.** By adding an administrative distance parameter to the end of a static route entry, you can change the default AD.

39. **B.** The `show version` command displays the current setting of the configuration register.

40. C. Even though a newer technology is probably a better choice at this point for home-to-corporate-office connections, Cisco's answer to this question is ISDN because of the periodic connection that is needed.

41. A. The priority of SwitchA is lower than that of the other two, and thus SwitchA will become the root bridge. The MAC address is relevant only if the priorities are all the same.

42. C. This is a hard one. To get the Local Management Interface (LMI) statistics for each Permanent Virtual Circuit (PVC) used on your router, use the `show frame-relay lmi` command. However, LMI uses a separate DLCI number between the router and Frame Relay switch, and this can be seen only with the `show interface` command.

43. B. This command assigns an IP address to the switch, which will be used to manage the switch. A switch does not need an IP address to work, but it will need one if you wish to telnet to it, for example.

44. A. Each PVC is assigned a Data Link Connection Identifier (DLCI) that uniquely identifies the virtual circuit over the connection between the router and the Frame Relay switch. The DLCI is only locally significant.

45. A. Broadcast and non-broadcast multi-access networks perform DR and BDR elections.

46. A, B. The split-horizon rule states that routers cannot send updates out on the same interface on which they were received. The route-poisoning rule dictates that routers must send out an update stating that the destination is unreachable when the link fails.

47. C. A crossover cable between the two switches, properly configured with a trunk link, will allow all users within any VLAN to communicate with each other. A router is only needed to communicate between separate VLANs, not within a single VLAN.

48. C. When you enter an enable secret password, it is encrypted and cannot be viewed in the configuration file. In addition, it will override the enable password, causing all users to use the enable secret password when attempting to enter privileged EXEC mode from user EXEC mode.

49. A, B, C. You can use the `portfast` command only on switchports with hosts or servers attached.

50. A. If the router cannot find a startup-config file, it will start the setup process.

51. B. In this case, all addressing and RIP configuration is correct. The most likely problem is IP subnet zero. If you notice, the 192.168.0.0 network has been subnetted using a /30 mask. The subnets in use on the WAN links are the first and last subnets.

52. C. When entering the line console command, you are entering the line mode where you can configure the console line. The only option presented that is a valid line-configuration task is creating a password.

53. C. The Transport layer is responsible for segmenting the data. The Network layer packetizes the segments received from the Transport layer. The Data Link layer is responsible for encapsulating the packet with framing information. The Physical layer is responsible for converting the bytes of the frame into bits and transmitting the bits across the physical media.

54. C. The default baud rate for the console port on a Cisco router is 9600bps. If the setting of the factory-default configuration register is changed, a lower baud rate can be selected. Data bits, parity, stop bits, and flow control are always set to 8, N, 1, and None and cannot be changed by modifying the configuration register settings.

55. A. In order to communicate between VLANs, you need a router.